Mid-century women's writing

Manchester University Press

Mid-century women's writing

Disrupting the public/private divide

Edited by
Melissa Dinsman, Megan Faragher,
and Ravenel Richardson

MANCHESTER UNIVERSITY PRESS

Copyright © Manchester University Press 2024

While copyright in the volume as a whole is vested in Manchester University Press, copyright in individual chapters belongs to their respective authors, and no chapter may be reproduced wholly or in part without the express permission in writing of both author and publisher.

Published by Manchester University Press
Oxford Road, Manchester, M13 9PL

www.manchesteruniversitypress.co.uk

British Library Cataloguing-in-Publication Data
A catalogue record for this book is available from the British Library

ISBN 978 1 5261 6977 8 hardback

First published 2024

The publisher has no responsibility for the persistence or accuracy of URLs for any external or third-party internet websites referred to in this book, and does not guarantee that any content on such websites is, or will remain, accurate or appropriate.

Typeset
by Deanta Global Publishing Services, Chennai, India

Contents

Introduction: politicizing the domestic and domesticizing politics – Melissa Dinsman, Megan Faragher, and Ravenel Richardson   *page* 1

Part I: Professionalizing the domestic

Introduction to Part I – Megan Faragher   17
1. Professional identity and personal space in Mary Renault's *Kind Are Her Answers* and *Return to Night* – Victoria Stewart   20
2. Talking shop: Celia Fremlin and invisible work – Luke Seaber   35
3. 'Some thoroughly tiresome housekeeping crisis': Rebecca West's wartime journalism – Debra Rae Cohen   51
4. 'Coldly kind': calculated care in post-war British women's writing – Emily Ridge   66

Part II: Nationalizing gender politics

Introduction to Part II – Melissa Dinsman   85
5. New world women and the Labour Party win in Marghanita Laski's *The Village* – Sarah E. Cornish   89
6. Beyond 'companionate marriage': Elizabeth Taylor's gendered critique of post-war consensus in *A View of the Harbour* and *A Wreath of Roses* – Geneviève Brassard   108
7. Dissident friendship and revolutionary love in the novels of Sabitri Roy and Sulekha Sanyal – Sabujkoli Bandopadhyay   128
8. 'The political theory of heaven': religious nationalism, mystical anarchism, and the Spanish Civil War in Sylvia Townsend Warner's *After the Death of Don Juan* – Charles Andrews   146

Part III: Women beyond the nation

Introduction to Part III – Ravenel Richardson   165
9 'A woman is always a woman!': British women writers and refugees – Katherine Cooper   169
10 Families in a time of catastrophe: Anna Gmeyner's *Manja*, 1920–33 – Phyllis Lassner   185
11 'Some other land, some other sea': Attia Hosain's fiction and non-fiction in *Distant Traveller* – Ambreen Hai   202

Bibliography   223
Index   235

Introduction: politicizing the domestic and domesticizing politics

Melissa Dinsman, Megan Faragher, and Ravenel Richardson

Anglophone women's lives were dramatically impacted by seismic domestic, national, and international political shifts of the mid-century. They responded to these changes in a variety of ways – insight, nuance, excitement, alacrity, rage, dismay, and poignancy – and in a variety of mediums – letters, diaries, news journalism, radio broadcasts, poetry, fiction, and non-fiction. Hailing from different continents, religions, nationalities, and political persuasions, their writing does not fall into neat categories, such as public/private or progressive/conservative, but rather demonstrates that, whether they were writing about dictators or diapers, women were keenly attuned to the ways that politics impacted their lives. This volume, in large part, is an effort to take up the very problem of the public and private divide that undergirds many of the standard historical narratives of the mid-century, a narrative that continues to stealthily frame the work we as scholars do in the space of women's literature. The goal of this collection is to expand beyond the many bounds of modernism, intermodernism and post-modernism to examine women's writing – across classes, genres, and nationalities – during one of the most tumultuous periods of modern history. By choosing the term *mid-century* to describe the women writers in the volume, we seek to open the tent of literary representation to include writers of different races, ethnicities, classes, sexualities, and religious orientations. Through this expansion, we show that domesticity and politics, from the local level to the global, were of central importance to women writers worldwide.

The mid-century, which in this volume we are defining as 1930 to 1960, was an era of nationalism, autocratic governments, war, declining empires, and a reordering of geopolitical power and alliances. The global and economic crises that defined this time period had substantial impacts on women's lives, impacts which they sought to address through a broad range of fictional, non-fictional, and personal writing. One part of these momentous political and cultural changes was women's rights, which saw both an increase and decline in the years surrounding the Second World War. For women living in Britain specifically, the traditional narrative of these years is that of an expanding and constricting wave. With the swelling of economic and political freedoms for women in the 1930s, the cresting of women in the public sphere during the Second World War, and the resulting break as employment and political opportunities for women dwindled in the 1950s when men returned home from the front. But while women across Britain and the commonwealth certainly experienced changes in both the public/political sphere and the private/domestic sphere during the mid-century, the neat analogy of a wave of women gaining and then losing freedoms needs re-examination. Each of the chapters in this volume rejuvenates, and in some cases resuscitates, the work of mid-century women writers, journalists, broadcasters, and public intellectuals living in or working in Britain or under British rule. This expansion beyond Britain's borders and British writers is essential to any re-examination of mid-century writing, but certainly one that seeks to challenge the existing ways in which scholars approach women's writing of the period.

The period in question was one of extreme historical significance, with the formation of new (and often authoritarian, and even fascistic and genocidal) political parties, landmark elections, and global re-alliances impacting not only the interactions between nations, but also daily life at home. War and reconciliation are two of the major topics dealt with by authors in this volume, including the Spanish Civil War (1936–39), the Second World War (1939–45), the Nuremburg Trials (1945–46), and the establishment of the State of Israel (1948). Some authors in this volume focus specifically on the rise of fascism in the 1920s and 1930s – the formation of the British Union of Fascists (1932), Hitler being named German Chancellor (1933), and the increased violence of antisemitism throughout the 1930s and 1940s, culminating in the Holocaust. Still others approach the post-war domestic politics of women's writing with an eye toward rebuilding the nation, including the rise of the Labour party and Britain's post-war welfare state, which started with the Social Insurance and Allied Services Report (better known as the Beveridge Report) in 1942 and the landslide election of Clement Attlee in 1945. Yet others consider British colonialism and imperialism, and the larger global realignment that saw the decline of the British Empire, starting with Indian independence (1947), the Indo-Pakistani War (1947–48), and the beginning of the Windrush Generation that brought many Caribbean workers to Britain in search of work, starting in 1948.

On the surface, the relationship between women and such events is unilateral. After all, the world-historical figures alluded to above – Mosley, Chamberlain, Churchill, Hitler, Franco, Beveridge, Attlee – were all men. So, while many women were subject to the changing material conditions that came with these wider world-historical changes – for example, managing wartime rationing and moving themselves and their families to avoid danger – the larger cultural narrative has conceptualized women not as agents of change, but victims of it. More often than not, these assumptions have positioned women outside the political sphere and limited in political agency. In fact, while Virginia Woolf famously claimed that as 'a woman, I have no country. As a woman I want no country', women across the globe were aligning themselves with nationalist agendas and the opportunities they offered them, even when those agendas marginalized and subjugated other individuals.[1] Even representing the changes of the mid-century in terms of world history, as we do above, elevates public politics and reifies the division between public and private, which risks a similar sidelining of women's roles in the global and national political changes of this period.

Already in the mid-century, writers recognized the ways in which the evolving divide between public and private disproportionately harmed women and argued that such a system was fundamentally flawed for all citizens. Historically, the classical division between public and private is already co-constructed; as Hannah Arendt noted in 1958, the realm of secrecy and privacy of the home from the *polis* stemmed from the understanding that 'without owning a house a man could not participate in the affairs of the world because he had no location in it' and that 'a man who lived only a private life [...] was not fully human'.[2] Isolation to the private sphere, she argues, classically connoted *de*privation; in other words, the value of any individual in the private sphere was only guaranteed through their recognition in the public, and a lack of relationship with the latter made moot the benefits of the former. Though Arendt concerned herself with classical distinctions between home and the *polis*, women were always at the centre of such distinctions; women, whose bodies represented the 'physical survival of the species' were 'hidden away' in privation and, with that, foundationally deprived of the power accessible in the public sphere, denying them the opportunities of full citizenship.[3] In the modern world, much of this remains, as 'the distinction between private and public' evolves to coincide 'with the opposition of necessity and freedom, of futility and permanence, and, finally, of shame and honor'.[4] But fundamentally, the divide between public and private is not just concerned with political agency, but also, as Arendt suggests, with conditions of citizenship itself. As Raia Prokhovnik has argued, it is necessary to 'recast' the division of the public and private to take into account '*how* people are citizens', further recognizing that for women in particular, private responsibilities cannot be separated from public life: 'one does not cease to be a mother (or father) in the public realm or in any other activity'.[5]

This work of recasting women's citizenship in the period covered in this collection was particularly prescient as the pressures of war forced the conflation of spheres, muddling the domestic space of care into the public space of politics.⁶ For example, during the Second World War, women's citizenship was tenuously expanded, though women had to engage in a precarious balance, 'expected to engage in wartime work but at the same time had to maintain their domestic responsibilities'.[7] Yet such expansion also came with new restrictions. As Sonia Rose points out, the emphasis on the 'common good' during the war also meant, for women, the politicization of previously privatized realms, including the upholding of 'moral standards' and 'fulfilling [...] state-enforced obligations'.[8] When women's work is subsumed into the sphere of the private, as it often is during war, it is not just a matter of suggesting women's work is trivial or apolitical; rather, it also suggests the denatured status of women's citizenship if such categories hold sway. And as nations negotiate crises – whether those of the mid-century or those of the 2020s – we find the claims of national 'necessity' not only pushing women homeward, but also actively attempting to rescind their privileges to status as full citizens.

The long road to recovering women writers in the mid-century

Though the crises of the mid-century have often led to scholarship on the public-facing work of politically committed male writers, scholarly interest in mid-century women's writing has recently increased, as is evidenced by books like Sue Kennedy and Jane Thomas's *British Women's Writing, 1930 to 1960* (2020), as well as Maroula Joannou's contribution to *The History of British Women's Writing* (2013). Additionally, by moving away from standard constraints of high modernism, efforts like the Edinburgh University Press's book series 'Midcentury Modern Writers' and Oxford's 'Mid-Century Studies' series have expanded to include neglected writers, particularly women. Our collection aligns with this more expansive, inclusive approach.

But the path to this point has been a long and circuitous one, often privileging masculinity, whiteness, linearity, and formal experimentation. One of the earliest scholarly texts on mid-century writers was Valentine Cunningham's *British Writers of the Thirties* (1989). A study of a decade, Cunningham presents a linear narrative about post-Second World War writing that privileges male authors and the canon. However, he also opens up studies of modernism and the mid-century to consider history, politics, and ideologies, centralizing the cultural materialism that is now the cornerstone of many literary projects, including our own. Cunningham inspired interest in what would become known as 'late modernism' at the turn of this century. Foundational texts like Tyrus Miller's *Late Modernism: Politics, Fiction, and the Arts Between the World Wars* (1999) and Jed Esty's *A Shrinking*

Island: Modernism and National Culture in England, like Cunningham, took a linear approach to analysing writing of the late 1920s to the 1950s. Miller focuses on the earlier years of mid-century writing and uses the term 'late modernism' to describe the more political and self-aware work of the late 1920s and the 1930s as separate from the high modernism in and around 1922. Arguments emphasizing writers' evolving political commitments, emergent in the work of Cunningham and expanded by Miller, have since been challenged by those scholars who argue that middlebrow and non-canonical writing are underserved by a focus on writers' relationships to a public-facing audience. The chronological frameworks prominent in 'late modernist' scholarship, including works by Miller, Esty, and Marina McKay (particularly her 2007 book *Modernism and World War II*), were crucial for the establishment of the field of study. These vital works on late modernism paved the way for the boom in mid-century studies that we have seen recently, and have made possible collections, like ours, that challenge the accepted linear structure and muddy the divides between highbrow and middlebrow, canonical and non-canonical, nation and Empire.

Though many of the early studies of the late modernist period often worked outward from the rooted canonical figures, another stream of critical inquiry – one focused on the middlebrow, women, and the domestic – was also sprouting branches, starting with Margaret Crosland's *Beyond the Lighthouse: English Women Novelists in the Twentieth Century* (1981), Nicola Beauman's *A Very Great Profession* (1983), Alison Light's *Forever England: Femininity, Literature, and Conservation Between the Wars* (1991), and Nicola Humble's *The Feminine Middlebrow Novel: 1920s–1950s* (2001). These works, and others like them, represented a critical stage in the recovery of women writers and the transformation of the canon through feminist scholarly approaches.[9] Works like these inspired yet others, who articulated how middlebrow writing might be particularly valuable in the study of gender and domestic politics. One such crucial early work in the study of domestic politics and middlebrow writing is Chiara Briganti and Kathy Mezei's *Domestic Modernism, the Interwar Novel, and E.H. Young* (2006). Using the term 'home culture' to describe the everyday events of the domestic sphere, Briganti and Mezei offer techniques of reading interwar novels that are not traditionally considered 'modernist' – meaning they supposedly lack the formal experimentation that marks the modernist form. As an alternative, Briganti and Mezei offer a definition of the domestic novel as 'written by middle-class women for middle-class women about middle-class life and often middle-aged women's daily and inner lives', which has helped shape our own thinking about the formation of this collection.[10] This book seeks to explore what is uncovered if we take seriously the centralization of women's daily and inner lives in the period. What we find in the chapters that follow include a bevy of women writers, all of whom, in the words of Briganti and Mezei, are in 'search for and creation of the self and a subtle pursuit of the art of living'.[11]

In taking seriously the lived experience of women in the mid-century, it was necessary to eschew the standard historical framing and find an alternative method to consider the writing of women on the terms of women's lived experience. And, as much work on middlebrow fiction, domestic fiction, and home studies has suggested, an emphasis on space and place can be particularly insightful – even if particularly fraught; as Leonore Davidoff claims, 'space is an often-unacknowledged element in the public/private divide'.[12] After all, many of these women authors found themselves tied to (whether willingly or not) the domestic sphere, a social distinction only understood through a spatial limitation, but which has also been critically placed in opposition to the public sphere, a traditionally more masculine and amorphous space. Virginia Woolf's *A Room of One's Own* is an urtext for thinking through the importance of place and space for women in the early twentieth century. Her rallying cry for a room within the domestic space, however, also shows that the domestic sphere was far from being under feminine control. Instead, even within the home, the politics of patriarchy and the public shape the nature of life within the domestic sphere. For recent scholars of mid-century and interwar middlebrow fiction, the domestic space, and the experiences of such spaces, has become an increasingly important lens through which to read women writers. For Briganti and Mezei, the 'deliberate attentiveness to domestic objects, interiors, rituals and their validation of the everyday' in interwar British women's fiction required their own 'inventive narrative strategies in dialogue and focalization' to reveal 'the extraordinary in the ordinary'.[13]

Recent scholarship on the mid-century has begun to assert the political ramifications of the commonplace or the everyday, as demonstrated by works like Thomas Davis's *The Extinct Scene: Late Modernism and Everyday Life* (2015) and Nick Hubble's *Mass Observation and Everyday Life: Culture, History Theory* (2006). For example, Davis focuses on late modernist texts that 'describe the particulars of everyday life and arrange those particulars in a way that expresses some feature of world-systemic disorder'. For Davis, then, the prevalence of the everyday in late modernism 'is not primarily aesthetic or ethical; it is simultaneously aesthetic *and* political'.[14] Thus, the focus on the everyday and the domestic scene muddies the line between what we traditionally think of as the public (political, worldly) and private (domestic, local) spheres. We find an example of this in practice in *Reconstruction Fiction: Housing and Realist Fiction in Postwar Britain* (2020), in which Paula Derdiger's analysis of housing in post-war British literature reveals not only a real historical domestic issue, but also the politics of a nation that is undergoing a transition into a welfare state and realigning itself geopolitically with the United States as the new world power.

This turn towards politicizing the everyday and domestic in critical approaches to late modernism has also reframed the work around women's fiction, as the politics of the quotidian likewise transforms conventional understandings of the domestic sphere. Of course, politics were directly felt in the domestic sphere in more overt ways. This included the specific cultural politics and events of the time – the aftermath of the First World War, mass production, government policies like the marriage bar, and the increase in the publication of women's magazines. Alternatives to this overt representation of politics in the domestic, yet still very much invested in the home and women's culture, include Terri Mullholland's *British Boarding Houses in Interwar Women's Literature: Alternative Domestic Spaces* (2017) and Martina Plock's *Modernism, Fashion and Interwar Writers* (2017). Each of these texts focuses on community within and through a cultural space and/ or item often considered feminine. In this volume, we include both overt and subtle representations of a politicized domestic and the everyday. As a result, what emerges throughout the chapters in this collection is a historically attuned 'domestic' that works in two different directions: first, as a representation of the home and everyday life that *is*, at its very core, political, national, and global; second, as a means to explore the ways in which politics were a part of women's ordinary and local lives.

Seminal critical studies of British women's writing of the Second World War recognized how permeable the binary of public and private became as fascism's root grew into mass genocide, precipitating a global conflict the reach of which – whether through brute violence or public policy – left no area of individuals' lives unscathed. Texts such as Karen Schneider's *Loving Arms: British Women Writing the Second World War* (1997) and Jenny Hartwell's *Millions Like Us: British Women's Fiction of the Second World War* (1997) brought British women's writing of the Second World War, which with the exception of Woolf had been largely ignored or forgotten, to light as a complex body of fiction. Gill Plain's *Women's Fiction of the Second World War: Gender, Power and Resistance* (1998) revised the received binary of women being associated with peace and men with war, a binary that historically excluded examinations of women's engagement with wartime and its attendant political ideologies. Phyllis Lassner's *British Women Writers of World War II: Battlegrounds of their Own* (1998) draws attention to women's domestic fiction that erased the distinction between the battlefield and the home front by demonstrating that the political ideologies and violence which shaped the former were brutally enacted on the familial level. Lassner's recognition that women writers, who were conscious of their own precarious subject position as women, used their fiction to address how Europe and Britain's treatment of Others (namely Jews, refugees, and evacuees) was reflective of the precarious state of English and European civilization is revisited with this collection. Collectively, these critical texts were significant for their recuperative scope, and also for providing nuanced examinations of how the personal experience of living in the Second World War directly shaped British women writers' representations of the impact of political ideologies in the domestic sphere.

The above critical studies have paved the way for *Mid-Century Women's Writing*, but whereas many of these critics chose to define their work as 'interwar' (limiting the scope to between the First and Second World Wars), we have expanded the temporal range of this collection into the 1950s. In so doing, our collection demonstrates that rather than simply being pushed back into the home following the Second World War, women were increasingly participating in and reflecting on the political processes and movements of the time. We are far from the first to do this. Catherine Clay's *British Women Writers 1914–1945, Professional Work and Friendship* (2006) is one of the earliest recovery projects of forgotten British women's writing of the mid-century.[15] Setting an expansive date range that encompasses both World Wars, Clay's work focuses on a single network of women writers, which included Naomi Mitchison, Storm Jameson, Vera Brittain, and Winifred Hotby, among others, allowing her to engage with a variety of genres and writing forms. While our collection is more varied in authorial subjects and goes deeper into the mid-century, like Clay we also emphasize the value of looking at writing across genres and argue that by doing so we gain an even richer understanding of women's literary output in the years surrounding the Second World War and the post-war peace.

The turn from chronology towards space also tends to be more holistically reflective of women's lived experiences. To impose the cessation of the war in 1945 as an immutable nodal point of literary historical transition is also to suppose that the impact of geopolitical transition necessarily impacts all audiences the same. As this book expands its scope to writing of the 1950s, we follow works like Gill Plain's *Literature of the 1940s, Postwar and 'Peace'* (2013). Plain's book signalled a departure from previous critical studies that marked 1945 as a unique historical break between war and peace. By reading the 1940s as a decade, Plain paves the way for other mid-century scholars to rethink the arbitrary temporal boundaries we set on our work. In fact, Plain suggests that two other temporal time periods might be better used to understand the mid-century: 1933–45 and 1939–56. Our book takes up Plain's challenge and expands it by covering modernist and middlebrow literature of three decades (1930s–50s). By doing so, we show that the path to war and post-war reconstruction were long intertwined realities explored in women's narratives across Britain and her crumbling Empire.[16]

In order to capture the capaciousness of this period and purposely move away from preconceived notions of the thirty years that this book covers, the term 'mid-century' seems the most appropriate. We recognize the value of many efforts to provide alternative modalities for understanding the literary networks outside of high modernism, and our use of 'mid-century' does not suggest that terms like 'late modernism', 'interwar', and 'intermodernism' are not useful. On the contrary, these expansive visions of the literary field are foundational for this volume. 'Intermodernism', for example, is a particularly prescient one for our volume in its effort to 'deconstruct *multiple* binaries' that are emphasized through the dominance of modernist studies, including oppositions between 'elite and common, experimental and popular, urban and rural, masculine and feminine, abstract and realistic, colonial and colonized'.[17] And, to the extent that, as Kristin Bluemel writes, intermodernism is a praxis – a process of 'discovery' and 'theorizing', inviting us to do our work in 'new terms' – this book is at home with the intermodernist project. But, as Bluemel admits, it is not our writers who are 'intermodernists', but rather our approaches.[18] So while the scope of our work captures the spirit of the intermodernist project, the book retains the 'mid-century' as the most capacious and generous scope through which to view our work, particularly as our temporal framework and breadth in genres move so far beyond the 'modernist' project that even its use as a counterpoint might suggest unnecessary impositions on the works at hand.

Women taking up space

Our approach to the structure of this book has been heavily influenced by spatial feminism, and, in particular, Susan Stanford Friedman's *Mappings: Feminism and the Cultural Geographies of Encounter*, in which she argues that feminism should be approached spatially *and* temporally. As Friedman explains:

> The feminism in the singular that I advocate assumes a locational epistemology based not upon static or abstract definition but rather upon the assumption of changing historical and geographical specificities that produce different feminist theories, agendas, and political practices. A locational approach to feminism incorporates diverse formation because its positional analysis requires a kind of geopolitical literacy built out of recognition of how different times and places produce different and changing gender systems as these intersect with other different and changing social stratifications and movements for social justice.[19]

This localized approach to women's politics is a driving force of this volume; thus, we take seriously the call to address the unique kinds of domestic politics that emerges in different parts of the world at specific historical moments. But focusing on women's literature in specific places at specific times does not mean that we are only interested in a locally focused feminism. Instead, as Friedman writes, we seek to show that 'thinking geopolitically means asking how a spatial entity – local, regional, national, transnational – inflects all individual, collective, and cultural identities'.[20]

Because of the significance of local, national, and global politics in women's writing and because we acknowledge the value of feminisms based on spatial and temporal conditions, we have rejected an artificial linear chronology as the volume's overarching structure. We have, of course, still set temporal boundaries on the texts included, determined by our definition of mid-century, but temporality takes a backseat to locality. As a result, we have divided this book into three parts based on place and space – local, national, and global – rather than decades. By intermingling chapters across three decades and putting them in conversation, and by using a scalar organization rather than a neat chronology, we hope to illustrate the heightened complexity of women's engagement with, and labour in, the public sphere. This structure is also used to help us avoid and undermine the well-known centre/periphery and Britain/Empire dichotomies, which are increasingly being called into question by critics, but are still used to help define the modern and the mid-century. Instead, the categories of local, national, and global allow us to analyse local and national politics across national borders as well as to explore similar and contrasting concerns about the new geopolitics that emerged during this time period.

It is usually in this part of the introduction that a summary of each contributor's argument occurs. However, in order to heighten the spatial organization of this text, we have chosen to provide brief introductions preceding each part. That being said, a brief roadmap of how the collection is laid out seems appropriate. This volume is divided into three distinct, but related, spatially oriented categories. The first part, 'Professionalizing the Domestic', re-imagines how women in the professions – as sociologists, journalists, doctors, and caregivers – engaged with the pressures of domesticity throughout the mid-century, with specific attention paid to depictions of labour and the home. The second part, 'Nationalizing Gender Politics', focuses on the fraught relationship between gender, the nation, and political identities and examines the transformation of the role of the nation and nationalism during and after the Second World War and its impact on women and the home. 'Women Beyond the Nation' is the final part of this volume and examines the writing of women authors, many of whom had hyphenated national identities, who were particularly concerned with the threats that fascism, nationalism, and imperialism posed for vulnerable and marginalized populations globally before, during, and after the Second

World War. By approaching mid-century women's writings through scalar categories of the domestic, national, and global, this collection, which both revisits canonical writers and contributes original research on largely unknown authors, provides a new and more expansive perspective on women's writing of the mid-century.

The need for a volume like this seems even more urgent now than when we first conceived of the idea in 2019. Since that time, we have seen the global explosion of the #MeToo movement, which was started in 2006 by Tarana Burke in order to support women who had survived sexual violence, result in the United Nations International Labor Organization ratifying a treaty against workplace violence and harassment in 2019. We have also seen a more intersectional feminism emerging, with women's rights organizations supporting the advances of LGBTQIA+ rights around the world as well as placing a spotlight on the disproportionate impact climate change has on women. Helmed on the local level by organizations like the Women's Collective in India and the Women in Rural Development Network in Northern Uganda, among many others, the focus on climate change by localized women's rights groups is the essence of the global being local and the domestic being political. We have also witnessed the gains and losses of women's reproductive rights worldwide, including the restrictions and bans increasingly occurring across the United States, and even in states where some of our editors and contributors reside. More recently, the global stage has watched as Iranian women fight back against gender violence, oppression, and the policing of women's bodies by the Iranian State; their rally cry 'Women, Life, Freedom' has gained global traction and has been echoed by women around the world.[21] This list is, of course, only the tip of a very large iceberg of human rights issues that have impacted women on both the local and global levels. Yet these events show just how intertwined feminisms are locally, nationally, and globally and how, as we declare with this volume, the domestic is always political and politics are always domestic.

Notes

1 Virginia Woolf, *Three Guineas* (Oxford: Oxford University Press, 2015), p. 125.
2 Hannah Arendt, *The Human Condition* (Chicago, IL: University of Chicago Press, 1998), pp. 29–30, 38.
3 *Ibid.*, p. 72.
4 *Ibid.*, p. 73.
5 Raia Prokhovnik, 'Public and Private Citizenship: From Gender Invisibility to Feminist Inclusiveness', *Feminist Review* 60 (1998), p. 97.

6 The question of citizenship and whether or not someone had access to the public/political sphere was also a major topic of discussion during the mid-century, especially as it concerned race and national identity. See, for example, Patricia Chu's *Race, Nationalism and the State in British and American Modernism* (Cambridge: Cambridge University Press, 2006); Daniel Gorman's *Imperial Citizenship: Empire and the Question of Belonging* (Manchester: Manchester University Press, 2010); and Kathleen Paul's *Whitewashing Britain: Race and Citizenship in the Postwar Era* (Ithaca, NY: Cornell University Press, 1997).

7 Caitríona Beaumont, *Housewives and Citizens: Domesticity and the Women's Movement in England, 1928–64* (Manchester: Manchester University Press, 2013), p. 136.

8 Sonya O. Rose, *Which People's War? National Identity and Citizenship in Britain 1939–1945* (London: Oxford University Press, 2003), p. 108.

9 See also Phyllis Lassner, *British Women Writers of World War II* (London: Macmillan, 1998); Elizabeth Maslen, *Political and Social Issues in British Women's Fiction, 1928–1968* (London: Macmillan, 2001); Penny Summerfield, *Women Workers in the Second World War: Productivity and Patriarchy in Conflict* (Dover, NH: Croom Helm, 1984); and Jenny D. Hartley, *Hearts Undefeated: Women's Writing of the Second World War* (London: Virago, 1994).

10 Chiara Briganti and Kathy Mezei, 'Introduction: Living with Strangers', in *Living with Strangers: Bedsits and Boarding Houses in Modern English Life, Literature and Film*, ed. Chiara Briganti and Kathy Mezei (London: Routledge, 2020), p. 1.

11 *Ibid.*, p. 1.

12 Leonore Davidoff, 'Gender and the Great Divide: Public and Private in British Gender History', *Journal of Women's History* 15.1 (2003), p. 13.

13 Briganti and Mezei, 'Introduction', p. 2.

14 Thomas S. Davis, *The Extinct Scene: Late Modernism and Everyday Life* (New York: Columbia University Press, 2016), p. 6.

15 Maroula Joannou, *The History of British Women's Writing, 1920–1945* (vol. 8) (London: Palgrave Macmillan, 2013) offers readers a similar temporal timeframe to Clay. In this overview, Joannou demonstrates how, regardless of genre or context, women's literary production during this time was marginalized due to its associations with low-status writing and writing for commercial or mainstream audiences.

16 Sue Kennedy and Jane Thomas's *British Women's Writing, 1930 to 1960: Between the Waves* (Liverpool: Liverpool University Press, 2020) also seems to take up Plain's temporal call to action. Remixing Kristin Bluemel's 'intermodernism', Kennedy and Thomas shape their collection around the term 'interfeminism' to describe women's writing in an era that is frequently 'dismissed as a culturally insignificant "no man's land" between modernism and postmodernism' and first and second wave feminism (p. 1).

17 Kristin Bluemel, 'Introduction: What Is Intermodernism?', in *Intermodernism: Literary Culture in Mid-Twentieth-Century Britain*, ed. Kristin Bluemel (Edinburgh: Edinburgh University Press, 2009), p. 3.
18 *Ibid.*, p. 6.
19 Susan Stanford Friedman. *Mappings: Feminism and the Cultural Geographies of Encounter* (Princeton, NJ: Princeton University Press, 1998), p. 5.
20 *Ibid.*, pp. 109–10.
21 To learn more about these events and movements, visit the Global Fund (www.globalfundforwomen.org/) for Women and Human Rights Watch (www.hrw.org/topic/womens-rights).

Part I

Professionalizing the domestic

Introduction to Part I

Megan Faragher

What unites the chapters in 'Professionalizing the Domestic' is the evidence of the longstanding impacts of the multi-faceted notion of 'privation' on women's work and writing. As noted in the introduction, the privation of the woman writer – a decoupling of her from any relation to the public sphere – does not just deny her relation to social or political spheres, but also denies her a full stake in humanity, which requires involvement in both. For the writers covered in this part, including Elizabeth Taylor, Celia Fremlin, Daphne du Maurier, Rebecca West, and Muriel Spark, many of the forms of labour imaginable for women sat at the precarious boundary between domestic and professional spaces, rendering the limit utterly permeable and recognizing the necessary ambiguity that encompasses the lived experiences of these women. Labour in the service of social welfare and care, perhaps unsurprisingly, emerges throughout this part, in novels that recognize the direct impact of professions on the private lives of women. In highlighting the professionalization of care in the works of Mary Renault, Victoria Stewart provides just one example of women centralizing the emergent tensions evoked by the fungibility of professional and personal realms. We find similar dynamics in a work like Elizabeth Taylor's *Mrs Palfrey at the Claremont*. Stewart's chapter highlights the way that Mary Renault's novels, in focusing on the professionalization of the medical profession, allow the author to map the 'domestic sphere, the workplace, and the points of contact between the two'. Similarly, Emily Ridge reads the hotel in the opening of Taylor's novel as a staging ground for a popular theme of 'calculated care' in post-war fiction. Though Ridge focuses primarily on professions of care, even in cases where the professions themselves are not care-oriented, women in the occupations similarly realize the fluidity between the spheres of professionalism and privacy. As Luke Seaber identifies, Celia Fremlin's contributions to sociology speak, perhaps most overtly and productively, to the way that professional work *about* the domestic sphere is necessarily sensitive to the impacts of the incursion of professionalism on those very domestic spaces.

In what follows, the domestic spaces of literary fiction – when viewed through the lens of the increasing transmutability of the domestic and professional spheres – become increasingly associated with dread and anxiety. Novelists featured in this part did not just focus on this as thematic concern; they likewise rendered it formally. This becomes obvious when we find the formal elements of the literary gothic emerging in the works featured throughout this part. Fremlin's *The Hours Before Dawn* and Elizabeth Taylor's 'Apple Tree' (1952), for example, suitably describe narratives of the everyday gothic and domestic noir, and articulate private spaces increasingly encroached upon by the pressures of capital and the professions. The convergence of the gothic and these post-war reflections on women's labour is revelatory. Traditionally, the gothic has represented the sublimation of social anxieties, particularly those born of a challenge to gendered norms. As an example, we can look at transformations of gendered norms around care which, as Emily Ridge outlines, emerge in gothic domestic spaces like those in Daphne du Maurier's *Rebecca*. The same dynamic emerges in *Kind Are Her Answers* by Mary Renault where, as Victoria Stewart argues, the gothic emerges as a working metaphor for women balancing between professional and domestic spaces. This dynamic of domestic unsettling is further exacerbated in wartime, as Debra Rae Cohen demonstrates in her analysis of Rebecca West's journalism. If the mid-century allowed women into more areas of the workforce – and particularly the emergent care economy – the reconciliation of this with a post-war commodification of that culture stands as a foundational challenge to the conventional understandings of domestic space and its purpose for women.

If the chapters in this part detail the works of a wide array of authors exposing the foundational indeterminacy that undergirds domestic and professional boundaries, they also understand the impacts of the 'privation' of women's labour as it pertains to the professional spaces of writing. Just as the pressure of capitalism alters the relationship between women and the professions, the profession of writing is likewise subject to that very same pressure. This is perhaps evident in the fact that many of the writers here lack a breadth of academic attention – as is the case of writers like Elizabeth Taylor, Mary Renault, and Celia Fremlin. As Luke Seaber suggests, the invisibility of women's social labour – like that of Fremlin's multiple studies undertaken at the behest of Mass-Observation – continues to hold sway over the scholarship that surrounds them. To the extent that genres like the domestic noir are held as peripheral – and to the extent that mid-century literature continues to be held extra-canonically – scholarship will continue to overlook the works of women whose literary work expands and challenges traditional boundaries of space and gender.

What follows are four chapters that provide new insights into how intrusions of professionalism into the domestic sphere provide new insights into tensions faced by women who negotiated the tenuous boundaries between the two. Chapter 1, Victoria Stewart's 'Professional Identity and Personal Space in Mary Renault's *Kind Are Her Answers* and *Return to Night*', argues that Renault's experiences in the medical profession, and her depictions of medical professionals in the novels under study, reveal the increasing difficulty of distinguishing between public and private life both during the war and after it. This ambiguity of boundaries, in Stewart's reading, is only reinforced by the medical profession itself, a public-facing profession attending to the most private and intimate of subject matters. In Chapter 2, 'Talking Shop: Celia Fremlin and Invisible Work', Luke Seaber demonstrates how the often-invisible professional work of women writers impacts scholarly work long beyond their lifetimes. In establishing how Celia Fremlin's professional work in the field of sociology was underrecognized in her lifetime, he also emphasizes that the privation of Fremlin's work has long-lasting impacts on scholarship that seeks to reverse this unfortunate trend. Debra Rae Cohen continues the discussion of invisible work in Chapter 3, '"Some Thoroughly Tiresome Housekeeping Crisis": Rebecca West's Wartime Journalism'. In this case, Cohen demonstrates that West, in chronicling the 'mundane struggle of the everyday' in women's lives, also aids in challenging the 'myth of the Blitz' itself. Finally, this part turns to the post-war with '"Coldly Kind": Calculated Care in Post-War British Women's Writing'. Here, Emily Ridge returns to the professions of care, specifically contending that the increasing incursion of the state into matters of private care facilitates the emergence of a paradoxical distance in the depiction of, and practice of, care professions. Exploring the interwar novels of Daphne du Maurier, Elizabeth Taylor, and Muriel Spark, Ridge identifies moments of ambiguous care, tinged by the control of the state and institutionalized professions.

1

Professional identity and personal space in Mary Renault's *Kind Are Her Answers* and *Return to Night*

Victoria Stewart

Mary Renault is best known for a series of six novels set in ancient Greece, beginning with *The Last of the Wine* (1956) and culminating in *Funeral Games* (1981). Prior to this, however, she wrote novels with contemporary or near-contemporary settings, a number of which have medical professionals as their protagonists. Having taken an English Literature degree at Oxford, Renault enrolled at the city's Radcliffe Infirmary as a trainee nurse in 1933, and she continued to work in hospitals until her emigration to South Africa in 1948. She thus had a grounding in both medical procedures and the relationship dynamics that were liable to arise in the hospital workplace. She met her long-term partner, Julie Mullard, while at the Radcliffe, and her first novel, *Purposes of Love* (1939), has a nurse living in a nurses' home at its centre. There are particularly striking parallels between the plots and characters of *Kind Are Her Answers* (1940) and *Return to Night* (1947), the two novels that will be my focus here. In the former, Kit, a married doctor, has an affair with Chrissie, an aspiring actress who is the niece of one of his elderly patients. *Return to Night* sees Hilary, a female doctor, embarking on a relationship with Julian, a younger man with theatrical ambitions, after treating him for a head injury.

It might be tempting to explain this switching of genders as evidence of Renault using these taboo heterosexual relationships as encoded explorations of same-sex desire. But in these early works, as in her later novels set in the classical world, Renault did not shy away from depicting same-sex relationships in a relatively explicit manner for the time of writing. As I will show, *Kind Are Her Answers* and *Return to Night* contain gender-specific explorations of the intertwining of personal and professional identity which intersect with Renault's mapping of the domestic sphere, the workplace, and the points of contact between the two. Nicola Humble observes that the Victorian model of the bourgeois home as a 'source of feminine identity designed to soothe and soften the culture's aggressive materialism' was 'in the process of disintegration' by the inter-war period.[1] This sense that the domestic sphere was 'in a state of flux' is compounded in Renault's novels by both the difficulty that the protagonists have in separating their working and personal lives and by the intermittently present threat of an international conflict.[2] By the time *Kind Are Her Answers* and *Return to Night* were published, the exigencies of the war effort, especially the mobilization of civilians under the banner of the 'Home Front', had further problematized the separation of private and public life. *Kind Are Her Answers* contains only very passing references to its pre-war setting, while *Return to Night* is located more firmly in 1937–8, and both engage obliquely with the socio-cultural pressures that would have been recognized by their first readers, and their female readers in particular.

Working from home

The relationship between work and the domestic sphere is a complicated one for members of the medical profession and has gender-specific elements. Elaine Thomson has considered how women were situated within medicine in Britain during nineteenth-century campaigns to allow them to undertake full medical training. She comments:

> Medicine as a profession sits in an ambiguous position with regard to the public and private worlds. Medical authority is based on knowledge of private bodily functions, while knowledge of the body and medical evidence about personal health and illness necessarily involve an opportunity for those who create that knowledge to monitor and regulate private behaviour.[3]

Letting a doctor into your home involves surrendering a degree of privacy in the hope of a cure, a negotiation that also has class ramifications. Thomson notes that early female doctors were frequently involved in preventative medicine, with a domestic and often working-class focus, situating themselves 'as the intermediaries between the public and private worlds', a socially acceptable role for women to undertake, not least because of its relatively low professional status.[4] The doctors in *Kind Are Her Answers* and *Return to Night* are both in general practice and are therefore expected to visit the homes of their patients, a fact that has particular significance for the plot of the earlier novel. Equally importantly, in each novel, the doctor's home arrangements are affected by and entangled with their working life.

In *Kind Are Her Answers*, Kit lives with his wife Janet in a building that has been converted and contains not only their own living quarters, and the flat where Fraser, Kit's partner in the practice, lives with his wife, but also Kit and Fraser's shared consulting rooms, where they see their patients.

From the outset, the question of space and privacy is a pressing one for Kit and Janet, whose marriage has not recovered from the loss of their child:

> There was very little room in their home for getting away from one another. [...] They shared with the Frasers a solid, two-story Georgian house, taking the upper floor and the front garden. [...] Kit slept in the room which had been meant for the nursery, a fact which Janet, he knew, always silently remembered; she seldom entered it. They had only one guest room, a living-room, and a small dining-room not adapted for anything else. There remained the consulting-room downstairs; it was cramped and rather bleak [...] but it was useful as a last resource. Unluckily, Janet knew, by now, the times when he really needed to be there.[5]

Though this might sound like an enviable amount of space for two people to have at their disposal, the allocating of rooms to specific purposes – the guest room, the dining room 'not adapted for anything else' – makes it difficult to go into any of them simply to be by oneself. Kit is even under semi-surveillance if he goes down to the uninviting consulting room, because of Janet's knowledge of his work schedule. This description, from Kit's perspective, emphasizes the difficulty he has of finding his own space, and, by extension, being his own person. However, the reader's sympathy for him has already been tempered by the visit he makes to his wife's bedroom just before these reflections, an encounter that has more in common with a medical consultation than with marital or romantic intimacy: 'he went on allowing for her convalescence long after it had passed'.[6] When he leaves her, he smokes a cigarette out of his bedroom window. This reads as a minor, even adolescent, boundary infraction, but could also be an ironic reference to stereotypical post-coital behaviour. In either case, it acts as a small warning of what is to come.

Hilary, the central protagonist of *Return to Night*, also inhabits accommodation that has been adapted – 'two rooms of a house which, though friendly, was not her own' – but she at least has 'freedom from domestic fuss' even if she is, as she describes herself 'a glorified lodger'.[7] Later, we are told that the house is 'a newish one built round an old core; Hilary's two rooms, in the irregularly thick-walled part at one end, were almost self-contained, her sitting-room having its own glass door onto the garden, and, in one corner, a steep, crooked staircase leading into the bedroom upstairs'.[8] She and Lisa, who owns the house and lives in the other part of it, can have relatively sequestered lives, and the glass door means that Julian can come and visit Hilary without entering the main part of the house and being observed. Whereas the spatial arrangement of Kit and Janet's flat serves to underline and even exacerbate their growing estrangement, Hilary's status as a lodger has come about partly because of the curtailing of her previous professional and personal hopes. Passed over for a traineeship in surgery in favour of her boyfriend, David, who had previously expressed little interest in that specialism, Hilary has broken from both David and her ambitions to be a surgeon. Like Kit, she visits patients in their homes, and she is also attached to a cottage hospital, a small, local institution offering a range of care, operating, prior to the establishment of the National Health Service in 1948, on a charitable basis.

The hospital is where we first encounter Hilary. It has, we are told, been 'adapted from one of the huge, impracticable rectories of the 1860s'.[9] This prejudice against Victorian aesthetics, and by extension 'Victorian values', not uncommon for the mid-twentieth century, is echoed in *Kind Are Her Answers*.[10] Kit first meets his lover Chrissie because she agrees to act as a nurse to her elderly relative Miss Heath, who lives in Laurel Dene, 'a smallish Victorian-Gothic castle [...] in what had been, 60 years before, the best part of town'.[11] While most of the houses have been turned into 'offices or maisonettes [...] behind the wrought-iron gates and spiked brick wall of Laurel Dene, nothing had altered much'.[12] The scene is set for Kit to rescue a maiden from this 'smallish [...] castle', though Chrissie hardly seems helpless, and this is one of the points at which Renault invites the reader to see Kit as a rather earnest and self-regarding individual rather than to admire him as a tortured romantic hero.

The spatial arrangement that facilitates Chrissie's role as Miss Heath's carer is also what enables her affair with Kit, and Renault marks this conjunction as a troubling one. Once Chrissie arrives to stay at Laurel Dene, she takes the 'old drawing-room' to use as a bedroom, to be within easy reach of Miss Heath. When Kit asks whether she finds the room 'eerie', Chrissie explains that she likes it because she can 'have the big doors open straight onto the garden'.[13] Kit stops himself from expressing concern that someone might get in and do her harm if she leaves the doors open at night, not wanting to worry Chrissie, and this serves to foreshadow the fact that he himself will use the garden doors to visit her once their affair begins. There is also a parallel here with *Return to Night*, where the door in Hilary's sitting room allows Julian access to her rooms. For Julian and Hilary, this arrangement enables discretion and preserves a degree of privacy. But in the early part of *Kind Are Her Answers*, Kit is conducting his affair in a house where a woman lies dying, a fact which hardly bodes well. It also means that on at least one occasion, he has to switch from being Chrissie's lover to being Miss Heath's physician simply by stepping across the hall from one room to another.

While Hilary ostensibly has more freedom of movement than Kit, like him she is subject to the intrusion of work-related concerns while at home, because of the 'on call' system. Both are liable to be telephoned and required to come and attend emergencies, and if they cannot be reached are required to account for their whereabouts. Kit reflects on the relative ease with which even his movements between one place and another can be monitored: 'the town was a small one, and he and his car were known everywhere'.[14] Once his affair with Chrissie has begun, Kit uses being on call as an alibi for going out at night to meet her, and they also devise a method of communicating, involving tapping on the telephone receiver, so that he knows she is calling without her having to speak. Meanwhile, in the early stages of her relationship with Julian, Hilary uses being on call as a reason to return alone to her own rooms so that she can think through the implications of becoming further involved with him. The particular ways that, for an on-call doctor, work can infiltrate the home are employed expediently, though differently, by each medical protagonist. For Kit, home is somewhere to be escaped from; for Hilary, it is a place she can sometimes escape to.

Workplace romance

As well as confronting these logistical difficulties, each protagonist has to engage with ethical issues prompted by their romance. Kit's lover Chrissie is the relative of a patient rather than a patient herself, and by the time Hilary begins her sexual relationship with Julian, he has been discharged from the care of the hospital. But each protagonist shows, to varying degrees, an awareness of how their private actions could affect their professional lives. Renault's consideration of these issues is grounded in contemporary medical ethics, and her first readers might well have been aware of what was at stake for the doctors in these novels. A glimpse of the workings of the disciplinary committee of the General Medical Council (GMC), the organization that is still responsible for overseeing doctors' education and regulation in Britain, can be found in an article by Margaret Lane that was published in *The Daily Mail* in 1937. Being removed from the medical register, or 'struck off', and forbidden to practise is described as 'a sentence of professional death'.[15] Lane notes that half the disciplinary cases before the GMC are for motoring offences, particularly drink driving, and that in such cases the doctor might well be placed on probation by the Council, offering a chance of rehabilitation. No such leniency is likely to be shown for '[a]dvertising and canvassing', that is, attempting to poach patients from other practitioners. Hilary alludes to this in *Return to Night*, telling Julian that 'seducing patients from another doctor ranks nearly as high' as an accusation of rape, presumably because advertising would undercut doctors' supposed objectivity and undermine the GMC's underwriting of all registered doctors as equally professionally competent.[16]

Hilary's use of the word 'seduction' to refer to enticing another doctor's patient to your practice indicates the extent to which maintenance of the professional standards outlined by the GMC involved the scrutiny – and self-scrutiny – of doctors' behaviour in their private lives. In her article, Lane suggests that the public may not wholly condemn a doctor who is struck off after being cited as correspondent in a divorce case where the respondent is a patient: 'Judgments are fresh in the memory of most of us, which have seemed harsh at the time, which have been called the cause of loss to the medical profession, punishment out of all proportion to the crime.'[17] For the GMC, she explains, the question is one of the maintenance of trust in the profession as a whole. A case that may have been a prompt for Lane's article was covered by the *Daily Mail* just a few days later: Dr Douglas Chetham Pim was struck off for, in the GMC's formulation, misconduct with a woman 'while he stood in professional relationship with her'.[18] The *Mail*'s reporter describes how Dr Pim had 'endeared himself' to the inhabitants of the Buckinghamshire village he would now be obliged to leave, and cites several villagers' dismay at the GMC's verdict.[19] The tenor of this article, like Lane's comments on the GMC's proceedings, is that professional competence should take precedence over personal morality. Implicitly, if Pim's patients were willing to forgive him and continued to trust his medical judgement, then his private infraction should be forgivable. In this context, one might suspect that a reader in the 1940s could be minded to be sympathetic to Kit's predicament rather than straightforwardly condemnatory, though Renault does not simply set to one side the ethical questions that his behaviour raises.

Interestingly, although Kit's professional relationship with Chrissie is a more indirect one than Hilary's with Julian, because Chrissie is not herself Kit's patient, Kit's concern for his professional standing is more strongly expressed than Hilary's. On his way home after his first sexual encounter with Chrissie, the worries that Kit had brushed aside in the heat of the moment creep into his consciousness:

> At the time, the purely professional aspect of what he had done had seemed distant, fantastic, even, to the point of humor. Now, hideously lucid and concrete, it began to emerge. He could see it set out, in neat clear sentences of neat small type, in the lower half of a right-hand column in the *British Medical Journal*:
> *While visiting the house of a patient in a professional* –[20]

The half-finished sentence at the end of this quotation is Kit's imagining of how his actions might look if described from the perspective of the *BMJ*, the doctors' weekly journal of record, which printed summaries of the GMC's twice-yearly disciplinary hearings. But this is not just an indication of the construction that an objective authority might put on his private life. It is Kit's acknowledgement that what he might have bracketed off as 'fantastic' in order for the encounter to happen at all should actually have been the principle informing his behaviour. That he reaches for the language of the professional body to frame his actions in his private life indicates the extent to which he has internalized these principles even while choosing not to abide by them. Kit also has the added concern of the effect he believes any revelations could have on his practice partner, Fraser:

> It was no new idea to him that, if he and Chrissie were caught together at Laurel Dene, nothing could possibly prevent him from being struck off the register. [...] It had not occurred to him before that a public scandal would nearly kill Fraser. He had brought his standards of propriety intact from the 1880s. Moreover, he liked Kit and trusted him.[21]

Being struck off and therefore not allowed to be a doctor any more is the ultimate sanction Kit believes he faces, but his comments here about Fraser's Victorian 'standards of propriety' indicate the split between the standards that Kit is required to uphold as a member of his profession and his personal view of what is or is not acceptable. The implication is that the standards by which Fraser lives, and which also govern doctors' behaviour, have not caught up with the wider social context, and this echoes some of the sentiments expressed by Margaret Lane in her article. Kit's main anxiety is not about betraying his wife but about being publicly shamed. The biggest specific threat he perceives, and which he articulates to Chrissie, is that Miss Heath's elderly servant Pedlow might attempt to blackmail him.[22] At the climax of the novel, Pedlow does indeed send letters revealing her suspicions about Kit to both Fraser and Kit's wife Janet, but with Fraser on his deathbed and Janet away in South Africa, Kit manages to intercept both missives, and is relieved that Pedlow 'has just not known enough to write to the General Medical Council'.[23] As I will show, Kit's narrow escape from public exposure does not necessarily mean that the issues the threat raises are resolved by the end of the novel.

In *Return to Night*, Hilary's concerns are differently configured, though, like Kit, she feels constrained by the judgement she believes a member of an older generation is passing on her. When Julian is brought into the hospital after a riding accident, Hilary is obliged to lay down ground rules for his mother Mrs Fleming's contact with him, and Hilary is immediately aware of Mrs Fleming's gender-based prejudice against her. Arriving to see her son, Mrs Fleming initially approaches the Matron: 'Hilary stood ready for her turn; and was aware that her presence was being felt as an unexplained intrusion. If she had been a man her function would have been instantly apparent; she had ceased to think about such things, but, under the skin, continued to feel them.'[24] Ceasing to think but continuing to feel implies that Hilary has become resigned to, if not accepting of, such attitudes, and when she perceives Mrs Fleming's 'dismay' on learning that Hilary is indeed a doctor, she feels first 'resentment' and then shame.[25] Given that this is how her relationship with Mrs Fleming begins, it comes as little surprise that Hilary's relationship with Julian can only really start when his mother has gone away from the house that she and her son share, and that it can only be cemented when Julian has literally and symbolically separated himself from her influence.

Although there are moments at which Kit and Chrissie occupy the roles of doctor and patient in their private dealings with each other, most notably during a conversation when he advises her against using under-the-counter abortifacients if she believes herself to be pregnant, telling her, 'you're not to mess about with these patent poisons', it is in Hilary and Julian's relationship that the lines become more blurred, not least because Julian has actually been under Hilary's care.[26] Her first physical contact with him comes when she assesses his injuries after the accident, and the first night they spend together follows in the wake of him getting into a fight with a stranger and her treating his wounds, a sequence David Sweetman describes as 'a strange and violent rite of passage'.[27] Even before this, Julian, involved in an amateur dramatic production, asks Hilary if she has a skull he could borrow to use as a prop, and when she indicates on the skull the line that was cut during his operation after the accident, he asks her to locate the scar on his own head:

> She [...] drew her fingers through the heavy dark sweep of hair across his forehead. Faintly she traced the elliptical edge of the incision [...] As she explored it with the delicate stroking movements that were necessary to find so slight an outline at all [...] she felt a difference in his weight and pressure, and saw that he had relaxed sleepily and closed his eyes. Abruptly she took her hand away.
>
> 'Don't stop', he murmured placidly. 'It feels nice.'
> 'Don't be such a baby.' She laughed, and pushed his head away.[28]

The uncomfortable mixing of the sensual and the medical – the 'delicate stroking' of the 'incision' – is defused when Hilary frames Julian's behaviour as infantile. She is eleven years older than him and is situated not only in a position of medical authority but as a mother substitute, roles that ought to be kept separate, though both have a caregiving aspect. The climax of the novel, as I will show, sees Julian undergoing a form of rebirth before finally resolving to defy his mother and throw his lot in with Hilary.

This blurring of Hilary's status in psycho sexual terms is potentially more troubling to the reader than what the professional consequences of her actions might be. Indeed, despite the struggles she has experienced in her professional life – she tells Julian that her father 'thought that besides being unwomanly it was perfectly pointless, being in a job in which no woman ever gets to the top' – her attitude to potentially having to give up her career is a largely pragmatic one.[29] These reflections come as she is deciding whether or not to sleep with Julian for the first time:

> [S]he wasted no time on obvious practical considerations, such as the effect on her private practice if it got about, as sooner or later, in the country, it inevitably would. Even a very small private income, possessed since girlhood, lends a powerful if adventitious fortitude in matters of this kind. To the social aspect she felt indifferent, having had a love-affair in hospital, where such affairs are, within weeks, the property of almost everybody one knows.[30]

A reader who has sympathized with Hilary's struggles in a male-dominated world – in 1938 there were just over sixty thousand registered doctors in Britain, of whom six thousand were women – may well feel deflated by this easy dismissal of the potential consequences of the loss of everything she has worked for.[31] The bottom line seems to be that she would still be able to pay her bills in any case. It is also striking, however, that she places so much less store on public perceptions of her private life than Kit does. Both are living in similar small towns, but she is much less concerned about the making public of her private life than he is. This does not mean, though, that the resolution of *Return to Night* is any less ambivalent about Hilary and Julian's future prospects than *Kind Are Her Answers* is about Kit and Chrissie's.

Happy endings?

Left alone in Julian's bedroom after dressing the wounds he sustained in the fight, Hilary tidies away the bandages and iodine she has used; like the skull, the dressings were lent to him by her to be used as props in the play he staged. Opening a drawer, she finds three books put away in there: 'a famous theatrical autobiography [...], *Married Love* by Dr Stopes [and] a thin gaudy little pamphlet with a young man in a flying-helmet on the cover, and a title in red, white, and blue: *The Royal Air Force, To-day and To-morrow*'.[32] The concealment of the first of these books indicates the suspicion with which Julian's mother views his wish to be an actor; the second makes Hilary aware that Julian is not naïve, sexually speaking, alleviating her concern that she could be exploiting his innocence; and the final one is a reminder that the action of the novel is unfolding in 1937–8, foreshadowing, for readers in 1947, the fate that might await Julian. In fact, each of these publications is concerned to some extent with possible futures, to be embraced or averted. Hilary's landlady Lisa becomes pregnant during the course of the novel, having reconciled with her husband, a journalist who spends much of the novel away on assignments in Europe. Lisa broaches the subject with Hilary in a manner that appeals to Hilary as both a friend and a professional: '[I]f a woman came to you who'd lost two babies in succession, would you call her a fool to be starting another?'[33] Hilary offers Lisa her support, reassuring her that the outcome may not be the same this time. In a later twist, it emerges that, because Lisa's husband has made only flying visits to her, there are rumours locally that the father of her child is actually Julian, and Lisa's pregnancy and a desire to preserve Lisa's reputation is therefore one precipitating factor in the regularization of Hilary and Julian's own relationship.

Hilary's exchanges with Lisa also stand as a positive counter to the incident that occupies part of the opening of the novel, when Hilary assists at the birth of a premature baby which dies soon after. The mother, in that case, is a working-class woman with several children, who, Hilary reflects, 'had tried to stop this one [...] by every means short of the criminal', behaviour that Hilary sees as pitiful rather than condemning.[34] When Julian mistakenly believes that Hilary is pregnant, he is willing to take the blame but also places some of the responsibility at her feet, specifically because of her professional knowledge: 'It was my fault, I suppose [...] I'm bad at talking about these things. I thought, being a doctor, you'd probably warn me if … well, there's no point in going into all that now.'[35] But any recriminations or regret give way to a renewed proposal of marriage, though one that is shadowed by Julian's admission of what Hilary has already discovered: that he has been investigating the possibility of joining the Royal Air Force.

Unlike Lisa and her husband, Hilary and Julian do not end the novel facing an uncertain future together but with a baby on the way to cement their bond. Julian cannot be united with Hilary until he manages to break away from his mother. This separation also involves confronting issues of personal and public identity, though these are different issues from those with which Hilary grapples. Julian's desire to be an actor has been tempered, over the course of the novel, by an anxiety centring on the fact that his successes at university and in amateur productions have been based on him playing grotesques, or 'character' roles, tied up with his self-consciousness about his good looks. But his mother also objects to him embarking on what she considers to be a frivolous career, and the climax of the novel involves her revealing what really lies at the root of her concerns. While a Voluntary

Aid Detachment nurse during the First World War, she had an affair with a Canadian soldier who was an actor in civilian life and who, having made her pregnant, married her, only for it to emerge that he already had a wife. She was rescued from this situation by the man Julian has hitherto believed to be his father, who was being treated in the hospital where she is stationed. Julian understands that the Canadian is the source of both his good looks and his acting ambitions, and his response on learning this news is to accept biology as destiny: 'I'm sorry. It must have been a pretty depressing job for you all these years, trying to lick me into a gentleman. I wish I could have done more about it. But I'm afraid what's come out, in the end, is just another cad of an actor.'[36] This deprecatory self-characterization, emerging in the wake of his mother's confession, is followed by his blunt announcement that he will marry Hilary, and, in the context, this seems less a bold assertion of independence and more a confirmation of his mother's fears that, having bad blood, he won't amount to anything.

But Jesi Egan's characterization of Renault's first novel *Purposes of Love* as 'inhabit[ing] the conventions of the romance genre novel' with 'ambivalence' applies equally to *Return to Night*, and the latter's climax seems to turn away from the wider socio-cultural factors that have surfaced over the course of the narrative, focusing instead on seeking a resolution for the psycho-sexual aspects of Hilary and Julian's affair.[37] Hilary returns home to find that a distressed Julian has visited in her absence, and she believes that she will be able to find him at the cave system he took her to on one of their early outings together. Overcoming her fears about descending into the caves, she finds Julian stripping himself naked, with the intention of immersing himself in a subterranean pool. Hilary has just returned from attending an 'obstructed delivery', which ended in the safe arrival of a baby boy, and Julian, unbeknownst to her, is dealing with the revelations about his own parenthood. It is therefore difficult to avoid reading this incident in the cave as a form of symbolic rebirth. More discomforting are Hilary's reflections as she cradles Julian in her arms: 'She would never bear a child to him. It would be too long before she could spare for its needs the love of which his own need had never been satisfied; before his mind was ready, her body would be too old.'[38] Having shown a degree of maturity and independence in telling his mother about his intentions towards Hilary, Julian is here resituated in the position of child, and the consequences of Hilary, potentially, occupying the space in Julian's psychic life from which his mother has just been displaced are not dwelt on.

The conclusion of *Kind Are Her Answers* is equally ambivalent, at least where Kit is concerned. Indeed, if anyone reaches a 'happy ending' in this novel, it would seem to be his wife Janet. Janet becomes involved with the Oxford Group (also called Buchmanites after their founder Frank Buchman), described by Robert Graves and Alan Hodge as '[t]he only notable revival of simple Christianity' in the interwar years.[39] A non-denominational religious movement aimed at encouraging spiritual self-awareness and enlightenment among its members, it focused on 'practice more than preaching', and for Janet it provides an opportunity for self-fulfilment that goes beyond the spiritual. During a visit to South Africa with her new friends, she finds, as Kit reflects, 'someone to take his place. The new relationship was likely to be free from the inconveniences of the last, for it was with a woman.'[40] Kit views this as a positive outcome, notwithstanding that it will still not be possible for him and Janet to divorce because of the strictures of the GMC regulations. For this reason, although Chrissie returns to Kit after her own marriage prospects are blighted by Pedlow's interference, Chrissie and Kit's relationship will have to remain on an insecure footing, and the implication is that, as has previously been the case, Chrissie will not remain faithful to him. Mutatis mutandis, Kit is likely to occupy the position in the ongoing relationship with Chrissie that Janet occupied in their marriage; it is Chrissie who seems likely to have the greater freedom. Thus, although the immediate threat of exposure to the disciplinary processes of his profession has been fended off, Kit's relationship with Chrissie nevertheless seems compromised, and the closing words of the novel, uttered by Chrissie, have a hollow ring: 'You're never going to be unhappy any more.'[41]

Kind Are Her Answers was published in May 1940, and, given the exigencies of the historical moment, it is perhaps not surprising that, as Sweetman observes, it was 'barely noticed' by reviewers.[42] One review that Sweetman cites condemns the novel as 'completely divorced from the everyday world'.[43] But this divorce is not as absolute as the reviewer, Anthony West of the *New Statesman and Nation*, implies, especially if one allows the 'everyday' to encompass matters other than the explicitly political or the conduct of the war. *Return to Night* had a higher profile on its publication in July 1947, not least because it won the MGM Award, given by the film company to a novel in the expectation that they would then make a film based on it. (The award, in its third year when Renault received it, was curtailed in 1948, and no film was ever made of *Return to Night*.[44]) Perhaps inevitably, some critics saw the awarding of a financial prize by a film company as bearing inverse relation to the novel's literary qualities. Michael Sadleir, writing in the *Sunday Times*, suggested that the reader could be forgiven for thinking that *Return to Night* was a first novel and that the author's work would improve once she 'learnt to simplify and leave out', before reflecting facetiously on the mismatch between MGM's verdict and his own:

> Yet not only is *Return to Night* not a prentice effort: it has been awarded a prize of £40,000 by M.G.M and is to be filmed. Clearly something is badly

wrong with the responses and critical judgment of the present writer. So be it: each of us has a blind spot and can only grope in the darkness of an individual unenlightenment.[45]

Sadleir, a champion of neglected Victorian writers and the author himself of a popular best-seller, *Fanny by Gaslight* (1940), describes Julian as a '"Peg's Paper" Adonis'. This is a reference to the popular story-based women's magazine that had ceased publication in 1940, and which was critiqued by George Orwell in his essay 'Boys' Weeklies' for offering its working-class target readership 'a pure fantasy-world', despite its surface realism.[46] The implication is that in her depiction of Julian, Renault draws not only on a stereotype with a sub-literary pedigree (even given that Sadleir might be expected to have a broader sense of the category of 'literature' than some other commentators), but on one that is outdated.

But the mixing of fantasy and reality, and the difficulty, if not impossibility, of reconciling the two, is precisely what is at stake in Renault's novels. This difficulty is signalled by their inconclusive endings, and by the move, criticized by Sadleir, from technically exact descriptions of operations to scenes of romance (or the segue Hilary makes from examining Julian's incision to stroking his hair). These transitions may indeed be awkward for the reader, but it is an awkwardness which reflects the challenges of balancing professional and personal aspects of identity. What becomes painfully apparent is that these aspects, which one might wish to keep separate, are intricately and indissolubly woven into each other; nor can they be segregated from the additional pressures of gendered expectations. As Renault's first readers would have known all too well, in the face of war, the scrutiny of private life and the pressure to place duty over and above desire would become even more pronounced, and not only for members of the medical profession.

Notes

1 Nicola Humble, *The Feminine Middlebrow Novel, 1920s to 1950s: Class, Domesticity, and Bohemianism* (Oxford: Oxford University Press, 2001), p. 109.
2 *Ibid.*, p. 111.
3 Elaine Thomson, 'Between Separate Spheres: Medical Women, Moral Hygiene and the Edinburgh Hospital for Women and Children', in *Medicine, Health and the Public Sphere in Britain, 1600–2000*, ed. Steve Sturdy (London: Taylor and Francis, 2002), p. 108.
4 *Ibid.*, p. 109.
5 Mary Renault, *Kind Are Her Answers* (London: Virago, [1940] 2014), p. 18.

6 *Ibid.*, p. 8.
7 Mary Renault, *Return to Night* (London: Virago, [1947] 2014), pp. 3–4.
8 *Ibid.*, p. 76.
9 *Ibid.*, p. 1.
10 Victoria Stewart, 'Objects, Things and Clues in Early Twentieth-Century Fiction', *Modernist Cultures* 14.2 (2019), pp. 178–9.
11 Renault, *Kind Are Her Answers*, p. 14.
12 *Ibid.*, p. 14.
13 *Ibid.*, p. 27.
14 Renault, *Return to Night*, p. 63.
15 Margaret Lane, 'Life or Death for Your Doctor', *Daily Mail*, 27 May 1937, p. 12.
16 Renault, *Return to Night*, p. 328.
17 Lane, 'Life or Death', p. 12.
18 Anon, 'General Medical Council: Disciplinary Cases', *British Medical Journal Supplement*, 19 June 1937, p. 398.
19 Cyril Martin, 'Struck-Off Doctor Leaves His Home', *Daily Mail*, 31 May 1937, pp. 13–14.
20 Renault, *Kind Are Her Answers*, p. 53.
21 *Ibid.*, p. 94.
22 *Ibid.*, p. 128.
23 *Ibid.*, p. 128.
24 Renault, *Return to Night*, p. 35.
25 *Ibid.*, p. 36.
26 *Ibid.*, p. 247.
27 *Ibid.*, p. 108.
28 *Ibid.*, p. 113.
29 *Ibid.*, p. 145.
30 *Ibid.*, p. 246.
31 Anon., 'Numbers of the Profession', *British Medical Journal*, 3 September 1938, p. 488; Anon, 'Women in Medicine', *British Medical Journal*, 3 September 1938, p. 524.
32 Renault, *Return to Night*, pp. 247–8.
33 *Ibid.*, p. 336.
34 *Ibid.*, p. 17.
35 *Ibid.*, p. 362.
36 *Ibid.*, p. 402.
37 Jesi Egan, 'Cultural Futurity and the Politics of Recovery: Mary Renault's Ambivalent Romances', *MFS: Modern Fiction Studies* 62.3 (2016), p. 475.
38 Renault, *Return to Night*, p. 417.
39 Robert Graves and Alan Hodge, *The Long Week-End: A Social History of Great Britain, 1918–1939* (New York: Norton, [1940] 1994), p. 194.
40 Renault, *Kind Are Her Answers*, p. 285.
41 *Ibid.*, p. 291.
42 David Sweetman, *Mary Renault: A Biography* (London: Pimlico, 1994), p. 88.

43 Ibid., p. 88.
44 The other British winner of the award was Elizabeth Goudge. The film adaptation of her historical novel *Green Dolphin Street* (1944) was released in 1947. The remaining three winning novels also had nineteenth-century settings. They were Elizabeth Metzger Howard's *Before the Sun Goes Down* (1946), Ross Lockridge's *Raintree County* (1948), and Esther Forbes's *The Running of the Tide*, the 1947 winner, which was unpublished at the time of the award but appeared in 1948. The adaptation of *Raintree County* was released in 1957, but like the proposed adaptation of Renault's novel, the other two were not produced. Anon, 'MGM Drops Story Prize', *New York Times*, 26 May 1948, p. 29.
45 Michael Sadleir, 'A La Carte', *Sunday Times*, 31 August 1947, p. 3.
46 George Orwell, 'Boys' Weeklies' [1940], in *The Complete Works of George Orwell: A Patriot After All, 1940–1940 (XII)*, ed. Peter Davison (London: Secker and Warburg, 1998), p. 73.

2

Talking shop: Celia Fremlin and invisible work

Luke Seaber

The history of the study of literature is, amongst other things, the history of the rediscovery of authors and of attempts, successful or otherwise, to add their work to the canon, however that canon may be conceived.[1] In the case of the novelist Celia Fremlin (1914–2009), this work, which yet awaits canonicity, would appear to comprise the nineteen volumes (sixteen novels and three short-story collections) published between 1958 and 1994. This chapter will not aim to bring Fremlin into the fold of canonicity, however. This is not because her work does not 'merit' it, whatever that may mean; rather, it is because to focus first on explaining *why* one should consider a writer's work is to have a tacit acceptance of a state of affairs where, as Patrick Collier warns against in a different – though related – context, 'we are content to write off the majority of literary production as beneath our notice or to relegate it to the status of "context"'.[2] If we are interested in exploring the various factors and forces, both synchronic and diachronic, that meet at the intersections of public and private, text and life, then we should show ourselves open to reading without straining to justify *a priori* whom and what we are reading. What follows will examine Celia Fremlin as a case of how the marginalization of a particular woman writer operated (and indeed continues to operate). It will focus on how work by and about women can be made invisible, both at its mid-century moment of creation and in its continuing absence of a critical afterlife. In doing so, we shall explore how the lack of recognition in the 1940s of Fremlin as a professional is paralleled by and elucidated by her later lack of canonicity as a writer (and indeed vice versa).

This chapter will interweave biographical material with analysis of Fremlin's work, examining chiefly the twin central question of her professional role as a sociological investigator on the one hand and why she has been so forgotten on the other. This will put this chapter in dialogue with Megan Faragher's examination of Fremlin in her book on public opinion polling in mid-century British culture and her analysis of how 'the new field of quantitative public opinion research was an a priori exclusionary one'.[3] Analysing her professional life will shed light not only on her canonical exclusion but also, it is hoped, on that of women authors more generally.

Much of what follows will be based on Chris Simmons's general introduction to the 2014 reprinting by Faber and Faber of the nineteen volumes of Fremlin's fiction and *There Isn't a Snake in the Cupboard: A Review of the Life of JH Fremlin*, an online biography of Celia Fremlin's elder brother, the nuclear physicist John Heaver Fremlin, by his children. The accuracy of these non-academic secondary sources must for the moment be taken on trust, as more detailed biographical investigation into Fremlin is an ongoing process. It is worth noting at this point the question of the tacit rules governing the *forms* of academic writing itself, and how these may influence academic canonicity as much as content can. In a culture of relatively rigid word counts – so many for a monograph, so many for an article, so many for a chapter – it is often difficult to justify having to spend a significant amount of those words on biography. Yet the more overlooked the author, the more that biographical, non-analytical, non-theoretical material is necessary. In that sense, bringing more overlooked writers to light as objects of study – which means more women, people of colour and those otherwise underrepresented – is discouraged in *practical* terms by the very fact of their being unknown.

Celia Margaret Fremlin was born on 20 June 1914 to Heaver Fremlin, a physician and researcher, and his wife Margaret (née Addiscott) in Hendon, then in Middlesex, now part of Greater London.[4] The family lived in Finchley in north London until 1920, when they moved to a farmhouse outside the village of Bedmond in Hertfordshire.[5] In 1923, John Fremlin began as a 'train boy' (that is, not a boarder) at the nearby Berkhamsted School, which was then under the headmastership of Charles Greene, Graham Greene's father.[6] Later that year, to be nearer the school, the family moved to the town of Berkhamsted itself, and Celia soon began at Berkhamsted School for Girls.[7] After Heaver Fremlin's retirement and move to the village of Ryarsh in Kent, Celia began boarding, remaining at Berkhamsted until going up to Somerville College, Oxford, in 1934 with a £60 Scholarship for Distinction in General Work to read Classics ('Greats').[8]

As she recounted later in life, when Nick Stanley interviewed her in 1981 due to her time working for Mass-Observation, after she came down from Oxford she took a path that greatly differed from that which might have been expected:

> Well of course when you do Greats you land up with a Classics degree which is of no use to man or beast unless you're planning to teach. The one thing I was determined not to do was teach. So I thought 'right, the thing I'm qualified in isn't a qualification for anything I want to do, therefore I must treat myself as unqualified, like any fourteen year old'. So what can you do if you are unqualified? – You can do low grade catering jobs. I saw an advertisement

in The New Statesman for a girl who wanted to share a nine shilling flat in Fulham with another girl – so we paid 4/6 each per week. So I got that and just went along and looked at noticeboards outside newsagents and just applied for the first job I saw, of some low grade catering nature. It so happened that the first job I got was as a counter hand at an Express Dairy.[9]

On the one hand, this may be fitted in to a wider 1930s phenomenon in Britain of middle-class youth 'going over' to the proletariat, as Valentine Cunningham has called it.[10] However, Fremlin's elder daughter Geraldine would in 2005 tell Chris Simmons that 'her mother was notorious within the home for embroidering the truth and was quite often caught out by her family for telling "little white lies"', which she attributed to her mother's creative streak and an almost ludic habit of self-fashioning.[11] It is in light of this trait (which should be read as a general underlying complication to nearly all discussion of Fremlin's life) that it is most valuable to consider Fremlin's account of her life in the late 1930s. According to the magazine produced by the Berkhamsted School for Girls, in 1938 'Celia Fremlin, who now has a flat in Oxford, in the intervals of her domestic duties is just finishing her thesis for B. Litt.'[12] The B.Litt was a research degree, not an undergraduate degree (notwithstanding its name); Fremlin was therefore presumably starting out on what she hoped would be an academic career. This supposition is borne out by her having been awarded the previous year the 'Margaret Pollock Research Scholarship of £100 at Somerville College, Oxford [where she] hope[d] to research in Logical Positivism'.[13] Recent research by Michael Kremer has revealed that Fremlin not only began but completed her B.Litt, the title of which was 'A Logical Examination of Non-Propositional Forms of Thought with Special Reference to Aesthetics', having her examination on it on 31 October 1938.[14] She also published two short articles in the philosophy journal *Analysis*, later to become one of the most important in the field: 'Must We Always Think in Propositions?' (5:2; January 1938) and 'Dialectical Grammar' (6:1; November 1938). This suggests her academic career was looking promising in 1938, and that her later account of her life after receiving her Classics degree is not accurate. Something happened to take her away from Oxford and research, and her later version misses out an important stage in her life.

What this was remains unknown, as do the 'domestic duties' in Oxford to which there is reference. This offers a further illustration of how doubly badly served non-canonical figures are. Whatever happened at this point in Fremlin's life is perhaps the single most important in terms of creating her career as a writer, but not only is her work little known and studied, the absence of research on her life means that important tools for approaching that work are lacking in their turn. Furthermore, the facet of Fremlin's character often makes engagement with the paratexts to her work frustratingly difficult – for instance, are the two minor biographical errors in the four and a half lines of the 'about the author' in the 1988 Pandora republication of *The Hours before Dawn* editorial carelessness or another example of Fremlin's often subtle self-fashioning?[15]

Although we should treat Fremlin's account of how she began doing 'low grade catering jobs' and similar in the late 1930s with caution, that she did these jobs is certain. It is out of them that there came her first book, *The Seven Chars of Chelsea*, published by Methuen in 1940.[16] This is an example of incognito social investigation, that is, works such as Jack London's *People of the Abyss* (1903), George Orwell's *Down and Out in Paris and London* (1933), or Barbara Ehrenreich's *Nickel and Dimed* (2001) 'detailing their authors' experiences whilst pretending to be poor'.[17] It can be divided into three parts: the preface and first chapter are theoretical, examining the nature of the author's project and middle- and upper-class views of women in domestic service; the four central chapters that follow contain accounts of Fremlin's work in domestic service of various types; the final seven chapters offer analysis of what Fremlin has experienced, as well as looking at the results of the 211 replies she received to a questionnaire that she sent out to mistresses of servants. The status of *The Seven Chars of Chelsea* is rather anomalous amongst Fremlin's work. It is not part of the fiction that makes up the vast majority of her literary output, but this (very rare) book is that which has received the most critical attention.[18] I have examined elsewhere how *The Seven Chars of Chelsea* 'deserves a place next to *The Road to Wigan Pier* as a masterpiece of insight into the problems of cross-class contact in Britain in the 1930s (and beyond)', and it is instructive in terms of canonicity and how it is constructed to consider these two works' different statuses.[19] Orwell's book is very much part of his oeuvre; Fremlin's is not. This is a related but separate question to that of canonicity. All of Orwell's work may be considered canonical due to Orwell's own canonicity, but within that such things as the great majority of his book reviews, for example, are not considered by the general reader as part of his oeuvre in the same way his novels or essays are.[20] Neither Fremlin nor her works are canonical, but her (non-canonical) oeuvre consists of her novels, leaving *The Seven Chars of Chelsea* not only outside the general canon but also not part of what one would find if searched for Fremlin's 'works' in the usual sense.

Tom Harrisson, one of the founders of Mass-Observation, either read *The Seven Chars of Chelsea* and was favourably enough impressed by it to contact Fremlin to offer her a job, or he read a review of the book with the same result; the record is unclear.[21] Fremlin performed various roles within Mass-Observation. She worked as an incognito social investigator, besides conducting interviews and collecting 'overheards'; as time went on, she also became more involved in the planning of surveys.[22] At least three publications coming out of her Mass-Observation work can be attributed to Fremlin, one of which would appear not to have been recognized as being part of her bibliography hitherto (although, as will be seen below, its attribution to her is not fully certain). The relationship between Fremlin's publications for Mass-Observation and Harrisson's deserves particular attention as a case study in how women's labour can be de-professionalized and made invisible. In 1943, the book *War Factory: A Report* was published. This account of life in a factory making secret electronics equipment had a signed introduction by Harrisson but was otherwise anonymous; however, it was all Fremlin's work. Earlier that year, 'Methods of Mass-Observation, with Particular Reference to Housing' was published in the periodical *Agenda: A Quarterly Journal of Reconstruction* under Fremlin's married name, Celia Goller (she had married Elia Goller in 1942). The only time that this appears with (hidden) reference to Fremlin is in Harrisson's rather disingenuous introduction to *War Factory*. He writes: 'The greater part of this investigation was undertaken by a highly trained and experienced Cambridge graduate, married, one child; she has worked with Mass-Observation for the past four years.'[23] This in itself is misleading: Fremlin was Oxford-educated and had been working for Mass-Observation since 1940, not 1939. Harrisson goes on to explain the normal workings of a Mass-Observation investigation, noting though that 'a team of trained objective observers working simultaneously' would be impossible 'owing to the small size of the unit and the difficult problems of "security" involved'.[24] Harrisson refers in a footnote to various recent papers offering 'critical accounts of Mass-Observation method'; one of these is that in '*Agenda* (Aug. 1943), by Celia Goller'[25] – which is to say, by the very woman of whom he is talking in the text above! The third work of Fremlin's for Mass-Observation is Chapter 5 of Tom Harrisson's posthumous *Living through the Blitz* (1976), as Harrisson himself noted (again, not without some disingenuousness, given that he speaks of a 'first draft').[26]

The case of 'Methods of Mass-Observation, with Particular Reference to Housing' and Fremlin's absence from the paratext of *War Factory* merits further consideration. Faragher notes that 'Fremlin never received recognition for her work as a professional sociologist' in *War Factory*;[27] this is true, but reading her article alongside the section in Harrisson's introduction headed 'Method: Quantitative or Qualitative?' suggests that this was not solely a *general* case of a male authority marginalizing a female voice. Something more specific and much more complex also seems to be happening here. Harrisson writes:

> It is easy to believe that by asking a 'random sample' of two thousand people what they think about the Prime Minister, you have achieved something socially scientific. Actually, at best you have found out what they say to a stranger in the street, which may widely differ from what they *think*.[28]

This is a summary of the opening section, a page and a half long, of Goller's article. She makes no reference to the prime minister in her article, however, only to what people say and what people think about 'existing leaders' in general, writing, '"Public" opinion about existing leaders, existing legislation, present indisputable facts, is almost always more favourable, more accepting, than "private" opinion.'[29] If we turn to the typescript entitled 'Methods of Mass-Observation, with Particular Reference to Housing' in the Mass-Observation Archive, we find, as it were, the missing link between Harrisson's summary and Goller's article. There, the opening section contains specific details of the sorts of differences that the published piece discusses in generalities:

> The history of Chamberlain, as recorded by Mass-Observation methods, shows a different development. [...] Private opinion and feeling against him was, in fact, steadily gaining momentum, while public opinion (as expressed to a street interviewer) remained predominantly in his favour.[30]

It would therefore thus far suggest that Harrisson is not only openly but disingenuously using Goller's piece to provide a theoretical support for Fremlin's work, but also directly working from the draft of it to make his own points. We meet here a problem, however. The archival typescript is attributed neither to Celia Goller nor Celia Fremlin, but to H.D. Willcock (who was placed in overall control of Mass-Observation by Harrisson on the latter's being called up for active military service, which took place when *War Factory* was already substantially underway).[31] Who, then, was the author of 'Methods of Mass-Observation, with Particular Reference to Housing'? Willcock certainly did write a piece on Mass-Observation methods that came out in 1943; this, 'Mass-Observation', appeared in the prestigious academic journal *The American Journal of Sociology*, and indeed was included in Harrisson's footnote list of 'critical accounts of Mass-Observation method'.[32] Without the complication of the attribution in the typescript heading, it would be very easy to read this as another example of the de-professionalization of the female writer, whose work appears in a less prestigious, less academic, forum. If Willcock was the true author of the Goller piece, though, this interpretation clearly cannot stand. This remains a mystery still to be resolved, but it once again highlights the difficulties inherent in working on an author to whom little attention has been paid.

There is very obviously something important happening here in terms of who publishes and who receives credit for that publication, but a lack of underlying *factual* research makes analytical research into texts and events something that must always come with a caveat: we very often simply do not yet know enough to make firm statements.[33] Such a caveat, of course, is in its frustrating indeterminacy yet another factor discouraging work on those who are already overlooked.

War Factory marked the end of the period of Fremlin's near-full-time work for Mass-Observation.[34] She settled down into the life of a Hampstead housewife, writing and publishing the occasional short story; it would, perhaps, be fair to presume that hers was to be another case of a woman whose early academic and literary promise had all too sadly been subsumed into caring for children and a husband and the labour of housework. As we shall see, even if Fremlin had never written or published anything again after 1943, this reading would be problematic in Fremlin's view in its implicit dismissal of the housewife's importance, but return to publishing she did, and triumphantly so.

In 1958, she published her first novel, *The Hours before Dawn*. It was a success, winning the Edgar Award for best mystery novel of 1959 (its US publication date) in 1960. She continued publishing novels and short stories to critical and commercial success for the next thirty-six years, her final novel being *King of the World*, which came out in 1994.[35] Having outlived her two husbands (Elia Goller committed suicide in 1968; in 1985 she had married Leslie Minchin, who died in 1999) and three children, Fremlin died in a nursing home in Bournemouth in 2004, very much a forgotten figure; she had an obituary written by her niece published in the *Guardian*'s 'Other Lives' feature of obituaries for the non-famous[36] and a short obituary in *The Times*, but otherwise her passing went unremarked.[37] Her obituary in *The Times* suggests the subject matter of her novels as well as pointing to a reason why she may have become overlooked: 'Publishers by then [1981] sometimes treated her novels as mere precursors of the "woman in jeopardy" genre that Ruth Rendell exploited with such success (when writing as Barbara Vine).'[38] Fremlin's novels are thrillers focusing on middle-class women, usually housewives; novels like those of Ruth Rendell/Barbara Vine, with their grittier tone and more explicit psychological rather than sociological focus, I would argue, led to Fremlin's work looking overly lower-middlebrow, as it were, and unadventurous in its domestic settings and relationships that were generally neither particularly happy nor unhappy but simply *quotidian*. This is obliquely hinted at in Fremlin's preface to the 1988 Pandora re-publication in the Women Crime Writers series:

I'd like to assure readers that I did *not* mean the husband to be any kind of a 'monster'. In fact, although this is a crime story, I did not intend *any* of my characters to be monsters of iniquity. Rather, they are ordinary, well-intentioned people caught in a dilemma that is too big for them.[39]

It is, in many ways, ultimately the *dilemma* that interests Fremlin, I would argue. This is not to argue that she is uninterested in character drawing, or at all incapable of it. Rather, I would suggest, her novels are interested in intersecting social and societal pressures in terms of individuals' responses thereto more than they are in those responses themselves. Judy Giles has written that *The Seven Chars of Chelsea* 'is unusual in that its structures and modes of expression blur the conventional disciplinary boundaries between sociology and literature'.[40] This though, as I have explored elsewhere with reference to *Appointment with Yesterday* (1972) is true above all of Fremlin's fiction: it offers a perhaps unparalleled sociology of middle-class British women, above all with regards to housewives (including, importantly, those who are no longer housewives, with all that that implies) in the second half of the twentieth century.[41]

In this sense, Fremlin's scope can be seen as (deliberately) restricted, focusing overwhelmingly on middle-class housewives. Of course, the very fact that such an in-depth body of work on so large and important a group of people could be considered as 'restricted' is in itself indicative of the problems faced when discussing a figure like Fremlin. However, it is also this domestic scope of Fremlin's novels that has led to some rediscovery of her work with the increased popularity of, and interest in, 'domestic noir'. This label was coined by the novelist Julia Crouch in 2013,[42] and her 2018 definition of it is extremely relevant to Fremlin, who is very much a writer of it *avant la lettre*, although Fremlin also offers much more besides: 'Domestic noir puts the female experience at the centre. The main themes are family, motherhood, children, marriage, love, sex and betrayal. Setting is important: the home a character inhabits, and the way they inhabit it, can tell us as much about them as what they say or do.'[43] This centring of the *female* experience is of course key not only to Fremlin's novels and short stories – her 'domestic noir' – but also to her sociological work.

In terms of academic attention, no single novel of Fremlin's has received the – admittedly very limited – attention that *The Seven Chars of Chelsea* has.[44] *Appointment with Yesterday* (1972) has been examined in terms of how it offers a fictionalized version of the incognito social investigation that she carried out for her first book and for Mass-Observation;[45] Megan Faragher has explored how *The Hours before Dawn* 'emphasizes [the] same discrepancy between the supposed experts and the authentic experiences and feelings of women' that Fremlin chronicles in *War Factory* and elsewhere in her Mass-Observation work.[46] Other than these two cases, Fremlin's novels remain massively under-explored by literary scholars. This lack of academic attention paid to Fremlin's literary output mirrors, in a different field, her de-professionalization by Harrisson, and its implied overlooking of works centring the female experience also mirrors wider questions of female-centred methodologies in Fremlin's work, as we shall now examine.

Although Fremlin never published any further sustained non-fiction other than the occasional article in publications such as *The Ethical Record*, the journal of the Conway Hall Ethical Society (Fremlin was active in the work of Conway Hall and the Progressive League), in the late 1970s and early 1980s, she began working on a new research project. She began walking the streets of London by night, particularly areas like Hackney and Brixton that were deemed to be especially dangerous.[47] As she recounted it in 1987, 'She began out of curiosity. Later her experiences developed into a book'; this, it would appear, was called *The Mugging and the Myths*, but it never found a publisher.[48] Sadly, this was almost certainly destroyed, as her archive 'was cut down twice, once when she moved from a large flat to a tiny warden-assisted one, and again at her death, no one having the space to store such a massive archive'.[49] Once again, we see how the marginalization of an author is a vicious circle: there was clearly not enough interest in Fremlin for her archive to be saved; this in turn means that to work on her academically now is to have that work hampered by lack of archival material, thus making it not only more difficult for academics to produce it but also less likely that they will do so.[50]

This gendered question of what is considered a suitable object of study is mirrored in Fremlin's own views on what she was doing in her work for Mass-Observation. Harrisson's presentation of what Fremlin and Mass-Observation were doing in *War Factory* focuses on what is (potentially) *discovered*. That is, the ultimate interest of the material lies not in the material itself but in what it tells those analysing it and those reading that analysis. For example, on the one hand, he stresses what comes out of the evidence collected by Fremlin: 'the *results* suggest certain mental conditions among a number of female workers';[51] on the other, when he compares *War Factory* favourably with Marie Jahoda's 1941 'Some Socio-Psychological Problems of Factory Life' and does talk of that evidence, he more or less explicitly valorizes it because of how it can be used rather than because of any inherent interest: 'Such imposing vocabulary [Jahoda's] might carry the weight if supported by correspondingly elaborate *evidence*.'[52] This results-focused stance of Harrisson's, where (so to speak) one may throw away the ladder of evidence gained by the observer after one has climbed up it, is implicitly countered in what Fremlin wrote for the 1987 Cresset Library republication of *War Factory*. She begins by noting her unawareness that her results were to be handed on to factory management, and that had she known, she would have felt somewhat more uneasy about what she was doing. Nonetheless, she would, she thinks, still have carried out the project. The reason why, though, she would still have thought it valid and important work – and by extension thought, and thinks, the same of Mass-Observation's work in general – is revealing:

> In any case, this all seemed to me to be of only passing significance in comparison with the historical perspective within which M-O was operating. I felt we were providing unique material for future historians. I still do. How exciting it would be if we had a record of the Trojan war through the eyes of an ordinary housewife or trader within those walls, and not solely through the eyes of warrior-kings and heroes, as interpreted by tragic poets.[53]

Pace Harrisson, the importance of the material that Mass-Observation collected lies not in what is done with it, but in the very fact of its having been collected. There is something in what Fremlin suggests here that we might almost call an academic negative capability: she sees the merit in gathering information without reaching after analyses thereof; unlike in Harrisson's view, the ultimate interest of the material lies in itself rather than in what it may lead to. Fremlin feels no need to make what she discovers her own, as it were; this belief in the importance of what she was doing is – unexpectedly, paradoxically – denied Harrisson, whose need to make protestations of the usefulness of Fremlin's anonymous work belies those very claims. Fremlin is happy to be an ancillary, and the etymological gendering of that word is of course relevant: the handmaid, the *ancilla*, can bring the same otherwise absent insights to the methodologies of historians and sociologists as the Trojan house*wife* can to the contents of their work.

This brings us to something that may go some way towards suggesting why Fremlin has been so overlooked a figure, not only amongst Faragher's 'supposed experts whose failure to hear women's stories leaves them blind to the truths under their noses',[54] but also amongst the various waves of feminist critics and academics who have also tended not to engage with her work. Fremlin was for many years active in giving talks at Conway Hall; she also on occasion provided written summaries of them for *The Ethical Record*. She gave one such talk on 9 November 1965, with a written summary of 'A Housewife Looks at Affluence' appearing in the March 1966 number of the journal. This examines why, labour-saving appliances and material plenty notwithstanding, 'the housewife today, who has so much more of everything than her grandmother, complains as she has never done before'.[55] She begins with a veiled criticism, not so much of 'experts' as of their relationship vis-à-vis those whom they would describe, that confirms

Faragher's thesis: 'First, I must explain how it is that a mere housewife should venture to tackle a subject which you may feel to be the province of qualified experts – sociologists, economists, psychologists and so forth.'[56] In this, and in the brief but dense analysis that follows, Fremlin is clearly setting the record straight, so to speak, giving a housewife's voice to counter those external (male) 'experts' who presume to talk for her and other women – not for nothing does she set out her stall at the very beginning as a '*mere* housewife'. It may appear, though, that there is a touch of disingenuousness here; by 1965 she had already published five novels, after all. I would argue that to read that 'mere' in this way would be to fall into a trap Fremlin is laying. Later on in her piece, she goes on to say, 'I don't want to give the impression from all this that the lot of the modern affluent housewife is a miserable one; on the contrary, it is a most challenging and exciting one, and many women enjoy it immensely.'[57] She in no way conveys any impression that housework, that the housewife's job, is any way something that a woman should not have to do, that it is not work that can be enjoyed in itself as any other job can. 'Mere' cuts both ways as a piece of irony: it is most obviously levelled at presumed (male) experts who would not listen to a housewife, but it is also implicitly levelled at (female) experts of a different type who would relegate the *work* of a housewife to the status of something not deserving of discussion except insofar as 'we housewives have been forced into a position of vast and unsought importance in the economy'.[58] In other words, we have here a similar view to that expressed in the 1987 *War Factory* preface: just as the non-elite minutiae genderedly collected by Mass-Observation hold importance and interest in their own right, so too does the non-elite gendered work of the housewife hold *intrinsic* importance and interest.

The key word here, ultimately, is 'work'; female work and its invisibility is central to Fremlin's life, thought, and writing. Just as her presence in her work for Mass-Observation was made invisible and the work itself discussed in a way inimical to her own desires and hopes regarding it, so does housework appear as invisible as something important in its own right, something husbands in her fiction expect to take place without noticing it, and, when 'society' notices it, it is to discuss it in a way inimical to housewives' possible desires and hopes. These two cases of invisible work are different in their proximate causes: Fremlin's work was *made* invisible due to the fact that she was not given authorial credit for her 1940s work; housework in her novels (and society more generally) is taken for granted and noticed only in its absence without anyone else taking the credit for it. The ultimate cause, though, surely lies in a shared devaluing of women and their work. Thus, Fremlin observes women's work in *War Factory*, but the woman's work of writing that makes this otherwise invisible labour visible is in turn made invisible by Harrisson. Housework too is invisible, except when the housewife is either a role to be marketed to regardless of how much the individual may dislike it or to be abolished however much the individual may enjoy it. Perhaps the most succinct statement of Fremlin's position on this comes in *The Hours before Dawn*. The protagonist, Louise, is a housewife and mother, and it is very clear from Fremlin's description of her that these two states may as well be one. They are both, ultimately, part of the same job. Early on in the novel, Louise stops herself from talking too much about her children to her new lodger: 'To talk shop if you are a mother is not socially permissible as it is if you are a typist or bus conductress.'[59] Fremlin believed that the stereotypical, archetypal woman's work *was* work, work of intrinsic value. Her insistence on this but refusal to play by others' rules and make it *too* explicit herself has, I would argue, led to work on her falling victim to the same process that she describes and quietly and subtly bemoans. Fremlin's literary work has become invisible as part of the same process that she describes in her non-literary work (itself made invisible) of physical work that too many people consider invisible. This chapter is an attempt to begin the triple unearthing that Fremlin (like so many other unjustly forgotten figures) deserves.

Notes

1 Some of the research leading to this chapter has received funding from the People Programme (Marie Curie Actions) of the European Union's Seventh Framework Programme (FP7/2007–2013) under REA Grant Agreement No. 298208.
2 Patrick Collier, *Modern Print Artefacts: Textual Materiality and Literary Value in British Print Culture, 1890–1930s* (Edinburgh: Edinburgh University Press, 2016), p. 233.
3 Megan Faragher, *Public Opinion Polling in Mid-Century British Literature: The Psychographic Turn* (Oxford: Oxford University Press, 2021), p. 18.
4 For information on her parents, John Fremlin and Margaret Fremlin, *There Isn't a Snake in the Cupboard: A Review of the Life of J. H. Fremlin*, http://margaret.fremlin.org/one.html (accessed 23 July 2021); for her place of birth, www.freebmd.org.uk/cgi/information.pl?cite=OIvmG7%2FPEuMS759dJ5FC0w&scan= (accessed 23 July 2021).
5 http://margaret.fremlin.org/two.html (accessed 23 July 2021).
6 *Ibid.*
7 *Ibid.*; http://margaret.fremlin.org/three.html (accessed 23 July 2021); Chris Simmons, 'Preface', in Celia Fremlin, *Uncle Paul* (London: Faber and Faber, 2014), pp. 1–6, pp. 1–2.

8 http://margaret.fremlin.org/four.html (accessed 23 July 2021); 'Prizes and Certificates', *Chronicle of the Berkhamsted School for Girls* (July 1934), pp. 10–12, p. 11.
9 Mass Observation Archive, Brighton, The Keep, SxMOA32/32/5. Reproduced with permission of Curtis Brown, London on behalf of the Trustees of the Mass Observation Archive, © The Trustees of the Mass Observation Archive.
10 Valentine Cunningham, *British Writers of the Thirties* (Oxford: Oxford University Press, 1988), pp. 241–55. See also Luke Seaber, *Incognito Social Investigation in British Literature: Certainties in Degradation* (Cham: Palgrave Macmillan, 2017), pp. 62–3 and Luke Seaber, 'Kings in Disguise and "Pure Ellen Kellond": Literary Social Passing in the Early Twentieth Century', in *Working-Class Writing: Theory and Practice*, ed. Ben Clarke and Nick Hubble (Cham: Palgrave Macmillan, 2018), pp. 81–98, pp. 92–3.
11 Simmons, p. 1.
12 'Oxonians', 'Old Girls' News and College Letters: News from Oxford', *Chronicle of the Berkhamsted School for Girls* (July 1938), p. 62. Reproduced by permission, Berkhamsted School 2020.
13 'Editorial', *Chronicle of the Berkhamsted School for Girls* (July 1937), pp. 1–3, p. 2. Reproduced by permission, Berkhamsted School 2020.
14 Private correspondence with Michael Kremer and Christoph Schuringa, to whom I am extremely grateful. This and other information came to me as this chapter was being readied for publication, unfortunately too late to explore here of its further implications.
15 Her work for Mass-Observation was *not* in its archives, and she did *not* begin her writing career in the 1950s.
16 In his notes to his 1980 interview with Fremlin, Angus Calder notes the unfortunate timing – the book came out 'just as the war broke out – and sank it'. Mass Observation Archive, Brighton, The Keep, SxMOA32/32/4. Reproduced with permission of Curtis Brown, London on behalf of the Trustees of the Mass Observation Archive, © The Trustees of the Mass Observation Archive.
17 Seaber, *Incognito Social Investigation*, p. 1.
18 There are two sustained academic engagements with Fremlin's first book: Judy Giles, *The Parlour and the Suburb: Domestic Identities, Class, Femininity and Modernity* (Oxford and New York: Berg, 2004), pp. 81–7; Seaber, *Incognito Social Investigation*, pp. 189–201.
19 Seaber, *Incognito Social Investigation*, p. 203.
20 See Luke Seaber. 'Private Faces in Public Places: Auto-Intertextuality, Authority and 1930s Fiction', in *The 1930s: A Decade of British Fiction*, ed. Nick Hubble, Luke Seaber, and Elinor Taylor (London: Bloomsbury Academic, 2021), pp. 183–206, pp. 191–2 for the argument that what is canonical in Orwell's work changes over time.
21 In Angus Calder's interview of 17 March 1980, he notes 'But Tom Harrisson saw a review of it and wrote to her' (Mass Observation Archive, Brighton, The Keep, SxMOA32/32/4); in Nick Stanley's interview of 18 September 1981, she states 'What happened was that Tom Harrisson had read my book about

the Seven Chars of Cholera and he wrote a very nice review of it in *The News Chronicle* and then he wrote to me and said "you seem to be the sort of person that I want for studying the attitudes to A.R.P. Would you like to come and talk to me?" I said "yes"' (Mass Observation Archive, Brighton, The Keep, SxMOA32/32/5).

22 James Hinton, *The Mass Observers: A History, 1937–1949* (Oxford: Oxford University Press, 2013), pp. 171–2.
23 Tom Harrisson, 'Industrial Survey', in *War Factory: A Report* (London: Faber and Faber, 2009), pp. 5–11, p. 6.
24 Ibid., pp. 6–7.
25 Ibid., n. 1 to p. 6.
26 Tom Harrisson, *Living through the Blitz* (Faber and Faber: London, 2010), p. 17.
27 Faragher, *Public Opinion Polling*, p. 162.
28 Harrisson, 'Industrial Survey', p. 7; emphasis in original.
29 Celia Goller, 'Methods of Mass-Observation, with Particular Reference to Housing', *Agenda: A Quarterly Journal of Reconstruction* (August 1943), pp. 255–65, p. 256. I owe thanks to Victoria Stewart for identifying this journal for me.
30 Mass Observation Archive, Brighton, The Keep, FR 1626–7, p. 4; emphasis in original.
31 Hinton, *The Mass Observers*, p. 296, p. 308.
32 Harrisson, 'Industrial Survey', n. 1 to p. 6.
33 For what it is worth, the style of the piece attributed to Goller reads much more like Fremlin to me than it does Willcock. In terms of the question suggested at various points in this chapter about what is and what is not considered 'academic' when looking at a figure like Fremlin, though, note that I leave this observation to the obscurity of a learned endnote.
34 Faragher, *Public Opinion Polling*, p. 162.
35 It was not her last book published. In 1996, she and her second husband, Leslie Minchin, published *Duet in Verse: Some Occasional Poems*.
36 Margaret Kettlewell, 'Other Lives: Celia Fremlin', *Guardian* (7 September 2009), www.theguardian.com/theguardian/2009/sep/06/celia-fremlin-obituary (accessed 25 July 2022).
37 This is at least the case for the UK. Research is still ongoing on media in other countries and languages, although Fremlin's fame and reputation in the German-speaking world (greater than in the English-speaking world) suggests that there her death may have received more attention.
38 'Celia Fremlin', *The Times* (9 September 2009), p. 66.
39 Celia Fremlin, Preface to *The Hours before Dawn* (London: Pandora, 1988), pp. vii–viii, p. viii.
40 Giles, *The Parlour and the Suburb*, p. 27.
41 Seaber, *Incognito Social Investigation*, pp. 204–7.
42 Julia Crouch, 'Foreword: Notes from a Genre Bender', in *Domestic Noir: The New Face of 21st Century Crime Fiction*, ed. Laura Joyce and Henry Sutton (Cham: Palgrave Macmillan, 2018), pp. v–viii, p. vii.

43 *Ibid.*
44 It should be pointed out that the favouring of *academic* attention here continues (unavoidably given the context of this publication?) the marginalization of Fremlin and writers like her. There are various non-academic discussions of many of Fremlin's novels online on blogs devoted to crime fiction and in literary/cultural magazines, including one of the best things written on *The Hours before Dawn*, by an American academic in an online magazine 'of ideas, art, and scholarship': Leah Price, 'B-Sides: Celia Fremlin's "The Hours before Dawn"', *Public Books*, www.publicbooks.org/pb-staff-favorites-2017-b-sides-celia-fremlins-hours-dawn/ (accessed 30 July 2021). I am of course complicit in this spurious distinction between 'academic' and 'non-academic' sources that contributes to keeping marginalized writers marginalized by relegating Price's work to an endnote.
45 Seaber, *Incognito Social Investigation*, *ibid.*
46 Faragher, *Public Opinion Polling*, pp. 165–72, p. 165.
47 Steve Clarke, 'Scorning the Dread of Night', *Evening Standard* (22 January 1987), p. 23.
48 *Ibid.*
49 E-mail from Margaret Kettlewell, Fremlin's niece, 26 March 2013.
50 The only exceptions to the loss of Fremlin archival material of which I am aware are the very many pieces – collected though for reasons unrelated to the figure of Fremlin herself – in the Mass-Observation archive and, in the Howard Gotlieb Archival Research Center at the University of Boston, the manuscript for the novel *Prisoner's Base* (1967) and a holograph draft of a chapter from *The Spider-Orchid* (1977) written on the verso of the draft of a short story ('Test Case', first published in *A Lovely Day to Die* [1984]).
51 Harrisson, 'Industrial Survey', p. 8; emphasis mine.
52 *Ibid.*, p. 11; emphasis in original.
53 Celia Fremlin, 'Preface to the Cresset Library Edition', in 'Mass-Observation', *War Factory* (London: The Cresset Library, 1987), pp. vii–ix, p. viii. There are interesting parallels here with Bertolt Brecht's great poem of 1939, 'Fragen eines lesenden Arbeiters', which begins 'Wer baute das siebentorige Theben? / In den Büchern stehen die Namen von Königen. / Haben die Könige die Felsbrocken herbeigeschleppt' (Bertolt Brecht, 'Fragen eines lesenden Arbeiters', *Gesammelte Werke*, vol. 9 (Frankfurt am Main: Suhrkamp Verlag, 1967), pp. 656–7) (Who built Thebes of the seven gates? / In the books are the names of kings. / Did the kings drag the great rocks into place?; my translation) and ends 'So viele Berichte. / So viele Fragen' (So many reports. / So many questions; my translation). This was first published in 1939, so is very much of the period in which Fremlin was working; one might wonder, though, whether the echoes of it in the 1987 piece are due to her knowing the poem through her second husband, Leslie Minchin, who worked as a translator from German ('Celia Fremlin', *The Times* (9 September 2009), p. 66).
54 Faragher, *Public Opinion Polling*, p. 163.

55 Celia Fremlin, 'A Housewife Looks at Affluence', *Ethical Record* 71.3 (1966), pp. 10–11, p. 10.
56 *Ibid.*
57 *Ibid.*, p. 11.
58 *Ibid.*, p. 10.
59 Celia Fremlin, *The Hours before Dawn* (London: Pandora, 1988), p. 23.

3

'Some thoroughly tiresome housekeeping crisis': Rebecca West's wartime journalism

Debra Rae Cohen

In 1941, the *Atlantic* magazine excerpted, over the course of five monthly issues, huge dollops of Rebecca West's magnum opus *Black Lamb and Grey Falcon*. As West completed this manuscript in the early months of the war, and overlapping its publication, she also issued a series of short pieces addressed to her American readership – brief vignettes on the Blitz, on rationing, on housekeeping during wartime. These pieces for the *New Yorker*, the *Saturday Evening Post*, and other venues partake, I will argue, of some of the formal elements of the larger work, in which (as I've described elsewhere), West stages the interplay between public and private discourses, mixing the domestic and the panoramic in order to derive a multiple witnessing persona.[1] In these articles, too, she turns back on England itself the evocation of national character from collective quotidian practice that marks the landscape of *Black Lamb*. Read in this context, the pieces serve to illuminate both West's compositional practice and her gendered vision of the nation.

West had finally discovered the central organizing metaphor for *Black Lamb and Grey Falcon* on her third trip to Yugoslavia, in 1938, when the need to capture what she could of a world fast disappearing – Hitler had already absorbed Austria and was threatening Czechoslovakia – felt ever more urgent.[2] The shape of the minatory whole fell into place when she witnessed the aftermath of a fertility sacrifice – dead lambs, a slab of stone shining with blood, a child's forehead marked with the fluid, a sickening smell. As she wrote to her husband, Henry Maxwell Andrews, 'the sacrifice on the stone is now the clou of my book'[3] – an extended metaphor about the dangers of totalizing myth around which centred her complexly woven divagations about history, gender, local custom, and the dangerous distortions of imperial thinking.

But the assembling of what she often referred to as her 'incubus of a book' dragged on beyond the appeasement of Munich, the dismemberment of Czechoslovakia, the unsettling calm of 'the great bore war' of 1939–40.[4] Even as she rehearsed many of its overt arguments in her political columns – using a March 1940 'Notes on the Way' column in *Time and Tide*, for example, to laud the exemplary small state nationalism of the Finns, or, in a later article, reading arguments for pacifism as manifestations of the death drive[5] – she evoked in her descriptions of the wartime home front (staged – like *Black Lamb* in its initial publication – with West's American audience in mind) many of its more deep-seated concerns.

Carl Rollyson, West's most thorough biographer, says of *Black Lamb* that '[i]t is [West's] contention that what occurs on the world stage is connected to the private heart';[6] though Rollyson is apt to flatten this into the suggestion that she sees the potential for world-redemption in the heterosexual marriage,[7] he's astute in identifying the extent to which, as we'd say today, the personal is political for West. From the early days of her suffrage activism, through her scathing journalism and variegated fiction of the interwar period, West homed in repeatedly on how the private both shapes and echoes the public, the ways that domestic politics, domestic tyranny, bespeak the nation writ large. In *Black Lamb and Grey Falcon*, it is most often in the position of women – women 'deformed by the slavery of [their] ancestors'; women dressed, by the dictates of 'masculine tyranny', in 'cumbersome' garments 'heavy enough to wear down the strength of a bullock'; women whose traditional crafts, once the site of verve and joy, have been denatured by the tastes of their oppressors – who most clearly represent the nation distorted, crushed, or 'corrupted' by empire.[8]

And it is, as well, in women's crafts, women's faces, that West sees the potential for national life surviving under the yoke of history. The wealth of meaning lavishly spilling from a pile of embroidered dresses West spies, on her travels through Yugoslavia, in a Macedonian market – so different from the 'commercial peasant art' of Central Europe, moulded to German taste[9] – represents the improbable survival of the spark of a people:

> That they should remember glory, after they had been condemned for so long to be inglorious, is not to be taken for granted, as an achievement within the power of any in their place. A tradition is not a material entity that can survive apart from any human agency. It can live only by a people's power to grasp its structure, and to answer to the warmth of its fires.[10]

A similar power resides in the faces of women who insist on the principle of life in the face of the deathliness around them, such as one she glimpses in a photo and dubs 'the officer of earth':

> Such women have to suckle their children too long, because the kings and magi of the world have never yet been ready to take them over at their weaning and give them a liberal diet from the fields, such women all their lives eat only when their husbands and sons have had enough; so they are spare. If she

had found life so meanly disposed, why did she condemn her children to suffer it? She could not tell us; but on that point she is inflexible.[11]

On a hillside in Montenegro, West encounters another woman, whose very inflexibility and insistence on persisting proves the answer to West's doubts about the capacity for life to survive:

> She took her destiny not as the beasts take it, nor as the plants and trees; she not only suffered it, she examined it. As the sword swept down on her through the darkness she threw out her hand and caught the blade as it fell, not caring if she cut her fingers so long as she could question its substance, where it had been forged, and who was the wielder.[12]

This woman, West intuits, wants to comprehend 'the mystery of process' in order to understand 'what her life might mean'. The word 'process' is key to *Black Lamb*, resonating throughout the text as a kind of shorthand for the binding force of community that constitutes both national and international civilization. It is identified, notably, by its absence, in a central speech ventriloquized, like so many of the object lessons of the book, through West's husband Henry. In it, 'Henry' articulates the fatal flaw that characterizes Gerda, the German wife of West's (Slavic, Jewish) guide Constantine, a flaw that comes to stand for the imperial mindset at its most basic: 'Gerda has no sense of process'.[13] The speech traces the consequences of this moral blind spot from the domestic – Gerda's desire to 'enjoy the position of a wife' without the willingness to do the work of marriage – to the economic: she believes that she is superior because she 'cannot bake a loaf', but can afford to buy them 'born in [their] virginity of cellophane', to enjoy the 'results of processes without being concerned in the processes themselves'.[14] (One can hear contemporary echoes of this argument in Senator Elizabeth Warren's 'you didn't build it' speech.[15]) This is, says Henry, 'the conqueror's point of view', and writ large it augurs poorly for the near future of Europe: 'for a little while the whole of our world may belong to Gerda. She will snatch it out of hands too well-bred and compassionate and astonished to defend it'. And yet although this imperial mindset of entitlement is adequate for conquest – 'To go up in an aeroplane and drop bombs is a simple use of an elaborate process that has already been developed' – 'you cannot administer a country on this principle'.[16]

Positioned two-thirds of the way through West's vast tome, the speech is doubled in a number of senses: it both encapsulates and explicates both the book's minatory function and its philosophical core; 'process' stands in both for the sensitivity to connectivity and collective life West sees in the small nations doomed to serve as the bloodlands[17] of Empire and for the way that life is evoked in her compositional process, in the vertiginous wedding of anecdote and history, individual chronicle and civilizational sweep. If 'process' thus represents the life-affirming values West is anxious to preserve, it also captures the way in which private, small-scale actions and manifestations of value are inextricable from the currents of history.

This multiply-valenced notion of process as both subject and address, form and content, shapes the wartime articles as well, and serves to mark West's increasingly nuanced reading of home front epistemologies. Wartime, at first notable only for and in its lacks – distinguishable only by its absence of 'order', its status as state of exception[18] – gradually becomes discernible *as* process, and the capacity for discernment once more an index of civilized humanity.

West details war not in its sweep and sacrifice – the terms of the rejected bargain of *Black Lamb* – but from within the mundane struggle of the everyday and the sphere of domesticity. She thus anticipates both contemporary approaches to 'wartime' that Beryl Pong details in her introduction to the recent *Modernism/modernity* Print Plus cluster on the subject.[19] Like Jan Mieszkowski and others, West (as *Black Lamb* testifies) is highly cognizant of the historical currents that redefine the *longue durée* of war culture.[20] And like Mary Favret, she recognizes wartime as primarily an *affective* mode; her early articles echo Favret's observation that 'war itself does not necessarily *make sense*. Indeed, wartime is often the experience of an undoing or damaging of rational sense – which is to say that war, even at a distance, works to dismantle the forms that prop up our sense of the world and our place in it'.[21]

Indeed, West's first home front piece, 'The First Fortnight', published in the January 1940 *Ladies' Home Journal*,[22] is a comparatively straightforward account of the dismantling of those forms over the weeks leading up to and following the declaration of war – the shuttling of various domestic servants and their dependents from London to the Andrewses' rented country home in Sussex,[23] the serendipitous descent of various refugees, the ill-sorted emotional responses of the household to the stresses of the news. While West chronicles her own visceral response to the announcement of the Hitler–Stalin pact – 'For a second my bowels slid about inside me'[24] – she largely shows the displacement of anxieties onto the mechanics of process, a metonymizing that becomes the central compositional technique of the articles that follow. It is not just that, as she says here, one cannot spend all one's time responding in horror to events because 'there is so much to do' – it is that the material conditions of home-front life themselves prove the best corollaries for dread.[25]

The character of the war, West concludes in this first piece, is that 'something is trying to make nonsense of life' – and, she says, 'The housewife is certainly going to experience this to the full.'[26] Far from being a sop to the *LHJ* readership, however, this line presages the extent to which housekeeping itself emerges in West's articles as an emblem of the nation attempting to assert and comprehend process in the face of what seems to be the 'nonsense' of its erosion. In the first of her wartime dispatches for the *New Yorker*, in December 1940 – a 'Reporter at Large' column titled 'Housewife's Nightmare' – she lays this out clearly:

> There are aspects of this crisis in world affairs which, I feel sure, historians of the future are going to neglect. They will tell you much that is terrible and much that is glorious, and both will be true. … It is true that when one's people are defending their right to live, their courage gives one an immeasurable exaltation, but at the same time something else is happening. If you want to imagine what this something else is, think back to some thoroughly tiresome housekeeping crisis – that time when you were just going to have a baby and the other children got measles, or when the Swedish cook went mad, or when you were snowed in and the heating system and the cookstove went out of order. That is the true analogue of life on the domestic plane in wartime England.[27]

This vertiginousness of home front life, manifested in Elizabeth Bowen's Blitz fictions as the uncanny, West articulates as 'seasickness': in a letter to her American friend Irita Van Doren in December 1940, at the height of the Blitz, she explained that the war was 'like the stage of seasickness when you are not sure you are seasick but realise that everything but seasickness has ceased to exist' – because 'the connective tissue of life has gone'.[28] West renders the affect of this eradication of 'connective tissue' in a host of phrases that conjure up an unstable zone somewhere between no-man's land and bohemia: 'camping out', 'domiciliary promiscuity', 'makeshift collectivism', 'the sluttish way of living that war forces on one' – each emphasizing the bourgeois household as itself the orderly norm.[29] This affective dishevelment is repeatedly contrasted to the 'shapeliness and definiteness' of (post-Dunkirk) military operations: 'From an airdrome behind some houses, a squadron of fighters was rising in battle formation, as precisely aligned and synchronized as an ideal *corps de ballet*.'[30]

It's important to recognize that this shift to domestic scale by West is in no sense a diminishment – no more than was her juxtaposition, in her 1928 critical manifesto 'The Strange Necessity', of James Joyce's poetry and shopping for hats.[31] Nor, despite the important corollary of the 'seasickness' metaphor – that it implies the ability to develop 'sea legs' – can it be simply comfortably folded into the myth of the Blitz. If the classic keep-calm-and-carry-on-ish media artefacts of Blitz life that we associate with that myth – the photos of the white-coated milkman striding through the ruins, bottles intact, the barber giving haircuts in a bombed-out building – demonstrate the continuity of masculine labour in despite, West's chronicle the increasingly arbitrary, circuitous, and often futile performance of 'housekeeping' as itself the assertive reconstruction of national culture. Women don't simply carry on; they carry *around*.[32] In other words, they practise into being the new processes that war entails. A number of West's dispatches are centrally concerned with errands, and the difficulty of fulfilling them;[33] she attempts to move materials from London to Ibstone House, to locate necessary goods in a denuded consumer landscape, to secure the means of continuing her work (she boasted to Alexander Woollcott in December 1940 that 'I got every book I thought indispensable on my pet Balkan subjects and brought them down here – if the London Library has not sense to evacuate themselves I must do it for them').[34]

West crafts these anecdotes of peripatesis around the kinds of domestic objects that some might dismiss as fripperies – as if to stress the connection with the hat-buying of 'The Strange Necessity' and the salience of Balkan embroideries (indeed, her own embroidery collection is noted among the items secured and transported). She alludes repeatedly to the importance of lampshades, which serve as a kind of hinge-commodity between the worlds of ornament and necessity:

> This is not trivial babbling, the escape of an overstrained mind into frivolities. I am, on the contrary, grimly keeping in touch with reality. None of the lampshades I already own can be used today. They are transparent, as lampshades usually are, and send out rays that might cost us our lives … I had therefore to be sure to buy special Air Raid Precautions lampshades before I left London – horrid objects made of opaque paper and molded in a cone that throws the light down in a straight beam. These are not easy to find, for the winter is coming, and we are all laying in such unappetizing stocks … At last I saw what I wanted out of a window of a taxi, in an Oxford Street store, and I resolved to buy three dozen. I was to find this literally the most difficult enterprise I have engaged in in my life.[35]

West's odyssey meanders on, through several air raids, the eventual securing of the lampshades, and the impossibility of deploying them because none of the rooms at Ibstone House have been made safe to show a light; all is topsy-turvy in 'this fantastic era', with 'what was formerly cheap and plentiful … now dear and rare' and what was 'dear and rare … now cheap and not nearly so rare as its buyers'.[36] Thus she sits, awaiting the air-raid siren, in a room furnished with 'magnificent yellow taffeta curtains trimmed with bottle-green ruching in the eighteenth-century style', a kitchen chair, an electric stove, and nothing else.[37]

Elsewhere, West describes the search for campstools, cushions, and garden mattresses for London shelter accommodations; the arduous and complex transportation of a basket of vegetables from her country house up to the city; and even more lampshades. It is impossible to avoid thinking of class in relation to these pieces, which are firmly rooted in the consciousness of privilege. West goes out of her way to differentiate her travails from those endured by the poor ('Nothing can express what is being endured by the people in the East End and the poorer suburbs of London'[38]), yet references her servants and possessions with an almost parodic insistence: the retrained Welsh miners who unpack her goods, 'innocents who knew all about Handel and Bach and nothing about Sheraton and Hepplewhite', the butler who asks to keep the shrapnel that smashes into the London kitchen as a souvenir, the (almost assuredly apocryphal) housemaid who asks permission to 'mend the master's underclothing' in the air-raid shelter, the bizarrely inadequate cooks with whom one must content oneself when the others have 'rightly taken up war work'.[39]

If the overall effect is to emphasize that there is now no longer such a thing as what Jenny, West's narrator in *The Return of the Soldier*, calls 'the impregnable fortress of a gracious life',[40] it's with the understanding that West, not Jenny, conveyed in that novel – that the fortress was always in some sense a prison. Yet West charts in certain, less comic, renegotiations of value – those based on the rewriting of past associations – an unravelling of civilizational ties:

> Everything we saw seemed a victim of a sudden, irreparable depreciation of value. It was no longer worth its price, because of the people who lay dead underneath the whorled laths and plaster of a hundred rag-and-bone shops. It was sometimes distressing, because of other, less corporeal deaths. We have a Rembrandt drawing, a minute, cunning, loving bit of magic, a few strokes of a pencil which show, receding into an immense distance, mile upon mile upon mile of Holland. We have a Dufy that shows Burgundy as it is after the vines have been sprayed with copper sulphate, a blue land, deep bright blue, delphinium blue. They had become portraits of enslaved countries, unvisitable, dangerous.[41]

West reads such objects not merely as possessions, but, like the Slav embroideries, active participants in meaning-making, their unravelling an index of the encroachment of 'nonsense'. 'A Day in Town' ends with West struck by the effect of concussion on a treasured Empire table:

> 'What has happened to it?' I asked. 'What has happened to it?' Each of the three panels that made up its top bulged unevenly, as if forced apart by some inner strain. Its two wide legs were thrusting clumsily outward, and the bar

that joined them was ready to drop out of its sockets. I went up and touched it, and saw that every joint was gaping. Nothing had hit it, but it stood there like something dead and unspeakably mangled. Under the gentlest blow, this honestly and beautifully made article of furniture would have fallen to pieces on the floor. I felt a sick yet distant anger that was extreme and not quite my own, an anger that might have been felt by the long-dead cabinetmaker who had made this table.

As for Elaine Scarry in *The Body in Pain*, for West, here, *making* (the union of love and process) serves as the antithesis of war – and *un*making loosens the cord between the present and the past that makes up a national culture.[42]

Though West's concern with class and possessions is thus not simplistically reducible to 'snobbery', it nevertheless renders her American-directed articles complexly problematic in relation to those of peers such as Mollie Panter-Downes, whose 'epistles to the *New Yorker*', says Angus Calder,

served, and were doubtless intended to serve, the aim of convincing US readers that Common People in Britain were united in a Common Cause, that 'unknown warriors' were bravely doing their duty, and that it was for them that the USA should provide help – that such help would not be diverted merely to serve the ends of snobs and exploiters.[43]

West's spiky observations and comic distortions, and her very differentiation of the wartime experiences and attitudes of rich and poor – charting the different patterns of sleep versus wakefulness in shelters between servants and their employers, for instance[44] – make her writings less congruent with the myth of the Blitz, less anodyne as propaganda at a time when 'any pronouncement by Britons, official or unofficial, published or broadcast' needed to be 'acutely mindful of the USA'.[45]

Part of this disparity is a formal one. Panter-Downes's letters, although she is quietly amusing, with a novelist's eye, are manifestly those of a journalist-observer. She does not appear in her own dispatches; her eye is on national occurrences and patterns of behaviour, and the 'ordinary people' she celebrates are always a distant *they*: 'The bravery of these people has to be seen to be believed. They would be heart-rending if they didn't so conspicuously refuse to appear heart-rending.'[46] Her occasional short stories – like 'In Clover', a tale of evacuee culture clash,[47] or 'Lunch with Mr. Biddle', about an air raid warden[48] – are formally and stylistically distinct from her column 'Letter from London', which features little snark and few characters other than the national.

West's articles, by contrast, perform a generic mélange that, although it now calls to mind some of moves of the 'New Journalism' of the 1960s, in fact partakes of the fictionality and staging of *Black Lamb and Grey Falcon*. The first-person protagonist is always both West-the-housewife, herself struggling with the exigencies of the historical moment, and West-the-erudite-observer, aware of the ramifications, in a manner reflecting *Black Lamb*'s meta-creation myth:

> This experience made me say to myself, 'If a Roman woman had, some years before the sack of Rome, realized why it was going to be sacked and what motives inspired the barbarians and what the Romans, and had written down all she knew and felt about it, the record would have been of value to historians. My situation, though probably not so fatal, is as interesting.' Without doubt it was my duty to keep a record of it.
>
> So I resolved to put on paper what a typical Englishwoman felt and thought in the late nineteen-thirties when, already convinced of the inevitability of the second Anglo-German war, she had been able to follow the dark waters of that event back to its source.[49]

Like the compound witnessing voice of *Black Lamb*, the home front West-persona is constructed as 'typical', but also deeply historically versed (discoursing with the head janitor in her London air raid shelter about historical massacres in Macedonia)[50] and sensitive to culture, interrogating the responses of her 'housewife' self as she witnesses history being made. The articles proceed by way of anecdote, irony, and staged encounter, with characters clearly subject to conflation, 'improvement', or outright invention in the service of illustrative fable. Thus the janitor exclaims at the horror of civilian massacre ('Good God, I call that a shocking story! ... Men and women and children, old and young, all killed together! Why, it's beastly! Who ever would have thought of such a thing?'[51]) at the moment bombs are heard falling across London; an extraordinary number of randomly met strangers vouchsafe their admiration for Hitler; her servants go vividly and entertainingly mad. One can see in these reports a sliding scale of fictionality; indeed, Katherine Cooper (one of the authors in this volume) treats 'Around Us the Wail of Sirens', one of West's *Saturday Evening Post* articles, *as* fiction, calling it a 'short story'.[52] But though the piece is obviously fictional*ized* – allowing West to mount an unpleasantly pointed attack on her older sister Lettie, who appears here as 'Cousin Eva', a Jellyby-like sponsor of 'lame ducks' – there is no reason to think of it definitively as *fiction*. Indeed, the article's layout signals otherwise: it is accompanied, like West's earlier *Saturday Evening Post* article 'Shocking', by wire service photographs from London – in this case a photo of worshippers in a church, with the caption 'London prays while the bombs drop', and the note that 'The censor banned identification of the church.'[53]

Both here and in 'Enemy', an even more peculiarly hybrid piece published in the *New Yorker*, the milieu, household, and material goods are clearly West's own, the winding chain of anecdote much the same as in her 'Reporter at Large' pieces, the first-person narration tonally identical. Nothing identifies 'Enemy' as fictional;[54] it refers quite obviously to Ibstone House, West's sister's attack of flu, and the contents of her own bookshelves, and yet in it West tells us of how she (or 'she') was aided in her gradual relocation of her material goods to the country by a clairvoyant anticipation of air raids – a talent that she finally realizes was the work of the devil. Is this scenario any less believable than the conversation in 'Shocking' or the conveniently pithy *bon mots* West ostensibly culls from her servants and neighbours in 'The Bright Face of Danger'? More to the point – is it more 'fictional' than the maunderings of the imbecile pacifist in 'Around Us the Wail of Sirens', the jaw-dropping rudeness of the refugee foisted on the household in the same story, the resistant imbecility of the cook West dubs 'Little Horror of War', or that cook's successor in 'Dinner for the Man Who Came to Dinner', who cooks poison soup for Alexander Woollcott?

All of them, I would argue, partake of the fabulistic, are carefully crafted fables of the encroachment of what's referred to in *Black Lamb and Grey Falcon* as 'Gerda's empire', the entitled insistence on self and blindness to cause and effect that's summed up as having 'no sense of process'.[55] Though in narration all these pieces are picaresque, defined by metonymy and peripatesis, they crystallize as fables around moments of willed ignorance in which characters reveal themselves as, in effect, Gerda: the pacifist's fatuous approval of her 'sensitive' son's absconding ahead of conscription; 'Little Horror of War' refusing the jam ration for the entire household as a means of flirting with the grocer; the recurrence, in several stories, of determined blindness to the rationale behind various wartime regulations and restrictions.

In this context, the fantastic plot of 'Enemy' makes perfect sense: West has fallen, she realizes, into exploiting clairvoyance for personal convenience ('The house in the country became not only habitable but amiable, and the furniture, which made it comfortable and welcoming, escaped a sordid doom'[56]), enabling her to short-circuit the new wartime processes that bind the nation together. In a small way, she has been tempted to embrace 'Gerda's empire', even if she tells herself she is doing so simply to rescue those books made newly irreplaceable by war: 'they were acquiring a new and tragic value. Many of [them] had been published in Paris and Berlin, Vienna and Prague, Rome and Belgrade. To order them now from a bookseller would be like asking him for the *Lunar Times*.'[57] Her possession of these German-language books, as well as her avoidance of the raids, provoke hostility and the suspicion that she could be a Nazi spy – a massive irony, given (as West splutters to herself) her long history of anti-fascist activism, including *Black Lamb and Grey Falcon* itself. But to recognize the analogy with Gerda is to understand that it is actually not, or not only, irony, but the dramatization of the allure of self-interest, played out on West's own body. Though her political *bona fides* mean she is in no danger from the imputations of espionage, she has had a warning as visceral as was her response to the Hitler–Stalin pact: 'It was as if I had put up my hand to my neck and found there a noose which somebody had slipped over my head when my attention was busy elsewhere.'[58]

Even West herself, she makes clear in this extension of her minatory project, is vulnerable to the wartime practices she identifies with Gerda: the inability to comprehend the changed world, the adherence to privilege and practice, to an inherited prewar taxonomy of behaviour. And there is no such thing as the 'merely' domestic. There are no limits, West implies in 'Enemy', to the ramifications of the blindness to process even as battles rage against this very mindset – it is, she says elsewhere, 'as ashes in the mouth of the world'.[59]

Notes

1 See Debra Rae Cohen, 'Rebecca West's Palimpsestic Praxis: Crafting the Intermodern Voice of Witness', in *Intermodernism: Literary Culture in Mid-Twentieth-Century Britain*, ed. Kristen Bluemel (Edinburgh: Edinburgh University Press, 2009), pp. 150–67.
2 She observed grimly in a letter from Pêc that 'They say Göring and Hitler are coming here on a triumphal tour in the autumn'. Bonnie Kime Scott (ed.), *Selected Letters of Rebecca West* (New Haven, CT: Yale University Press, 2000), p. 166.
3 Ibid., p. 166.
4 Ibid., p. 168; Carl Rollyson, *Rebecca West: A Life* (New York: Scribner's, 1996), p. 200.
5 Rebecca West, 'Notes on the Way', *Time and Tide* (9 March 1940), pp. 237–8; Rebecca West, 'Notes on the Way', *Time and Tide* (6 December 1941), pp. 1053–4.
6 Rollyson, *Rebecca West*, p. 211.
7 He echoes here Peter Wolfe's earlier comment that '*Black Lamb and Grey Falcon*, in addition to its other services, could do duty as a marriage manual'; see *Rebecca West: Artist and Thinker* (Carbondale, IL: Southern Illinois University Press, 1971), p. 148.
8 Rebecca West, *Black Lamb and Grey Falcon: A Journey Through Yugoslavia* (1941; New York: Penguin, 1982), pp. 403, 674, 673.
9 Ibid., p. 782.
10 Ibid., p. 784.

11 *Ibid.*, p. 818.
12 *Ibid.*, p. 1012. Loretta Stec identifies West's valorization of survival here as a demand for women to 'heroically submit to male domination for the sake of national security', in nostalgic return to essentialist gender roles; while Stec's argument is compelling, it misreads, I believe, West's complex rejection of the trope of sacrifice. See Loretta Stec, 'Female Sacrifice: Gender and Nostalgic Nationalism in Rebecca West's *Black Lamb and Grey Falcon*', in *Narratives of Nostalgia, Gender, and Nationalism*, ed. Jean Pickering and Suzanne Kehde (New York: New York University Press, 1997), pp. 138–58, p. 139.
13 West, *Black Lamb*, p. 799.
14 *Ibid.*, pp. 799, 802.
15 The 'you didn't build it' trope – later adopted by Barack Obama in his run for president – was first articulated by Warren in her 2011 Senate campaign (see https://www.youtube.com/watch?v=htX2usfqMEs). The speech affirms the 'basic social contract' and emphasizes interdependency and process: 'There is nobody in this country who got rich on his own. Nobody. You built a factory out there? Good for you. But I want to be clear: you moved your goods to market on the roads the rest of us paid for; you hired workers the rest of us paid to educate; you were safe in your factory because of police forces and fire forces that the rest of us paid for. You didn't have to worry that marauding bands would come and seize everything at your factory, and hire someone to protect against this, because of the work the rest of us did. Now look, you built a factory and it turned into something terrific, or a great idea? God bless. Keep a big hunk of it. But part of the underlying social contract is, you take a hunk of that and pay forward for the next kid who comes along.'
16 West, *Black Lamb*, p. 803. Again, the contemporary echoes are inescapable; think of the contemporary US Republican Party, or, for that matter, the post-Brexit Tories.
17 This is Timothy Snyder's term; see *Bloodlands: Europe Between Hitler and Stalin* (New York: Basic Books, 2012).
18 I mean this in the vernacular sense as well as Giorgio Agamben's.
19 Beryl Pong, 'Wartime', *Modernism/modernity* Print Plus 5.2 (2020), https://doi.org/10.26597/mod.0145
20 On the proliferation of war culture, see for example Jan Mieszkowski, *Watching War* (Stanford, CA: Stanford University Press, 2012); Mary L. Dudziak, *War Time: An Idea, Its History, Its Consequences* (New York: Oxford University Press, 2012); and Patrick Deer, *Culture in Camouflage: War, Empire, and Modern British Literature* (New York: Oxford University Press, 2009).
21 Mary Favret, *War at a Distance: Romanticism and the Making of Modern Wartime* (Princeton, NJ: Princeton University Press, 2009), p. 15.
22 Rebecca West, 'The First Fortnight', *Ladies' Home Journal* (January 1940), pp. 12, 68–9.
23 West lived at Possingworth Manor in Sussex in the early days of the war while her husband travelled to London and his war work at the Ministry of Economic Warfare; shortly afterwards they bought Ibstone House, in the Chiltern Hills,

which she described in a letter as 'a derelict farm' with a 'lovely house ... the sort of house you can imagine Alice in Wonderland living in'. See Scott (ed.), *Letters*, p. 168.
24 West, 'The First Fortnight', p. 12.
25 *Ibid*. One cannot but think here of Beryl Pong's identification of the Second World War as 'the tipping point where dread – previously orientated around wartime as *future* – becomes a way of understanding wartime as *present*'. See Beryl Pong, *British Literature and Culture in Second World Wartime: For the Duration* (New York: Oxford University Press, 2020), p. 17. Also see Melissa Dinsman, 'Mrs. Miniver Builds the Home Front: Architecture and Household Objects as Wartime Propaganda', *Modernism/modernity* Print Plus 3.1 (2018), https://doi.org/10.26597/mod.0049. Dinsman claims that 'in the new era of total war all structures – social, narrative, cultural, industrial, even architectural and domestic – were engaged in narrating wartime propaganda, even if at times these home front objects strayed from the prevailing message of the day'.
26 West, 'The First Fortnight', p. 69.
27 Rebecca West, 'A Reporter at Large: Housewife's Nightmare', *New Yorker* (14 December 1940), pp. 50, 52, 55–62, 50.
28 Scott (ed.), *Letters*, p. 168.
29 West, 'Housewife's Nightmare', p. 50; Rebecca West, 'Little Horror of War', *New Yorker* (15 November 1941), pp. 29–34, 29; Rebecca West, 'Another Man's Poison', *Harper's* (November 1944), pp. 507–11, 511, West, 'Housewife's Nightmare', p. 50.
30 West, 'Another Man's Poison', p. 507; West, 'A Day in Town', *New Yorker* (25 January 1941), pp. 36, 38–40, 36.
31 Rebecca West, 'The Strange Necessity', in *The Strange Necessity: Essays and Reviews* (1928; London: Virago, 1987), pp. 13–198. The pile-on from male critics defending Joyce's honour in response to West's essay – including a scathing Williams Carlos Williams – has been amply detailed. See Austin Briggs, 'Rebecca West v. James Joyce, Samuel Beckett, and William Carlos Williams', in *Joyce in the Hibernian Metropolis: Essays*, ed. Morris Beja and David Norris (Columbus, OH: Ohio State University Press, 1996), pp. 83–102 and Debra Rae Cohen, 'Sheepish Modernism: Rebecca West, the Adam Brothers, and the Taxonomies of Criticism', in *Rebecca West Today: Contemporary Critical Approaches*, ed. Bernard Schweizer (Newark, DE: University of Delaware Press, 2006), pp. 143–56. It's hard not to see in Rollyson's characterization of West's home front articles as 'self-contented' ('she conveys the impression that she enjoyed the war') a similar, if unconscious, dismissiveness (*Rebecca West*, p. 203).
32 Contrast the competitive exchange between two male commuters: 'They compared notes as to the easiest way from getting from point to point in the City, avoiding the damaged tube stations and the roped-off areas. "Ah, but you hadn't thought of Porkpie Passage. Never even heard of it, I shouldn't wonder", the one said triumphantly ... ' (West, 'A Day in Town', p. 36). That 'Porkpie Passage' is one of West's fabrications should not need saying.

33 As she wrote to Irita Van Doren, 'Everybody is living miles away from where they usually do … and if anybody gets ill the relevant doctors and surgeons aren't to be found, so if you have stayed in London life goes in endless odd jobs.' See Scott (ed.), *Letters*, p. 168.
34 Scott (ed.), *Letters*, p. 172, fn 1.
35 West, 'Housewife's Nightmare', pp. 50, 52, 55–62, 61.
36 *Ibid.*, pp. 62, 57.
37 *Ibid.*, p. 50.
38 *Ibid.*
39 *Ibid.*, p. 57; West, 'A Day in Town', p. 39; Rebecca West, 'The Bright Face of Danger', *Reader's Digest* (October 1940), pp. 77–8, 77; West, 'Little Horror of War', p. 29.
40 Rebecca West, *The Return of the Soldier* (1918; New York: Penguin, 1998), p. 58.
41 West, 'A Day in Town', p. 40.
42 See Elaine Scarry, *The Body in Pain: The Making and Unmaking of the World* (New York: Oxford University Press, 1985).
43 Angus Calder, *The Myth of the Blitz* (1991; London: Pimlico, 1992), p. 51.
44 Rebecca West, 'Shocking', *Saturday Evening Post* (26 October 1940), pp. 16, 48, 50, 48.
45 Calder, *Myth*, p. 50.
46 Mollie Panter-Downes, 'Letter from London', *New Yorker* (28 September 1940), pp. 40, 42, 40. In her next report, she added that 'The courage, humor, and kindliness of ordinary people continue to be astonishing.' Mollie Panter-Downes, 'Letter from London', *New Yorker* (5 October 1940), pp. 37–8, 37.
47 Mollie Panter-Downes, 'In Clover', *New Yorker* (13 April 1940), pp. 15–16. West herself opined that this mismatch could best be described as 'a conflict between artistic styles: a Modigliani couple have to put up with Rubens evacuees, and so on'. See 'Dinner for the Man Who Came to Dinner', *Harper's* (December 1942), pp. 20–7, 21.
48 Mollie Panter-Downes, 'Lunch with Mr. Biddle', *New Yorker* (7 December 1940), pp. 31–3.
49 West, *Black Lamb*, p. 1089.
50 West, 'Shocking', p. 50.
51 *Ibid.*
52 Rebecca West, 'Around Us the Wail of Sirens', *Saturday Evening Post* (8 February 1941), pp. 27, 48–51, 53; Katherine Cooper, 'Figures on the Threshold: Refugees and the Politics of Hospitality, 1930–51', *Literature and History* 27.2 (2018), pp. 189–204, 190.
53 West, 'Around Us', p. 27.
54 The *New Yorker* did not introduce a table of contents until the 1980s and did not label 'fiction' as such until later. 'Enemy' is currently designated as 'fiction' in the even more recently created *New Yorker* digital archive – but so is all of the prose in that issue, other than reviews.

55 West, *Black Lamb*, pp. 805, 799.
56 West, 'Enemy', p. 23.
57 *Ibid.*
58 *Ibid.*, p. 24.
59 West, 'Little Horror of War', p. 33.

4

'Coldly kind': calculated care in post-war British women's writing

Emily Ridge

In the opening pages of Elizabeth Taylor's *Mrs Palfrey at the Claremont* (1971), the last novel published in her own lifetime, the Claremont hotel receptionist is described as 'coldly kind, as if she were working in a nursing-home, and one for deranged patients at that'.[1] The line between hotel and nursing home is, indeed, soon revealed to be perilously fragile in the novel; we learn that this hotel plays host to a number of long-term elderly guests who live in fear of the next stage of residential care that awaits them beyond the Claremont. While the hotel in which they temporarily reside offers a modicum of protection without the loss of freedom, the nursing home, posited in a not-too-distant future, is conceived as a sheltered point of no return. The cold kindness of the receptionist captures something of the ambiguous overlap between these two forms of care. Where the hotel is concerned, it is an affective posture that points to the managed attention of the service worker who, as Arlie Russell Hochschild would highlight just over a decade later, can experience an *'emotive dissonance'* between displayed and internal feeling in a professional role.[2] In nodding to the locale of the nursing home, cold kindness is indicative of the quantifiable care distributed within private or state-run institutions. Either way, care is seen to be instrumentalized in its application; it is used in a way that is calculated to achieve certain ends, whether customer satisfaction or the proficient supervision and guardianship of the more senior members of a given society.

This descriptor – 'coldly kind' – is typical of the double-edged and complex discourse of care that emerged in British women's writing after the Second World War, a discourse this chapter sets out to illuminate. The chapter will focus on three writers whose works, though stylistically divergent, exemplify a wider fascination with the paradoxical facets of care, as well as its instrumentalization, that comes to the fore with a particular emphasis in the 1950s and 1960s. The mid-century works of Daphne du Maurier and Muriel Spark, alongside those of Elizabeth Taylor, are replete with representations of the strategic manipulation of domestic care and kindness. What follows will spotlight three cases in point from their wide-ranging *oeuvres*. Midge, in du Maurier's 'The Apple Tree' (1952), looks after her husband so punctiliously that her attention takes the form of a 'long-term reproach' for an earlier indiscretion on his part.[3] In Taylor's *The Soul of Kindness* (1964), the benevolent intrusions of Flora into the lives of those around her are shown to disguise an inherent narcissism, anticipating the ambivalent care rhetoric that recurs in *Mrs Palfrey at the Claremont*. And in Spark's *Memento Mori* (1959), Mrs Pettigrew uses her position as carer to exercise absolute domination over her charges to the point of blackmail. In each of these cases, care is used, whether consciously or not, to manage and control interpersonal relationships.

Such domesticated representations have, as I will further show, marked socio-historical implications. In her account of the longstanding contradictions of capital and care, Nancy Fraser identifies three key periods when the 'capitalist organization of social reproduction' underwent a major shift: the first pertains to 'nineteenth-century liberal competitive capitalism', resulting in an ideology of separate spheres of work and care; the third pertains to our current era of global 'financialized capitalism', made possible by, amongst other things, women's large-scale entry into the work force and the outsourcing of care from, more often than not, the privileged to the less privileged.[4] However, my concern here is with the second key period in Fraser's schema – the shift towards the 'state-managed' capitalism of the mid-twentieth century – involving the internalization of 'social reproduction through state and corporate provisions of social welfare'.[5] I am contending that the works of du Maurier, Taylor, and Spark coincide with this middle phase and offer responses to a more widespread process of institutionalizing and commodifying care, both as discourse and practice, in the years immediately following the Second World War. 'After the fifties are over', notes the chairman of a management committee for a care home in Spark's novel, 'everything will be easier. This transition period …'[6] I argue that these women writers variously and subtly document a transition period that sees the establishment of what Nikolas Rose has defined as a 'new rationale of government', one directed towards the subjectivity and 'soul' of the citizen.[7]

They are equally attuned to the beginnings of a process recent theorists of care have come to refer to as '*carewashing*': that is to say, the integration of a language of care within corporate and commercial infrastructures, a development which has, by extension, allowed for the implantation of 'market logics into traditional non-market realms, including those of health and education'.[8] More broadly, their works articulate a problematics of care in ways that complicate later feminist approaches, such as Carol Gilligan's pioneering work on relationality in the 1980s, raising questions not only about the efficacy of care as a moral framework but equally its capacity as a strategic mechanism of governance. To be clear, these are not polemics against care in and of itself; rather, these authors imagine different scenarios and possibilities involving care's misappropriation. With the notable exception of *Memento Mori*, the texts in question have been almost completely overlooked in literary criticism to date, even criticism specifically focused on du Maurier and Taylor.[9] I can only assume that such neglect is driven by a misreading of these texts as inward-looking domestic dramas of misapplied care, elegantly written though of limited import. On the contrary, as I will show, these are outward-facing texts that offer a penetrating and subversive commentary on post-war socio-political developments. Placing the texts in dialogue discloses the larger stakes and implications of these seemingly insular dramas.

Care as critique: Daphne du Maurier

The 1938 novel *Rebecca*, with its conniving housekeeper figure, might seem like a more obvious starting point for a discussion of Daphne du Maurier's interest in the controlling impetus of care. Yet her later story, 'The Apple Tree' (1952), brings this interest to bear on everyday domestic space in the context of what might be characterized as a kitchen sink or 'everyday' gothic narrative.[10] The story, despite its melodramatic elements, thus speaks more demonstrably to the political and cultural landscape of the post-war period. The third-person narrative is focalized through the perspective of a retired man who is haunted by the memory of his late wife – Midge – with whom he had a difficult and unfulfilling relationship, particularly towards the end of her life. The unhappy spirit of his wife comes to embody, or so he perceives, the form of a 'half dead',[11] freakish, ugly apple tree, yielding a 'monstrous' supply of 'rotten' apples.[12] He ultimately cuts the tree down. The story ends as this man, on a dark and snowy night, trips and becomes caught in the 'clutch of the old apple tree', his foot stuck fast in its 'jagged' stump.[13] 'He sank deeper, ever deeper into the snow', we are told in the last line, 'and when a stray piece of brushwood, cold and wet, touched his lips, it was like a hand, hesitant and timid feeling its way towards him in the darkness'.[14] This line suggests his final submission to the unrelenting grip of his late wife, exemplified through the figure of the advancing hand, though the ending retains an intentional note of uncertainty.

So far so *Rebecca* – except that this invisible hand is arguably more in the tradition of Adam Smith than Edgar Allan Poe, by which I mean that it has economic as much as psychodynamic significance. Smith set out to expose the wider benefits to the market of individual acts of selfishness. Du Maurier's focus, by contrast, is on the market benefits of self*less* acts or, as Fraser puts it, the 'way that the capitalist economy relies on – one might say, free rides on – activities of provisioning, care-giving and interaction that produce and maintain social bonds, although it accords them no monetized value and treats them as if they were free'.[15] This is a phenomenon that, in its reversal of Smith's original emphasis, Nancy Folbre has fittingly explored through the metaphor of the 'invisible heart'.[16] Yet du Maurier, in her continued fixation on the hand, stresses the physical over and above the emotive aspects of care. The male protagonist in her story is haunted by a woman who, when she was alive, looked after him and his household environment with impeccable attention to detail. The 'hesitant and timid' ghostly hand that feels for him in the darkness deliberately reincarnates an earlier hand that performs the labour of care. Midge's hands are shown to 'clear the dishes' from the table, 'carry' trays that are 'laden', draw on 'gardening gloves' for staking the flowers, and to tackle 'plugged up and choked' kitchen drains.[17] It is an on-going labour that her husband questions:

> He had ventured to ask once why so much cleaning of the house was necessary. Why there must be the incessant turning out of rooms. Why chairs must be lifted to stand on other chairs, rugs rolled up and ornaments huddled together on a sheet of newspaper. And why, in particular, the sides of the upstairs corridor, on which no one ever trod, must be polished laboriously by hand, Midge and the daily woman taking it in turns to crawl upon their knees the whole endless length of it, like slaves of bygone days.
> Midge stared at him, not understanding.
> 'You'd be the first to complain', she said, 'if the house was like a pigsty. You like your comforts.'[18]

On the contrary, her husband experiences deep and perpetual discomfort in reaction to what is described as the 'undercurrent of reproach, mingled with suffering nobly borne, [that] spoilt the atmosphere of his home and drove him to a sense of furtiveness and guilt'.[19] It becomes evident that, as with the sides of the upstairs corridor, this is an invisible care that is, as a whole, conducted 'laboriously by hand' rather than lovingly by heart. Midge is, in this respect, less than sympathetic as a character, despite her toiling devotion. As du Maurier's biographer Margaret Forster observes, '[i]t is very hard to decide quite how Daphne intended this story to be read: is the hatred of the man for his dead wife justified, or does he get his deserts?'[20]

At a surface level, Midge's suppressed resentment is linked to an incident in the early years of their marriage when, during the war, she apparently caught sight of her husband sharing a moment of intimacy with a land girl on a neighbouring farm. There is clearly a vengefulness to Midge's indefatigable domestic efforts in that they serve to prick the 'conscience' of someone who is not only idle but has proven himself to be disloyal.[21] It is also noteworthy that her husband betrays her with a young woman whose role – as land girl – defies traditional gender norms, while Midge herself is bound by them. Yet it seems to me that this passing lapse, on the part of the husband figure in this story, is used as a pretext to delve into a collective guilt that goes beyond a singular episode of casual infidelity. Before his retirement, Midge's husband was a businessman with a job in the City. If his hands are shown to be 'in his pockets' while Midge's are furiously scrubbing, this is also because pockets are signifiers of masculine self-sufficiency, repositories for money as well as for dormant hands.[22] This is a protagonist who confronts, for the first time, the economic logic as well as the injustice of a social structure of separate spheres which, according to Folbre, enables men to 'exploit women in the family' in order to 'compensate them for exploitation they may experience within the capitalist workplace'.[23] Indeed, it is not until retirement that he is conscious of his wife's labour at all:

> When he had been in business, it seemed different. He had not noticed it so much. He came home to eat, to sleep, and to go up by train again in the morning. But when he retired he became aware of her forcibly, and day by day his sense of her resentment, of her disapproval grew stronger.[24]

Midge's controlled rage is not, or at least not only, the rage of a woman scorned; it is the rage of women whose unacknowledged domestic work forms what Fraser calls the 'indispensable background condition for the possibility of economic production in a capitalist society'.[25] This is a form of anger that enacts a 'critique of the world', as described by Sara Ahmed in her account of emotion as mediated rather than immediate.[26] Moreover, it is an angry critique that is performed through care. For Ahmed, 'knowledge is bound up with what makes us sweat, shudder, tremble', and Midge's sweaty exertions and shudders of resentment are legible beyond the portrayed circumstances of her own bodily experience as such.[27] Her husband's is the unease of a man who comes to an oblique realization of the mediated nature of this rage; it unsettles his particular and narrow vision of the world just as his newspaper – *The Times*, naturally – is returned to him, after she has handled it, with its pages 'in the wrong order and folded crookedly ...'[28] Following her death, the apple tree comes to register the same collective disquiet; it towers over him like a 'mop, a giant mop, whose streaky surface had been caught somehow by the sun, and so turned bleached'.[29] The monumental mop envisioned here points to a distinct organizational logic, one shaped by and within the domestic sphere. This domestic logic has been instrumentalized to serve the broader capitalist economy, made manifest in the ordered pages of *The Times*; yet, as this story dramatizes so effectively, not least through the disarrangement of those pages, such compliance cannot be taken for granted.

Managing the 'soul': Elizabeth Taylor

Elizabeth Taylor is less interested in unsettling the longstanding economic logic of separate spheres in *The Soul of Kindness* than in observing the emerging transactions between those spheres on the levels of behaviour and discourse. Late in her novel, one of its minor characters, a playwright by the name of Geoffrey, is planning his next play. It is to be about Parliamentary issues and will not include any female characters. He explains: '"The moment a woman walks onto a stage, the audience thinks of love – who is she in love with? and who will fall in love with her? – I can't risk even a women [sic] M.P. doing that to my play. I wouldn't even take the risk of Edith, or Bessie, passing briefly by upstage."'[30] What Geoffrey suggests here is that a gendered separation of spheres involves a gendered separation of emotions, at least representationally. If this play is to be about professional life and public governance, it must exclude the feminine emotion of love, an emotion that is more suited to deployment within domestic settings. His wife Elinor is unimpressed:

> 'But a committee room', she said, contemptuously stressing the last two words. 'What a boring set to have to look at, for one thing.'
> [...]
> 'People sitting round a table', she went on. 'It simply won't work.'
> 'They will get up from it now and then', he said, as if he were talking to a child who would understand things better later on.
> 'But the struggle for power', Elinor protested, in a disgusted voice. 'Darling, we *know* it all. We've watched it all time and time again, the same intrigues, the same conclusions drawn from them. It's such old stuff, Geoffrey.'
> 'And so is love old stuff, and death, and all the other themes we've also seen time and time again.' He did not look up this time, and had stopped smiling. He wrote quickly, paused, then looked about him frowning, as if the thread of what had occupied him was lost.[31]

Elinor and Geoffrey are both right in their claims that power and love are old stuff. What neither appears to recognize, however, is the growing alliance between these two themes in post-war politics and society. *This* is the new stuff. According to Rose, it was in the aftermath of the Second World War that the 'minutiae of the human soul [...] emerged as a new domain for management', while also entering directly into 'political discourse and the practice of government'.[32] In other words, intimate feeling became a province of professional and political activity and vice versa. This is not simply a version of the well-known second-wave feminist slogan – 'the personal is political' – that would become popular only a few years after Taylor's novel. For Rose, the interpenetration, at mid-century, of the personal and the political was strategically implemented rather than something to be taken as self-evident.

In Taylor's novel, this interpenetration is manifested through language. *The Soul of Kindness* centres on a character called Flora. Like Midge in du Maurier's story, she is married to a businessman and uses care in a similarly purposeful way. Flora might be said to amalgamate aspects of Jane Austen's *Emma* (1815) in her propensity to benignly meddle in the lives of those around her, aspects of Bertha Young in Katherine Mansfield's 'Bliss' (1918) in her wilful yet short-sighted insistence on perfection and happiness, and aspects of her namesake in Stella Gibbons's *Cold Comfort Farm* (1932), Flora Poste, in her delight in finding solutions to the imagined problems she sees around her. Flora's interventions are essentially narcissistic. She 'bestow[s]' herself and her attention upon others in the manner of a gift and cannot conceive of any situation in which that gift would not be desired: 'Although as good as gold, she had inconvenient plans for other people's pleasure, and ideas differing from her own she was not able to imagine.'[33] What distinguishes Flora's inconvenient plans from those of her literary predecessors is her engagement, in putting them into action, of a vocabulary that pointedly blends the languages of care and capital, of love and work. Flora does not simply arrange her domestic affairs, she *manages* them, as one would manage an office or, indeed, a committee room. Taylor alerts us to the intersecting concerns of personal and professional worlds and discourses early on:

> She, who was able to do so much to solve other people's problems, settle *their* disorders, had had no success with her husband's health. She blamed his work, his business life – for most businessmen had ulcers, she often heard, and said. On the other hand, for his work to have such ascendancy over his home, that it possessed the power to upset his life with her, was an affront. On this score, she felt her confidence weakening. His other world had escaped her influence. She had a vague understanding of what went on in the factory and warehouses, had been once or twice to that grim district and walked through one department after another, all smelling of glue and french polish; had sat – feeling a guest, with his secretary as her hostess – in his office, waiting to be taken out to lunch, while he, Richard, was constantly interrupted, telephoned. All had been bustle and commotion. She came to the conclusion that he should be made more inaccessible, blamed his secretary, saw herself in her place, warding off callers, delegating.[34]

At first glance, Flora seems to be establishing clear boundaries between work and home; she has influence in one sphere and not in the other. Unlike Midge, she resents not the extent of her caring duties, but the extent to which the 'world' of her husband's work interferes so that she cannot carry out those duties to perfection. To invert Fraser's logic, it is this world of capital that, for Flora, forms the 'indispensable background condition' for perfect domesticity, not the other way around. The primacy of domesticity is central to this vision; for work to take precedence is seen as an 'affront'.

In fact, a closer study of this passage reveals that it is Flora herself who brings a corporate ideology into play in her own home. She treats her domestic and social environments with the professionalism of a managing director, solving interpersonal and infrastructural problems and striving for 'success'. She blames 'business life' for poor domestic performance in the same way that private life might, elsewhere, be blamed for poor business performance. Finally, both worlds are merged together as she imagines taking on the 'bustle and commotion' of her husband's office space and channelling her skills in a more overtly professional capacity through better organization and delegation. 'Delegate', we later learn, is 'Flora's word'.[35] If, as Rose describes, the 'management of subjectivity has become a central task for the modern organization' since the Second World War, then Taylor reflects on this phenomenon in *The Soul of Kindness* by implying that the outlook of the modern organization also came to underpin spaces of intimacy.[36] Instead of bringing love into the committee room, she brings the committee room to bear on the world of love. This type of inversion is also remarked upon by Hochschild in her influential study of the infiltration of emotion regulation techniques in the workplace and its potential consequences: 'Commercial conventions of feeling are being recycled back into individual private lives; emotional life now appears under new management.'[37]

Indeed, throughout the novel, Flora is shown to employ emotion and attention as a form of social capital; her influence is primarily affective and is fine-tuned for the purpose of 'accomplish[ing] something' for the recipient and, by reflection, herself.[38] When, for example, she is asked by her friend Patrick about her progress with one young protégé, Kit, who aspires to become an actor, she responds as follows: 'I think I managed to put new heart and hope into him.'[39] Note, again, the confluence of languages of work (*to manage*) and love (*heart* and *hope*) here. For Patrick, these words are 'like the warning sound of a maroon'.[40] We come to infer that a care that is calculated (and calculated with the idea of 'success' in mind) cannot be fully trusted. Certainly, Flora's acts of kindness are shown to do more harm than good. At the end of the novel, Kit attempts to take his own life when he finds that he cannot live up to Flora's expectations for his fledgling acting career. Kit's sister, Meg, indicts Flora for her role in this crisis in a line that might also be read as an indictment of corporate greed, except that Flora's main commodity is feeling: 'She has so much, and always wants more.'[41]

The novel thus sounds a note of caution about what can happen when care becomes a means to an end, when it becomes a technique or a tool. It is a caution Flora herself receives but chooses to ignore mid-way through the novel: '"Compassion's all right"', she is told by Patrick, but '"reason's better, you know"'.[42] This remark might seem to play into a rather sexist and stereotyped prioritization of reason (conceived as masculine) over emotion (conceived as feminine), but I posit that Taylor is more preoccupied, in this novel, with exposing the way that care and compassion can be coolly and carefully co-opted to further individual goals. Incidentally, Hochschild saw the 'false selves' produced by narcissism and altruism, which she also genders, as flip sides of the same coin: 'Whereas the narcissist is adept at turning the social uses of feeling to his own advantage, the altruist is more susceptible to being used – not because her sense of self is weaker but because her "true self" is bonded more securely to the group and its welfare.'[43] Flora, it would appear, combines aspects of the falsity of both figures in the way that she uses feeling. Her 'generosity' is, Taylor notes, 'self-conscious', her 'tender influence' interpreted by certain characters within the novel itself as part and parcel of a 'spurious' appeal.[44] It is a tender influence that equally seems to bring out the individualistic instincts of those on whom it falls. Kit, for example, wonders at his own responses to Flora's attentions: 'Was loving Flora, for instance, perhaps only loving himself? Because she was the only one who would tell him what he wanted to hear. She was his protection and disguise.'[45]

Care seems to take the place of responsibility here, both to oneself and to others. Indeed, when, in the wake of Kit's attempted suicide, Flora receives an anonymous letter that accuses her of interfering, she declaims responsibility both in the senses of accountability and ethical judgement. Her defence is, in effect, the evidence of her care: '"Why do they blame *me*? I've tried and tried and tried to do all I could for Kit. There's no one I've tried *more* over. I'm so fond of him."'[46] She later reiterates: '"I've never done anything to harm anyone in all my life."' '"No; of course not, darling ..."' her husband responds, '"... No one is kinder."'[47] In the end, as friends and family 'rally round', it is Flora who must be protected and disguised from herself.[48] Diane Freeborn offers a succinct description of this state of affairs: 'If Flora is at the heart of this novel, it is a near empty heart.'[49] This is a particularly acute appraisal given Flora's continued emphasis on heartfelt kindness as a key component of her own character. Not unlike some of the self-estranged subjects of Hochschild's study, the outward form and spectacle of an emotion is shown to supplant its very essence in Flora's case; her 'near empty' yet well-publicized 'heart' captures something of the narcissistic altruism that can emerge from the encounter between authentic feeling and commodification in cultures of advanced capitalism in which the heart is no longer invisible but publicly brandished for private gain.

Administrating care: Muriel Spark

In Muriel Spark's *Memento Mori*, the economic dimensions of care (in this case, elderly care) are set in stark relief. When a certain Mrs Mortimer sees a group of 'infirm and agitated' men and women arriving with 'difficulty' at her door, she asks herself: 'Where are their children? [...] or their nieces and nephews? Why are they left to their own resources like this?'[50] This is a world in which care has lost all familial or emotional valence; it is not posited as a provision of love, within or outside of the family. It must be paid for, either privately or by the state, and, even then, it is shown to be subject to manipulation. By extension, authentic emotion itself is seen as something of a valuable novelty, as evidenced by the thoughts of one old poet as he attends a funeral: 'each new death gave him something fresh to feel'.[51] This novel feeling is subsequently put to work in his poetic practice, draining it of any of the authenticity it might once have had, to the extent that a fellow funeral attendee observes the same poet to have '"no feelings"' at all.[52]

Memento Mori similarly features a key character – Mrs Pettigrew – who strategically deploys care as a tool, both to express resentment at injustice, like du Maurier's Midge, and for personal advancement, like Taylor's Flora. Mrs Pettigrew works as a carer for a well-to-do elderly couple, Godfrey and Charmian Colston. Having been written out of the will of a previous employer, she takes advantage of her new position to extort money, through blackmail, from those she is supposed to be looking after. Mrs Pettigrew is driven by her own 'plans for the future' and, it is implied, a 'furious envy' related to her social disadvantage.[53] She is, in fact, originally recommended for the position by Godfrey's sister, Dame Lettie Colston, precisely because of her '"domineering"' reputation: '"Charmian *needs* a bully. For her own good."'[54] Yet it is Godfrey who is more readily brought under Mrs Pettigrew's control, his past sexual and financial indiscretions, as corroborated by '"private papers"', used as leverage.[55] Charmian, unlike her husband, has the wit to protect both her secrets and assets:

> She considered whether she could bring herself to leave Godfrey in his plight with Mrs Pettigrew. After all, she herself might have been in an awkward situation, if she had not *taken care*, long before her old age, to destroy all possibly embarrassing documents. She smiled as she looked at her little bureau with its secretive appearance, in which Mrs Pettigrew had found no secret, although Charmian knew she had penetrated behind those locks. But Godfrey, after all, was not a clever man.[56]

The above passage is telling in its emphasis on one paradoxical facet of the meaning of 'care': that is to say, the uncomfortable slippage, etymologically and semantically, between a sympathetic form of concern and a guarded form of anxiety. To be subject to care is to be vulnerable, in that one is, willingly or not, placed in the hands of another; this is a condition that can, as such, demand a mode of *taking care* in the sense of watching out or defending oneself from care's potential abuses. In *Memento Mori*, such abuses range from the corporeal to the psychological. Charmian and Godfrey are as exposed to '[r]ough physical handling' by Mrs Pettigrew as they are to scheming and 'torment'.[57] In concentrating on a segment of the population that is in the process of cautiously transitioning from a state of independence to various modes of dependence, this is a novel about giving care and taking care at one and the same time; whether care is being delivered or received, the risks and rewards are blatantly calculated on either side.

Yet the real work of care calculation is shown to be conducted, in this novel, by the government as part of its new social welfare programme, a programme that famously sought to oversee the well-being of its subjects from the cradle to the grave but one that was also shaped by what Jordanna Bailkin has called a complex 'politics of expertise'.[58] As she notes, the 'welfare state required a constant flow of information [...] and it relied on an army of experts to provide this knowledge' and to make possible the 'administration of interpersonal relations'.[59] *Memento Mori* charts the process by which care enters the domain of structured administration and expertise, with wards run by management committees 'largely composed of recently empowered professional men and women' and sometimes headed by 'formidable' and 'subtle private welfare-worker and busybody' types, the latter scenario inducing fear and dread in committee members.[60] These are wards that invest in televisions purely to hold the '"attention"' of their 'senile' occupants whose beds are always already earmarked for the '"next lot."'[61] '[T]he time would surely come', reflects Jean Taylor, former companion-maid to Charmian and now resident of the Maud Long Medical Ward, 'for everyone to be a government granny or grandpa, unless they were mercifully laid to rest in their prime'.[62] Spark's most celebrated novel, *The Prime of Miss Jean Brodie* (1961), published just a couple of years later, would famously explore what it means to be in the prime of life; here, her focus is on the wider logistical management of those who are irredeemably beyond it.

Jean Taylor's reflections might suggest a horror at the prospect of being cared for by the state, 'forced by law into Chronic Wards'; but, read as a whole, the novel is more equivocal, presenting a range of divergent views.[63] Indeed, different systems of elderly care, the distinctive merits of private and state-run nursing homes, and the history of British democracy become talking points amongst characters at various moments in the book as if to highlight the emergent and still-evolving aspects of the welfare state at this juncture; it is a development that invites both discussion and disagreement.[64] Politically conservative and privileged characters like Dame Lettie look at Ward occupants as '"fortunate"', benefiting from '"[c]entral heating, everything they want, plenty of company"'.[65] She later queries, in surveying the 'decrepit women' of the Maud Long Ward, the '"purpose of keeping them alive at the country's expense"'.[66] For others, this new system appears to promise, at least at a surface level, a greater degree of fairness and transparency in the treatment of those within care homes. In this vein, a pronounced split between pre- and post-war approaches to care is discernible. The latter approach is shaped by a legislative framework, the language of which is put to use, however ineptly, by the patients themselves. For instance, Granny Barnacle, another occupant of the Maud Long Ward, takes issue with a new Sister on the basis that hers was a pre-war training: '"You can't never trust a ward sister over fifty. They don't study that there's new ways of goin' on since the war by law."'[67] When it becomes clear that this particular Sister will remain in post, Granny Barnacle threatens to discharge herself: '"I know my bloody rights as a patient."'[68] Putting the question of rights to one side, the nursing home also speaks of security. In the case of Charmian, the home in Surrey, to which she ultimately relocates, offers a vision of 'reassurance' in the face of Mrs Pettigrew's increasingly threatening behaviour within her own property.[69] Charmian's nursing home is, however, a private institution, the luxury of which is denied to employees like Jean Taylor on the grounds that she is '"entitled"' to public care, or, indeed, to the conniving Mrs Pettigrew, who must resort to underhand means to ensure her own future security.[70]

Through her attentiveness to the nuanced perspectives on these post-war 'days of transition', Spark exposes, as Suzanne E. England and Carol Ganzer point out, the 'provisions of a partially realized welfare state in which traditional class inequities are reproduced and in which bureaucratic values define human relations'.[71] *Memento Mori* addresses the complex implications of the wholesale redesign of the administration of social insurance, which, in its dependence on all manner of careful calculations, represents the very essence of cold kindness. Nevertheless, the overarching joke of the text is that no provision of care, however carefully calibrated or costly, can remove the fact of death, as conveyed by the singular message of a recurrent prank caller: '" – *Remember you must die* – "'[72]

Conclusion

The works of du Maurier, Taylor, and Spark thus register ambivalent attitudes surrounding care, and, in doing so, offer new ways of thinking about

Carol Gilligan's ground-breaking 'ethics of care' paradigm, first proposed towards the end of the second-wave feminist era in 1982. Gilligan sought to elevate a feminine conception of morality 'concerned with the activity of care' and based on an 'understanding of responsibility and relationships' rather than the more masculine 'conception of morality as fairness'.[73] This paradigm was embraced for its empowering possibilities across disciplines, but numerous criticisms (from within and outside of feminist scholarship) equally followed. As Kathy Davis has outlined, the arguments against Gilligan's ethics of care can be categorized as follows: scientific invalidity, or a reductive gendered approach to morality; the oppressive potential of an ethics of care; the selective consideration of psychological rather than sociological dimensions of care; and the questionable political value of proposing an essentialist gender-based morality.[74] Aspects of Gilligan's theory have since been reassessed from the anti-essentialist standpoint of third-wave feminism.[75] More recently, the sense of a wider care crisis has given rise to new interventions that seek to redress a longer history of care's devaluation, articulated most prominently by a group called the Care Collective, who published their own *Care Manifesto* in 2020.[76] The relationship between care and gender continues to provoke divergent opinions, particularly in the context of the physical and affective labour conducted within the domain of the home, discussions which intensified during the COVID-19 pandemic.

Earlier women writers, however, not only anticipated the terms and parameters of these later debates but also moved beyond them. If the socio-political concerns of Gilligan's critics largely pertained to the exploitative implications of an ethics of care for women on a grassroots level – in that to advance an ethics of care is to perpetuate its imposition as women's labour – the socio-political concerns of this earlier cluster of women writers went one step further. To be sure, their works, especially du Maurier's, manifest unease about the gender of care and its ethical affordances, while also critiquing the imposition of care as a form of exploitative labour, unevenly distributed within society. But, as I have established, their works share a more expansive interest in the relations between care, capital, and techniques of power that resonates just as much with Michel Foucault's commentary on biopolitics in the late 1970s and early 1980s as with the feminist and sociological theorizations of care and emotional labour that came to the fore during the same period. Foucault was fascinated by the 'kind of power which takes freedom itself and the "soul of the citizen", the life and life-conduct of the ethically free subject, as in some sense the correlative object of its own suasive capacity'.[77] The relationship between care and control plays a pronounced role in his discussions of new forms of biopower that were tasked with the 'administration of bodies and the calculated management of life', and thus fixated on problems of birth rate, general health and population.[78] The works of du Maurier, Taylor and Spark show an analogous fixation on the administration of bodies and the calculated management of life and together offer illuminating perspectives on the beginnings of a more strategic assimilation of care into political and economic practice in the post-war period.

Notes

1. Elizabeth Taylor, *Mrs Palfrey at the Claremont* (London: Virago, 2013), p. 2.
2. Arlie Russell Hochschild, *The Managed Heart: Commercialization of Human Feeling* (Berkeley, CA: University of California Press, 2012), p. 90. Emphasis in the original.
3. Daphne du Maurier, *The Birds and Other Stories* (London: Virago, 2004), p. 116. All further quotations from du Maurier's story will come from this edition.
4. Nancy Fraser, 'Contradictions of Capital and Care', *New Left Review* 100 (2016), pp. 103, 104.
5. Fraser, 'Contradictions of Capital and Care', p. 104.
6. Muriel Spark, *Memento Mori* (London, Virago, 2009), p. 111. All further quotations from Spark's novel will come from this edition.
7. Nikolas Rose, *Governing the Soul: The Shaping of the Private Self* (London: Free Association Books, 1999), p. 76.
8. Andreas Chatzidakis, Jamie Hakim, Jo Littler, Catherine Rottenberg, and Lynne Segal, *The Care Manifesto: The Politics of Interdependence* (London: Verso, 2020), pp. 11, 12. Emphasis in the original.
9. Existing literary critical scholarship on both Taylor and du Maurier is on the slight side; in this scholarship, 'The Apple Tree' and *The Soul of Kindness* are referenced in passing or discussed briefly at most. 'The Apple Tree' would align with Gina Wisker's account of du Maurier's 'everyday' gothic, though the story itself remains unmentioned and Wisker's account does not touch on the question of care. *The Soul of Kindness* is analysed at greater length in a doctoral thesis by Diane Freeborn, who reads it as an exploration of conflicting versions of the 'feminine', drawing on the theories of Simone de Beauvoir; likewise, the question of care is not dealt with here. Spark's novel has received more extensive attention, particularly since a 2008 *Modern Fiction Studies* special issue renewed interest in her work. Relevant studies of this novel have looked at its representation of aging and elderly care as well as its engagement with post-war politics and society. However, this is the first essay to approach its vision of care through integrating political and conceptual understandings in the context of a wider preoccupation with care's affordances in post-war women's writing. See Gina Wisker, 'Undermining the Everyday: Daphne du Maurier's Gothic Horror', *Revue Lisa* 19.52 (2021), https://journals-openedition-org.nuigalway.idm.oclc.org/lisa/13590#quotation (accessed 9 December

2021); Diane Freeborn, '"Is It Time We Move through or Space?": Literary Anachronism and Anachorism in the Novels of Elizabeth Taylor', 2014, University of East Anglia, PhD Thesis, pp. 213–28, https://ueaeprints.uea.ac.uk/id/eprint/49756/1/2014FreebornDPhD.pdf (accessed 10 December 2021); see also Allan Hepburn, '*Memento Mori* and Gerontography', *Textual Practice* 32.9 (2018), pp. 1495–1511; Eluned Summers-Bremner, '"Another World Than This": Muriel Spark's Postwar Investigations', *The Yearbook of English Studies* 42 (2012): pp. 151–67.

10 See Wisker for an analysis of du Maurier's 'everyday' mode of horror writing.
11 du Maurier, *The Birds*, p. 121.
12 *Ibid.*, pp. 141, 143.
13 *Ibid.*, p. 159.
14 *Ibid.*
15 Fraser, 'Contradictions of Capital and Care', p. 101.
16 Nancy Folbre, *The Invisible Heart: Economics and Family Values* (New York: New Press, 2001). For a further discussion of the 'invisibility of care', via Smith and Folbre, see also Madeleine Bunting, *Labours of Love: The Crisis of Care* (London: Granta, 2020), p. 17.
17 du Maurier, *The Birds*, pp. 116, 117, 118.
18 *Ibid.*, p. 118.
19 *Ibid.*, p. 116.
20 Margaret Forster, *Daphne du Maurier* (London: Arrow Books, 2007), p. 257.
21 du Maurier, *The Birds*, p. 117.
22 In recent years, the pocket has become a lightning rod in debates about gender politics in the popular press. Yet the association of the pocket with masculinity is longstanding, an association brought to the fore most prominently in James Joyce's *Ulysses*, in which, as Karen R. Lawrence has argued, the contents of Leopold Bloom's pockets serve to 'buttress' his masculine identity. See Karen R. Lawrence, '"Twenty Pockets Aren't Enough for Their Lies": Pocketed Objects as Props for Bloom's Masculinity in *Ulysses*', in *Masculinities in Joyce: Postcolonial Constructions*, ed. Christine van Boheemen-Saaf and Colleen Lamos (Amsterdam-Atlanta, GA: Rodopi, 2001), p. 163.
23 Nancy Folbre, *Who Cares? A Feminist Critique of the Care Economy* (New York: Rosa Luxembourg Stiftung, 2014), p. 13.
24 du Maurier, *The Birds*, p. 118.
25 Fraser, 'Contradictions of Capital and Care', p. 102.
26 Sara Ahmed, *The Cultural Politics of Emotion* (Edinburgh: Edinburgh University Press, 2015), p. 171.
27 *Ibid.*
28 du Maurier, *The Birds*, p. 115.
29 *Ibid.*, p. 138.
30 Elizabeth Taylor, *The Soul of Kindness* (London: Virago, 2010), p. 147. All further quotations from Taylor's *The Soul of Kindness* will come from this edition.
31 *Ibid.*
32 Rose, *Governing the Soul*, pp. 72, 2.

33 Taylor, *The Soul of Kindness*, pp. 9, 14.
34 *Ibid.*, p. 25. Emphasis in original.
35 *Ibid.*, p. 55.
36 Rose, *Governing the Soul*, p. 2.
37 Hochschild, *The Managed Heart*, p. 160.
38 Taylor, *The Soul of Kindness*, p. 203.
39 *Ibid.*
40 *Ibid.*
41 *Ibid.*, p. 210.
42 *Ibid.*, p. 138.
43 Hochschild, *The Managed Heart*, p. 195.
44 *Ibid.*, pp. 132, 79.
45 *Ibid.*, p. 81.
46 *Ibid.*, p. 211. Emphasis in original.
47 Ibid., pp. 212, 211.
48 *Ibid.*, p. 218.
49 Freeborn, '"Is It Time We Move through or Space?"', p. 215.
50 Spark, *Memento Mori*, p. 147.
51 *Ibid.*, p. 15.
52 *Ibid.*, 17.
53 *Ibid.*, pp. 62, 79.
54 *Ibid.*, p. 31. Emphasis in original.
55 *Ibid.*, p. 135.
56 *Ibid.*, p. 126. Emphasis added.
57 *Ibid.*, pp. 60, 125.
58 Jordanna Bailkin, *The Afterlife of Empire* (Berkeley, CA: Global, Area, and International Archive, University of California Press, 2012), p. 8.
59 *Ibid.*, pp. 13, 8.
60 Spark, *Memento Mori*, p. 110.
61 *Ibid.*, pp. 179, 30.
62 *Ibid.*, p. 11.
63 *Ibid.*
64 *Ibid.*, pp. 37, 71–2, 52.
65 *Ibid.*, p. 12.
66 *Ibid.*, p. 176.
67 *Ibid.*, p. 37.
68 *Ibid.*, p. 44.
69 *Ibid.*, p. 160.
70 *Ibid.*, p. 71.
71 *Ibid.* Suzanne E. England and Carol Ganzer, 'The Micropolitics of Elder Care in *Memento Mori, Diary of a Good Neighbour* and *A Taste for Death*', *International Journal of Health Services* 24.2 (1994), p. 359.
72 Spark, *Memento Mori*, p. 2. Emphasis in original.
73 Carol Gilligan, *In a Different Voice: Psychological Theory and Women's Development* (Cambridge, MA: Harvard University Press, 1993), p. 19.

74 Kathy Davis, 'Toward a Feminist Rhetoric: The Gilligan Debate Revisited', *Women's Studies International Forum* 15.2 (1992), pp. 219–31.
75 See, for example, Cressida J. Heyes, 'Anti-Essentialism in Practice: Carol Gilligan and Feminist Philosophy', *Hypatia* 12.3 (1997), pp. 142–63; Jahnavi Misra, 'Exploration of Ethical Debates Through Desai's *The Inheritance of Loss*, Ishiguro's *Never Let Me Go* and Smith's *On Beauty*', *Journal of Medical Humanities* 35.3 (2014), pp. 335–48; Yayo Okano, 'Why Has the Ethics of Care Become an Issue of Global Concern?', *International Journal of Japanese Sociology* 25.1 (2016), pp. 85–99.
76 See also Bunting's *Labours of Love*.
77 Colin Gordon, 'Governmental Rationality: An Introduction', in *The Foucault Effect: Studies in Governmentality with Two Lectures and an Interview with Michel Foucault*, ed. Graham Burchell, Colin Gordon, and Peter Miller (Chicago, IL: University of Chicago Press, 1991), p. 5.
78 Michel Foucault, *The History of Sexuality, Volume 1: An Introduction*, trans. Robert Hurley (London: Penguin, 1990), pp. 139–40.

Part II

Nationalizing gender politics

Part II

Nationalism under polities

Introduction to Part II

Melissa Dinsman

The politics of labour in the domestic and the professional spheres explored in the previous chapters are expanded upon in the second part of this volume, which widens the space of women's political and cultural engagements to the level of the nation. The decisions women made in the mid-century about home, childcare, marriage, and employment were influenced by nationwide politics and events, including the Spanish Civil War, the Second World War, the Beveridge Report, post-war reconstruction, and Indian independence, among many others. But the direction of influence was not oneway; instead, the means by which women engaged with the world (both domestically and professionally) also impacted the policies of governments and independence movements.

National identity became a focal point for many women writers from Britain and the colonies and is evident in the four chapters that follow. Sarah E. Cornish, for example, shows how challenges to Britain's class system and traditional gender dynamics were seen as threats to post-war national cohesion. Similarly, Geneviève Brassard analyses the dissolution of wartime national unity as women were asked to give up their newfound freedom and return to the home for the sake of remaking a 'strong' Britain. Questions of national identity and women's roles within the nation were also of central importance in colonized and newly liberated countries. As Sabujkoli Bandopadhyay shows, post-independence India saw a need for a clear national identity, one that did not always see women as equal citizens or the home as an important political space. Such an intense focus on the nation could, of course, become violently and ethically dangerous, as Charles Andrews explains in his discussion of Sylvia Townsend Warner's depiction of Spain's religious nationalism. Like the first chapters in this collection, each of the authors in this part uses close readings of lesser-known, non-canonical novels by women writers to explicitly point to the value that genres that were kept on the periphery in academic scholarship have in contextualizing the relationship between the domestic and the political at the mid-century. These authors show how more popular genre forms – realism, melodrama, domestic, historical – were used to covertly critique and subvert the creeping expansion of patriarchal national politics and government dictates into the private sphere.

But the prognosis for women in the mid-century was not simply bleak or oppressive. Indeed, throughout much of the mid-century, women experienced tremendous gains in freedom both at home and in the workplace. Women also found ways of pushing back against or circumventing the traditional gender expectations that re-emerged with the rise of nationalism, the end of the Second World War, and the establishment of new nation-states. Two of these methods, as the authors in this part argue, were female friendship and empathetic love. Despite writing about women writers from nations across the world, both Brassard and Bandopadhyay argue that friendship was not only an antidote to female isolation in the mid-century, but also politically radical. Female friendships can become alliances that allow women to find freedom from the gender politics in the home, and they can also lead to larger-scale action against colonial and patriarchal oppression and stringent class or caste systems. In a vocabulary similar to Bandopadhyay's 'revolutionary love', Andrews argues that Warner's representation of 'inclusive human love and broad economic justice' is a means to combat centralizing state and religious power. While Cornish also explores post-war female friendships in Marghanita Laski's *The Village*, the outcome is not as optimistic. Instead, through a close analysis of conversations between women in Laski's novel, Cornish suggests that female friendships in post-war Britain could be fraught and fragile due to the pressures of the nation, traditional gender expectations, and a class system that refused to die.

In Chapter 5, 'New World Women and the Labour Party Win in Marghanita Laski's *The Village*', Sarah E. Cornish explores how the transition from war to peace and the Labour Party win of 1945 are represented through Laski's fictional village of Priory Dean. By reading the conversations between female characters alongside the reforms promised by Sir William Beveridge's 1942 'Report' and put into motion by Clement Attlee's government, Cornish articulates the concerns prevalent for conservative and progressive women alike. With its plot tensions centred on star-crossed lovers of different classes, the novel falls categorically into middlebrow domestic fiction, a category Laski uses to produce an important indictment of class-based social hierarchies that would have made its readers reflect critically on this transitional period. Like Cornish, Geneviève Brassard also writes about the impact of the Beveridge Report and the policies of the new Labour government in Chapter 6, 'Beyond "Companionate Marriage": Elizabeth Taylor's Gendered Critique of Post-War Consensus in *A View of the Harbour* and *A Wreath of Roses*'. Focusing on two of Taylor's post-war works, Brassard shows how middlebrow novels about small towns, seemingly quiet domestic interiors, and plots about private betrayals of the romantic and sexual sort conceal critical engagement with the erosion of traditional ties between spouses, family members, long-time friends, and small-town communities. Brassard argues that within her middlebrow novels, Taylor depicts a Britain grappling with post-war fragmentation of national identity and gender politics, a fragmentation that saw women absorbing the shocks of social change the most.

In Chapter 7, 'Dissident Friendship and Revolutionary Love in the Novels of Sabitri Roy and Sulekha Sanyal', Sabujkoli Bandopadhyay demonstrates how mid-century female novelists represented the complex modalities of politics and identity formation during the last decade of British colonial rule in the subcontinent. Both Sanyal's *The Seedling's Tale* and Roy's *Harvest Songs* offer a rare glimpse into the evolution of gender subjectivity in relation to the anti-colonial struggles, peasant movements, famine, and subaltern uprising in 1950s Bengali literature. Through careful readings of the novels and the historical moment, Bandopadhyay illustrates how colonial Bengali women found new coordinates of their gendered belonging through their participation in socialist politics. Yet like Cornish and Brassard, this chapter shows that even within liberal politics, patriarchal oppression continues, often under the guise of national unity. For Bandopadhyay, the novels of Sanyal and Roy offer critiques of the systemic patriarchy within political institutions (both colonial and national) and its impact on women and the domestic sphere. More significantly, however, these novels, like many discussed throughout this part, offer new possibilities for subversion in the hopes of meaningful and lasting change.

The need for change is at the centre of the final chapter, '"The Political Theory of Heaven": Religious Nationalism, Mystical Anarchism, and the Spanish Civil War in Sylvia Townsend Warner's *After the Death of Don Juan*', in which Charles Andrews explores the merging of Catholicism and nationalist politics in 1930s Spain and Warner's search for an alternative. Whereas the previous chapters focus on marriage, care work, and family obligations within the domestic sphere, Andrews's chapter enlarges the parameter of the domestic to include religion, which, by its very demands, is both personal and public and often relies on female labour. Focusing on the rise of religious nationalism under Franco, Andrews contends that Warner's fictional and parabolic depiction of Spain is a mode of political theology. Her novel *After the Death of Don Juan* entertains a secular political theology which engages with Catholicism and anarchism while never becoming explicit propaganda. Warner, Andrews argues, uses the domestic to dwell on the possibilities of political alternatives to fascism and nationalism. Like Andrews, Cornish and Brassard also discuss novels that seek to offer options other than the retrograde national politics that emerged in the mid-century. Bandopadhyay takes this a step further and suggests that even the offered alternatives can be just as restrictive for women. Yet it is in the quest for an alternative to the domestic and political status quo that hope lies for mid-century women writers. And this is a hope that each one of these chapters explores.

5

New world women and the Labour Party win in Marghanita Laski's *The Village*

Sarah E. Cornish

In her 1952 middlebrow novel *The Village*, Marghanita Laski portrays a typical English village at war's end where residents struggle socially and ideologically to find their way into peacetime. In the opening pages, readers will detect Laski's indictment of class-based social hierarchies and a destabilization of social norms that had become all the more fragile with the end of the Second World War and the Labour Party's 1945 win. The novel generates its social analysis around the reception of the shifting political climate by contrasting British wartime national narratives of unity and 'good citizenship' with their contested aftermath on society. The novel fits into what Kristin Bluemel has called 'aftermath novels', not just because its mise-en-scène is infused with war's reverberations, but also because it 'confronts contradictions imposed by disruptions in national and global politics'.[1] Women writing aftermath narratives, Bluemel claims, 'found themselves living in a nation that was victorious but impoverished, in communities where women were empowered by war work but increasingly found in the home, in a culture emboldened by democratic ideals but hostile to active feminism'.[2] As Sonya O. Rose deftly argues in her study of national belonging during the 'People's War', women faced a challenge of locating themselves within a highly emotional discourse surrounding nationhood and 'good citizenship'[3] during the war that, as this chapter uses Laski's novel to show, created complicated and damaging attachments to national mythologies well into its aftermath.

The Village captures these competing ideologies by not only pairing radical feminist ambitions with the cultural fear of the end of Conservative values, but also by using the seemingly traditional and benign marriage plot between star-crossed lovers of different classes, a middle-class girl and a working-class boy. Laski's use of such a plot affirms Nicola Humble's observation that middlebrow fiction contributes to 'a powerful force in establishing and consolidating, but also in resisting, new class and gender identities, and that it is this paradoxical allegiance to both domesticity and a radical sophistication that makes this literary form so ideologically flexible'.[4] Indeed, the Labour Party win brought with it a social recalibration of class and gender identities, which are played out in Laski's fictional village, Priory Dean. *The Village* is Laski's most subtle and gentle of her six novels. Those reasons alone may have contributed to it being forgettable. Yet this chapter asserts that the novel is also her most politically pointed in its feminism, as Laski makes critical interventions into how women grapple with a simultaneous excitement for and fear of the post-war era and attends to both citizenship and nationhood in the new world.

The novel's setting, 1945, and publication year, 1952, neatly encapsulate the Clement Attlee years, 1945–51. Read as a piece of socio-political history, the novel reflects upon the specific impacts of the Labour Party win as it looks back at the initial shifts needed to put Britain's Welfare State into motion. *The Village* presents a rather abrupt cultural turn from the wartime objectives of unity, sacrifice for the good of the nation, and class-blindness to a more troubling and regressive desire for a return to rigid conservativism that would impede the advancements women and working-class people had made during the Second World War. Laski's Priory Dean can therefore be read as a microcosm of the British state, where debates about the emerging Welfare State play out and characters grapple with the impacts of the housing drive, squatters, and the encroachment of urban developers.[5] Underpinning the narrative is a deep fear held by the more conservative residents that their village will become a London dormitory for socialist urbanites seeking respite from the city. In the early post-war months, the residents of Priory Dean work to resituate themselves along class and political lines in the brave new world being shaped by Attlee's cabinet. In conservative characters, there is a distinct nostalgia for what they call 'Old England', a fear of communism, and anxiety about America's growing power. In the characters who support Attlee and the Labour Party, there is an excitement about the possibility of resisting old-fashioned, class-bound ways of doing business. Through characters' heated debates about housing, commerce, and especially marriage prospects for the village youth, Laski's novel warns against perpetuating the myth of lost greatness endemic to the British Empire's decline and cautions against narratives that cling to an elite nostalgia for maintaining a social hierarchy as the only option for preserving democracy.[6]

Such political stakes in Laski's novel, even one as unassuming as *The Village*, are not surprising as Laski was a politically invested writer well-known to the public. Born into a prominent Jewish family in London, she was the daughter of Seraphina Gaster and Neville Laski, and the niece of political theorist, economist, and Labour Party chairman (1945–46) Harold Laski. While her contemporaneous critics nearly always mention the fact of her infamous uncle, a stronger influence on her intellectual upbringing came from her maternal grandfather, Moses Gaster, a founder of the English Zionist Federation.[7] At a time when many of her female peers were not encouraged into advanced schooling, Laski's family prioritized her formal education and a development of independent, critical, political thought. Lexicographers and recreational wordsmiths may remember her for her prodigious contributions to the *Oxford English Dictionary*; many of the over 250,000 suggestions she made beginning in 1958 ended up in the 1989 version and came to shape the English language of the twentieth century. By the end of her life as a public intellectual, Laski's would have been a household name for many upper- and middle-class progressives. She was a contributor to *Vogue*, the *Times*, and the *Times Literary Supplement*, an advocate for the arts, and a supporter of nuclear disarmament in the 1960s.[8] Not only did her name carry weight, so too did her voice as she was a regular panellist on the BBC's *What's My Line*, *The Brains Trust*, and *Any Questions?*

Each of Laski's six novels, published between 1944 and 1953, serves up a searing dose of socio-political criticism of persistent class and gender expectations and is fertile ground for critical attention. Laski's fiction emerged during a period still somewhat neglected by scholarship and common readers alike and long-ago regarded by W.W. Robson as 'one of the worst periods in English Literature',[9] an assessment this collection of chapters seeks to redress. However, recent recuperation efforts of women writers from the interwar, Second World War, and post-war years have yet to include Laski. Perhaps this is because no two Laski novels are of the same genre. To this point, P.D. James claims, 'She was not a prolific novelist, nor was she a writer who repeated herself.'[10] Laski's first novel, an out-of-print political satire called *Love on the Super Tax* (1944), parodies Walter Greenwood's 1933 bestseller *Love on the Dole*. Reissued novels from Persephone Press include *Tory Heaven* (1948), which presents a 'scorching indictment of a hierarchical society'[11] through a character who wakes up in a dystopic alternative universe where the Conservatives, rather than Labour, have won the General Election of 1945. *The Victorian Chaise-Longue* (1953) also employs the narrative strategy of waking up elsewhere; in this case, the female character is trapped in a Victorian past. *Little Boy Lost* (1949) is a thriller about a man in war-torn, post-Occupation France seeking a refugee child who may or may not be his son. Of all Laski's novels, *To Bed with Grand Music* (1946) has received the most critical attention because its highly shocking protagonist's story calls feminist attention to the impact of austerity measures and wartime propaganda on women.[12] Despite their differences in genre, each of her novels are linked through characters navigating localized changes and daily concerns amidst massive national and global upset. Sue Kennedy notes that Laski's fiction carries a 'fascination with situations that oppose and destabilize the norm'.[13] It is this negotiation of conflicting possibilities across Laski's narratives that makes her fiction rich for a reassessment of women's experiences in the early years of the Second World War's aftermath.

This chapter is split into two sections. The first establishes the political backdrop of the Labour win in 1945, the Beveridge Report that provided Labour's platform, and how changes brought by that victory shape the experiences and social expectations for women. The second analyses the interactions of the women in the novels and demonstrates Laski's argument that feminist social change begins not just with progressive policy reform at the government level, but also with conversations between women about what it means to be a good citizen. Laski's female characters (Margaret Trevor, Wendy Trevor, Edith Wilson, Jill Morton, Martha Wetherall, and Miss Evadne) are caught in a space of contradictory messaging that comes from the government, their local communities, and even from each other about what it means to be 'good' in a post-war society. For example, the staunchly Conservative Wendy Trevor reminds Margaret that there is a distinction to be upheld between 'Poor People's children' and 'Nice Girls' like her.[14] Margaret Trevor yearns for a seemingly traditional life of a housewife, challenging the oversimplified notion that women in the post-war years were reluctant to return to the home. Yet she also wants to be a household cook, a profession restricted to working-class domestic servants pre-war; middle-class Margaret's desire shocks her mother, who forbids her to pursue it.[15] Laski presents her politics specifically through the conversations Margaret has with Jill Morton, Martha Wetherall, and Miss Evadne. Jill represents the aspirational girl who wants to move to the big city and work for *Vogue* but who expects to achieve her upward mobility through an upscale marriage. Martha is a well-meaning American who destabilizes social structures by getting involved in local politics and family dramas without understanding the British culture into which she has married. Miss Evadne, a spinster and the village's oldest, wealthiest, and most-esteemed female resident, serves as both the product of Old England, and as the inspiration for Margaret's break with her middle-class binds. Each of these female characters represent a specific political tension: democratic socialist possibilities within a new British society, the post-war relationship with America, and conservative nostalgia for Old England.

Beveridge reforms and women's return to the home

The public release of Sir William Beveridge's report in December 1942, under the title 'Social Insurance and Allied Services', promised reforms for daily life after wartime that would keep Britain from falling into the same kind of depressed post-war economy that the interwar years had suffered.

The colloquially named 'Report' set forth ambitious social reforms to alleviate what Beveridge saw as the 'five great evils' of the pre-war period, which, by all means, should be avoided once the war had concluded: want, disease, ignorance, squalor, and idleness. Historian Kenneth O. Morgan explains that the Beveridge Report

> became a spectacular best seller and a major political embarrassment for Churchill and other Conservative ministers. Beveridge himself, an austere civil servant turned academic, was propelled into the limelight as the new 'people's William'. Henceforth, the main framework of the Beveridge proposals, including such novelties as family allowances, along with its ancillary assumptions of the need for full employment and a national health service, became the foundation of all detailed social planning and policy-making for the post-war world.[16]

While there is no recorded evidence that Laski familiarized herself with the Report, she would not have been ignorant of it. The British Institute for Public Opinion surveyed the population after the Report's publication and found that 95% of respondents had heard of the report and the majority supported its recommendations.[17] National Archives archivist Chris Day notes that the Ministry of Information's 'Home Intelligence Weekly Report' showed evidence through mail censorship that most cases in which the Report was mentioned were favourable. Referencing the Home Intelligence Report of 10 December 1942, Day writes, 'Beveridge's plan was *the* most talked about topic in the country. A few weeks later people were said to be looking forward to bedding down during the Christmas break to really make a study of it.'[18] Laski's prodigious reading habits would likely have led her to do the same.

The Village's narrative arc is framed by both the social reforms that came about as a product of the Beveridge Report and the 'suitably apocalyptic' reactions to the General Election on 26 July 1945.[19] Upon the announcement of the Labour victory at a gathering of Priory Dean's middle- and upper-class residents, Laski's characters make their concerns clear in the following statements:

> 'It's the rank ingratitude! When you think of all Mr Churchill has done for us, then just throwing him away like an old glove. What they're going to think of us abroad, I shudder to think' [...]
> 'To think of being ruled by Communists like that Bevin. I'd like to string him up with my own hands' [...]
> 'Well, I suppose it's the end of people like us' [...]
> 'Yes, we'll just have to get used to being ruled by a lot of piddling clerks without an aitch to their names.'[20]

As the townspeople react, demonstrating staunchly anti-egalitarian positions and concern about how those abroad, specifically Americans, will perceive them, only Miss Evadne offers a balanced assessment. 'Well, after all, it is a *British* government – I mean they're all *Britishers*' – reminding her neighbours that it could have gone an entirely different way had the war *not* been won.[21]

The Labour victory came about in large part because of the 'sweeping change of mood during the war years', the party's support of the reforms presented by the Report, and a conviction on the part of the majority of British people that policies were needed to prevent a return to the mass unemployment that had plagued the 1930s.[22] The mood shift included an embrace of reforms that would solve the housing crisis and desperate poverty that would become wholly visible once austerity measures were lifted. Morgan explains, 'The 1945 [Labour] election manifesto was largely a reaffirmation of key sections of Beveridge, with added emphasis on such old Labour themes as a national health service and a big new housing drive.'[23] Looking back on the Labour win, it is now evident that the welfare reforms put in place during the Attlee years did not, in fact, result in a drastic change in wealth distribution or a more 'egalitarian or open society',[24] and it is more accurate that the Attlee government was the climax for the Labour Party. Yet as Morgan concludes in his assessment of its impact, 'if the welfare state proved to have its limits, it offered an essential base for future social advance. It extended, at least in theory, a new concept of citizenship, universal and comprehensive.'[25]

Morgan's research into the Labour win is foundational; his study is based on archives that had been closed to the public for several decades and offers a compelling assessment of both the practical matters of the Cabinet and the mood of the public about the changes. However, his study does not attend specifically to the impact on women coming back into the home after the war years, and the fact that Beveridge's Report named housewives as 'dependents'[26] was by no means directly progressive for married women in what became the Welfare State. As an archival description of a Welfare State poster notes,

> The Welfare State has always been closely connected with the development of the family, acting to reinforce and support it in significant ways. In this sense, it is as much a set of ideas as well as services. Welfare provisions help to maintain women's primary role as reproducers of the workforce, despite the fact that women make up a significant percentage of the paid workforce.[27]

The reforms actively encouraged women's service to the state to be in the form of reproducing the future workforce and keeping a safe, clean, and healthy home for them.

Laski's female characters' experiences in the transition to peace subvert the notion that for a woman to be a good citizen, she had to be a good housewife and a good mother while also fulfilling her social responsibility via her wartime efforts. Central to the war's mythology is that women were liberated from oppressive and sexist expectations by doing war work.[28] However, as Rose articulates, this is not the case. The 'good citizen' woman had to maintain her balance between domestic and public service, while keeping herself neat, tidy, and chaste.[29] A woman who slid too far in one direction or another would no longer hold status as a good citizen, but rather would be viewed as selfish and individualistic. Simplistic and polarizing messaging coming from the Ministry of Information and seeping into popular culture would have it that a woman who wore too much make-up was libidinous, and potentially lethal, while a woman who stayed too much at home was slacking in her war duties.[30] This contradiction permeated wartime media, and Laski uses it to demonstrate the rhetorical hold such messaging continued to wield over women in the post-war years. As the war wound down, 'Mass Observation, as well as local and national newspapers, the Wartime Social Survey, and feminist publications suggested that women "desire to return to domestic life as soon as it is reasonably possible".'[31] According to Rose, this attitude was channelled into courses in housewifery and homemaking for girls and young women, but it also 'provoked discussion about social and political reform that could potentially have changed what it meant to be a wife and mother'.[32] Armed with the ideas posed in the Beveridge Report, especially the guiding principle that 'A revolutionary moment in the world's history is a time for revolutions, not for patching',[33] women's associations and community groups began to progressively re-imagine the status of the housewife and mother in ways that suggested a more socialist modernity for the new world. Feminist activists advocated that women no longer be considered dependents of their husbands, but rather have their own status as employees of the state, thereby giving them full agency over their role as producers of the workforce. Rose's research shows that such ideas were controversial, especially in conservative arenas where there was an effort to reify clear divisions between men's work and women's work once the war ended.[34] Rose concludes her study at the war's end, which is where this chapter begins. As Laski's *The Village* illustrates, the revolutionary and feminist debates identified by Rose and others continued into the post-war peace and mid-century.

The political power of chat

When the novel begins on 8 May 1945, V-E Day, we meet Wendy Trevor and Edith Wilson on their last night of duty at the Red Cross Patrol. The conversation that opens the novel explicitly engages in what life will be like in the new post-war world. The women spend the evening talking about what is to come, their hopes for their nearly grown children, and their political positions:

> 'A lot of things are going to seem funny', said Wendy thoughtfully. 'I expect we'll see a good many changes. For one thing, I suppose we'll have a General Election now, though there can't be any doubt about who'll get in.'
> Edith said surprisingly, 'I'm not so sure.'
> 'You don't mean you'd vote *Socialist*, do you, Edith?' said Wendy, shocked.[35]

Edith explains that the Conservatives have never done much for working people and that during the war was the first time she and her husband were able to put something by. Edith's reference to the equalizing effects of austerity measures makes visible the novel's driving argument that the end of the war brings an opportunity to embrace a dissolution of class. From its introduction in 1940 by the Board of Trade, austerity regulated goods and services to be accessible across class lines and was a boon to the most impoverished.[36] It is through this conversation between the two women that we also learn that, prior to the war, Edith was Wendy's char. War has made them equals financially, though not ideologically.

As the women chat through the night, they reflect on each of their children. Edith's son Roy will '"make some girl a real good husband one of these days"', and her youngest daughter, Maureen, is '"the clever one of the family"', bound for university.[37] Wendy's Sheila is also university-bound and hoping for a scholarship, but it is Margaret about whom Wendy admits to Edith she's ever so worried. Without scholarly aptitude and with no marriage prospects in her own class, Margaret has become a problem. But the real problem is that Wendy and Gerald Trevor's chicken farm has failed, and they cannot afford to keep their daughter at home, let alone scrape together enough money to buy her some suitable clothing for attending '"tennis-parties and things"' where she might meet an eligible young man.[38] For the Trevors, no amount of ration-book coupons can help. They are out of money. Edith considers her plentiful clothing coupons and comfortable income and wishes she could buy Margaret a new dress, but she is held back by an awareness that Wendy would find such a suggestion utterly insulting.[39] Wendy muses that she had hoped Margaret would be called into the Services, which '"might solve the problem of clothes *and* a job *and* a husband all at once"', but the war's end has closed that window.[40]

As an introduction to the politics of the novel, this conversation does a lot of heavy lifting. It brings into relief the ways the end of the war will specifically change the lives of women. It introduces the possibility of a Labour win and indicates how shocking that win would be for those who assume Churchill's continued incumbency. It highlights how austerity could help hide financial ruin and that the end of it would mean that ruin would become visible. Lastly, it sets up the dynamic between what will become the two main families of the narrative, the Trevors and the Wilsons. Margaret Trevor will fall in love with Roy Wilson, undermining the rigid social structures that both Wendy and Edith seem to accept will return in a post-war society. For Wendy, this will mean utter shame and social disgrace. For Edith, it will mean a wonderful opportunity to see her son well-matched through happiness. Writing from the short hindsight of the impacts of the Labour win, Laski's marriage plot allows an interrogation into what sort of social changes must occur at the local level for the social reforms promised by the Beveridge Report and implemented by the Labour government to take hold.

Laski frames Wendy's daughter, the 'mild, gentle and innocuous' Margaret, as the rebel who will lead Priory Dean toward more progressive views.[41] Margaret seems to be inspired by the innocent and dutiful sacrificial lamb characters played by doe-eyed Patricia Roc in wartime propaganda dramas. Like Roc's character Celia in *Millions Like Us* (1943), Margaret's desires are simple. She wants a quiet life in the country with a husband, two children, a little home with a garden, and flowerboxes in the windows. Most of all, she wants a white wedding. However, in building a character who would feel familiar to many of her female readers, Laski takes the opportunity to fill Margaret with radical potential for upending systems that have held women in place for too long. It is through Margaret's conversations and personal interactions with other women – Jill Morton, Martha Wetherall, and Miss Evadne – that the politics of *The Village* unfurls.

Margaret and Jill Morton: variations on female liberation

Margaret's closest friend at the beginning of the novel is Jill Morton, who encourages Margaret to consider moving with her to London. Laski uses this friendship to show the contradictory possibilities for a girl just finishing school and reaching marrying age through both girls' differing perceptions of what female liberation looks like and their varying degrees of class consciousness. It is noteworthy that Jill also serves as a vehicle for the novel's critical awareness of persistent antisemitism within conservative British society. Jill's Jewishness is what makes Wendy Trevor apprehensive about the friendship between the two girls, evident when she says to a neighbour about Jill's family, '"I believe they're Jews, though naturally I've never liked to ask. Mind you, I've nothing against Jews as such, but they do tend to be a bit – well, you know.'"[42] As far as Margaret can see, however, Jill is a truly mobile and aspirational girl on her way to becoming a journalist for *Vogue*. If Jill does eventually marry, she tells Margaret, her pick must be a rich man who can afford housekeepers so she will never have to cook her own food.[43] Jill's aspirations attract Margaret to her. However, those same aspirations also embody a contradictory kind of feminism that Margaret does not detect. For example, Jill's father has landed her an entry-level job at *Meg's Magazine*, a periodical for 'servant-girls' full of advice for best housekeeping practices.[44] Moreover, Jill hopes to have a career of her own but still wants to lean on a man for her comfort, first a father who gets her a job and later a husband who will provide her a housekeeper. Jill suggests Margaret could go to secretarial school and take the same approach to liberated womanhood by finding a rich husband in the city. When Margaret insists that were she to join Jill in this liberatory venture, she'd like to live in a flat so they could do their own cooking, Jill responds, '"You know Margaret Trevor, what you ought to be is a wife, not a secretary. You seem to like all the things that bore me stiff. I bet you'd be happy in a little house somewhere, counting the laundry and washing out the nappies."'[45] While Margaret does not take Jill's barbed reproach as an insult in this moment, the friendship between Margaret and Jill becomes strained later in the novel once Margaret reveals that she is in love with working-class Roy.

Due to a lack of private phone lines and other complications, Margaret is unable to share her news about the developing relationship with Roy with Jill for many weeks. When opportunity finally arises, Margaret gushes:

> 'His name's Roy ... and he's an absolute darling. He wants all the same kinds of things that I do, and we think just the same about practically everything. We're going to have a little home with a garden and we've decided exactly how we're going to furnish it. Oh, and Jill, you *will* be my bridesmaid, won't you?'[46]

There is not a trace of Old England's class expectation here. Margaret likes Roy for Roy, and it does not occur to her that her friend might not be happy for her. Jill's response reveals deep class-consciousness and a misleading attitude of what female liberation might be when she asks, '"Who is he? Has he got any money?"'[47] These two questions fish for family name and upper-class status, but Margaret simply responds that Roy is a printer and makes enough money for the both of them. Jill is 'cast into a turmoil of confusion' and 'cold stupefaction' as it dawns on her that Margaret means Roy Wilson, Wendy Trevor's charwoman's son.[48] Internally she thinks about how her friendship with Margaret will have to end. For all the progressiveness Jill appears to have from Margaret's point of view, she is shocked and outraged that Margaret would demean her position by falling for a working-class boy who is only a printer and not an editor of a glossy magazine. In a last-ditch effort to save the scenario, Jill asks Margaret if Roy is at least a Communist. If he were, it would mean for Jill 'who was very quick at picking up social nuances' that his job as a printer was some kind of political intervention into the conditions for the working man.[49] But no, Roy voted Socialist and it is, as Jill feared and from her point of view, the worst possible situation for Margaret's future. Through this friendship, Laski shows that even within the younger generation, the class bindings that Labour's governance and social reforms seek to soften are still vice-grip tight. But even more compelling is the way in which, through these two girls, she reveals the pervasiveness of regressive, traditional values. Jill, for all her progressive talk of liberation and career, carries the expectation that a man will look after her financially and help her climb the ladder. Her appalling suggestion that Margaret have an affair with Roy until it fizzles out solidifies the end of the friendship between the young women. Ironically, it is Margaret, whose desires seem traditional on the surface, who shows herself to be genuinely progressive by marrying beneath her class instead of just having an affair.

Margaret and Martha Wetherall: an American's intervention

When American Martha Wetherall and her English husband, Ralph, move to the village from London to get away from overcrowding, Margaret has an opportunity to develop a new friendship with the slightly older, sophisticated, and truly progressively minded woman. This friendship makes it possible for Margaret to have two life-changing epiphanies: (1) she realizes sexual safety is the most important quality to have in a relationship with a man, and (2) she realizes her mother's conservative politics are deeply offensive. Martha facilitates both these epiphanies through an invitation to the Country Club dance and through several conversations with Margaret about the similarities between race and class consciousness in America and Britain, respectively. Martha's presence in the novel reminds readers of the abrupt end of Lend-Lease and the need to accept the terms of a 3.75-billion-dollar loan from the United States[50] and of the lingering presence of Americans, especially in British cities, after the war's end. The perceptions of Americans in Britain post-1945 was complex and contradictory; as David Kynaston observes, 'There was an element of gratitude, certainly, and many personal entanglements, together with a largely frustrated longing for American material goods, but at the same time resentment of a newly risen superpower that seemed unpleasantly inclined to throw its weight around.'[51]

Martha is unaware of her direct impact on Margaret, but her character's brazen Americanness is central to Laski's analysis of the villagers' post-war attitudes toward an America to which they are financially beholden.[52]

One contemporaneous reviewer's description of Martha directly links her character to the larger ongoing anxiety about America's rising status as a world power: 'Subtly and surely [Laski] shows the menacing advance of social change ... in an American newcomer with her friendliness and her smart parties and her penchant for Progress, who has to be passively resisted until she can be translated properly into English.'[53] Martha struggles with integrating herself into the village's local ways and the ways befitting of her upper-middle-class status. She hosts parties at the wrong hour. She invites people across class lines because she likes their company; '"one would have expected her to be a bit more discriminating, somehow. Still, I suppose that's American democracy"',[54] remarks Wendy upon hearing about one party's guest list. She serves too much alcohol, always at the wrong time of day, and is accused of being '"showy"'[55] by Margaret's father, Gerald. She attempts to make suggestions at the local council meeting and is shunned; '"What she suggests is very interesting and perhaps it would work very well in America, but I'm afraid it isn't the answer for Priory Dean."'[56] Eventually, she is deemed '"vulgar"'[57] by Wendy for the grave infraction of wearing a lime-green raincoat and scarlet lipstick to run errands in town. These two infractions in particular – speaking one's mind and wearing scarlet lipstick – situate Martha in the libidinous woman category of wartime messaging to which characters like Wendy and Gerald remain committed.

However, Martha finds good company with Margaret, whom she takes under her wing, offering to teach her American cooking and inviting her over for afternoon cocktails as well as on an outing to the Country Club in the next town over. For Margaret, Martha's 'vulgarity' is what attracts her:

> Everyone I really like is vulgar, she thought, Martha and Jill and lately Maureen [Roy's sister] and sometimes she added Roy to the list. Vulgar people seemed to stand up to things better than refined people, to be able to take in their stride difficulties that at home would have been quite overwhelming.[58]

Margaret finds joy and, more importantly, self-confidence in her newfound attraction to 'vulgar' words and deeds. Martha's implicit influence over Margaret's blossoming self-confidence is squarely located in her inability to understand the class politics that govern Old England. In hoping to help Margaret find a job she actually likes and for which she has skills, Martha suggests to her husband that they hire her to be a nursery governess. Ralph explains that to do so would offend the Trevors so deeply that the Wetheralls would have no chance of being accepted into the village's social structure:

'Don't you see, it'd be putting her in an inferior position to us in their own village; it would be different if she went away to some other nasty rich people elsewhere.'

'But surely they don't feel like that about us?' asked Martha.

'They would if you suggested Margaret coming to work for us', said Ralph grimly. [...]

'All right, I won't then', said Martha amiably, 'though it all sounds very silly to me. I thought that even in England all those old ideas about class were going by the board.'

'Officially they are', said Ralph, 'but actually they're as strong as ever, and don't you forget it. Even if they never talk about it, class is still the most important thing in the world to people like the Trevors.'[59]

In her explicit interrogation of Britain's class-politics, which she struggles to understand, Martha's character serves as an implicit representation of the complicated relationship between America and Britain. Like the United States, which refused to enter the war until 1941, she's a bit of a late-comer to the scene, but she holds the financial cards to offer solutions for what she sees as a healthier society. On a more global level, Martha's ideas about how things ought to be reflect another, darker, critique of Laski's; the well-inculcated point of national identity of British superiority is not only disappearing as the post-war's economic effects shift power, but also the 'rightness of large swaths of the globe being coloured red', David Kynaston's record of how Britain's Empire appeared on maps,[60] is not right at all. Indeed, it is immoral. Laksi employs Martha to directly say the things that no British character can or would say, even if they think it. Thus, Martha's role offers the reader imaginative space to consider how the shift away from the Empire's superiority and into economic dependency on the United States has altered British notions of community and citizenry, both locally and globally.

Though Martha cannot help Margaret with employment, she does offer social capital. Martha's invitation to Margaret to join them at a Country Club dance is in an attempt to help the Trevors and pair Margaret up with Roger, a boy fitting of her class. However, rather than the match leading to love, it leads to Margaret being violently kissed. The scene begins with Roger's perspective, an angry and resentful young man who is thinking about a different and wholly glamourous unattainable girl as he 'pulled [Margaret] against him and kissed her brutally and clumsily, determined to vent on her his passionate dissatisfaction'.[61] However, the scene leads to Margaret's most valuable epiphany. As she reels from the violation, she realizes that what she wants and needs most is safety, something she will not get from her friendship with Martha Wetherall, her parents, or her middle-class status.[62] Margaret's desire for safety can only be achieved by confronting and rejecting her mother's classism and engaging in the sort of socialist modernity progressive feminist activists were calling for during Labour's transition period. Ironically, it is Miss Evadne, the epitome of Old England, who motivates Margaret to fully embrace what she has to do.

Margaret and Miss Evadne: a spinster's call for courage

From the villagers' point of view, Miss Evadne represents traditional values and distinguished status, both of which are on the verge of annihilation in the new society where Labour ideals are threatening to flatten class distinctions. Miss Evadne has lived her entire life in 'the Hall', Priory Dean's most valuable estate, now threatened by the urban developers whose investigative visits pepper the novel. The fact that she never married is of no consequence to the villagers, who assume it is only that she was never matched with someone deserving of her aristocratic status. However, she shares with Margaret that the reason she never married was because she was not permitted to marry the man she truly loved, a local dentist. Because of the dentist's middle-class status, Miss Evadne's father refused to acknowledge the possibility of a match, and no further possibilities presented themselves. She tells her tragic story of lost love to compel Margaret to go ahead with her relationship with Roy and not let her parents get in the way:

> 'If they see that you are firm and resolute, and that nothing they say can change you, I'm sure they will [come round] in the end. And if you feel like wavering, you think of me and my lonely life, and remember it was just because I hadn't the courage to stand out for what I wanted.'[63]

Here, Miss Evadne employs the rhetoric of wartime propaganda: 'firm', 'resolute', 'courage'. In having Miss Evadne use these particular words, ones included on well-known posters developed by the Ministry of Information,[64] Laski subversively recalls and endorses the unifying classless ideal promoted during the war years. Through her sad tale, Miss Evadne captures the danger of regressive decisions that would undo the progressive strides women, in particular, made during the war years. It is essential that Miss Evadne, a symbol of Old England, is the one to convince Margaret to stick to her convictions and go ahead with Roy. With Miss Evadne's death by heart attack in the last pages of the novel, Laski uses this character to close a chapter of a certain kind of oppressive British nationalism and move into a new, more hopeful future where Margaret and Roy can defy restrictions and have a life together.

Armed with epiphanies – that she does not and need not share her mother's political views, that love should be a classless endeavour, and that she needs safety above all – Margaret confronts her family:

> 'You talk a lot about people like us and not letting down standards, and what do we get out of it? If I don't marry Roy, what is there ahead of me but working at a job I loathe that will never be any different or lead me to anything better? I slave at my beastly job all day and then I come home and I slave at home, and you none of you even thank me, you just take it for granted that I'm the stupid one and I'm not worth anything better. You never do anything for me, buy me pretty clothes or take me out where I could meet people, or even behave as if you love me.'[65]

Directing her criticisms squarely at her parents, she rejects their politics and their antiquated attitudes about what makes a 'Nice Girl'. She divorces herself from 'people like us' and courageously reveals her family's participation in perpetuating regressive values. Her outburst is a success. The previously 'mild, gentle and innocuous'[66] Margaret eventually garners her family's approval of the marriage, but only on the condition that she and Roy leave the country and move to New Zealand.

Conclusion

Laski's decision to ship Margaret and Roy off to New Zealand might suggest that she lets old ideologies win; Margaret and Roy, if banished, will no longer be an embarrassment to the Trevor family as they cling to their disintegrating status. However, the conclusion of the novel conveys that Laski intends something more complicated. Once the young couple has boarded the boat at Tilbury[67] and are safely on their way to a new life, the Trevors return home and convene with their friends to close the rift that has threatened their reputation and settle back into their roles. What they do not realize, and what only begins to dawn on them in the final lines, is that the developers have got hold of Miss Evadne's land. Old England is no more, and Priory Dean is on its way to becoming a London dormitory after all. Laski erases the protective and imagined boundaries that rooted the villagers' sense of autonomous governance and maintained Priory Dean as a distinctive locality. Through this, Laski highlights anxieties about the complete dissolution of the village as a way of life in the new nationalized Welfare State. However, the end of the novel offers space for the reader to consider whether or not village life is still possible if those in the community work for it together.

These examinations of the national climate through Margaret's interactions with the women of Priory Dean make evident the macro-level changes in society brought about by the Second World War. The economic overhaul promised by the Beveridge Report in 1942, its aftermath where class divisions reared up once again, and the shocking outcome of the General Election in 1945 had direct and consequential outcomes for the women who would have read the novel in 1952. Laski brings geo-political tension into *The Village* by contrasting the decline of the British Empire with the rise of the American Superpower. And, with a sub-plot about housing development, she captures an anxiety that will become central to the literature of the post-war period up through the Thatcher years about the loss of safe, protective, community-governed village life. For economically strapped middle-class readers clinging to a mark of status to protect them from becoming one of the 'Poor People', Laski's novel may have stung and been easy to toss off as just another age-old marriage plot. However, its literary-historical impact now rests in the fact that when it was published, the Conservatives had been securely re-elected. With Churchill once again at the helm, tradition was back on its way to dominating. Laski's middlebrow domestic novel is more than just a jab at the class wars; it is a warning to women readers especially to not lose hold of the progress made toward public equity and domestic agency during the war and its aftermath and to embrace both for a safer and happier future.

Notes

1. Kristin Bluemel, 'The Aftermath of War', in *The History of British Women's Writing 1945–1975*, ed. Clare Hanson and Susan Watkins (London: Palgrave, 2017), p. 144.
2. Ibid.
3. Sonya O. Rose, *Which People's War? National Identity and Citizenship in Britain 1939–1945* (Oxford: Oxford University Press, 2003), p. 13.
4. Nicola Humble, *The Feminine Middlebrow Novel, 1920s to 1950s: Class Domesticity and Bohemianism* (Oxford: Oxford University Press, 2001), p. 3.
5. See Paula Derdiger, *Reconstruction Fiction: Housing and Realist Literature in Postwar Britain* (Columbus, OH: Ohio State University Press, 2020).
6. Laski's writing may be read against nostalgia narratives that emerged in the post-war years such as Evelyn Waugh's *Brideshead Revisited* (1945), an enormously popular novel with anti-egalitarianism as a central theme.
7. The Centre for Jewish Studies, 'Moses Gaster Projects', University of Manchester.
8. Susan Brown, Patricia Clements, and Isobel Grundy (eds), 'Marghanita Laski Entry: Life & Writing Screen', in *Orlando: Women's Writing in the British Isles*

from the Beginnings to the Present (Cambridge: Cambridge University Press, 2006).
9 W.W. Robson, *Modern English Literature* (Oxford: Oxford University Press, 1970), p. 146.
10 P.D. James, 'Preface', in *The Victorian Chaise-Longue*, Marghanita Laski (London: Persephone Press, 1999), pp. v–ix, vii.
11 Brown et al. (eds), 'Marghanita Laski Entry'.
12 See Andrea Adolph, '"At Least I Get My Dinners Free": Transgressive Dining in Marghanita Laski's *To Bed with Grand Music*', *MFS Modern Fiction Studies* 59.2 (2013), pp. 395–415 and Sue Kennedy, '"The Lure of Pleasure": Sex and the Married Girl in Marghanita Laski's *To Bed with Grand Music* (1946)', in *British Women's Writing, 1930 to 1960: Between the Waves*, ed. Sue Kennedy and Jane Thomas (Liverpool: Liverpool University Press, 2020), pp. 73–90.
13 Kennedy, 'The Lure of Pleasure', p. 74.
14 Marghanita Laski, *The Village* (London: Persephone Press, 2004), pp. 28–9.
15 The notion of a middle-class girl working as a domestic was shocking, but it was happening. As Deborah Philips and Ian Haywood note, the 'Steep drop in the number of domestic servants [...] caused by gradually increasing affluence and wider opportunities for working-class women' results in the 'proletarianism of middle-class women, who were forced to undertake domestic labor that would have been unthinkable to a previous generation'. See Deborah Philips and Ian Haywood. *Brave New Causes: Women in British Postwar Fictions* (Leicester: Leicester University Press, 1998), p. 6.
16 Kenneth O. Morgan, *Labour in Power: 1945–1951* (Oxford: Oxford University Press, 1984), pp. 20–1.
17 Chris Day, 'The Beveridge Report and the Foundations of the Welfare State', *The National Archives* (7 December 2017), blog.nationalarchives.gov.uk/beveridge-report-foundations-welfare-state/
18 *Ibid.*
19 Morgan, *Labour in Power*, p. 42.
20 Laski, *The Village*, p. 48.
21 *Ibid.*, p. 49.
22 Morgan, *Labour in Power*, p. 44.
23 *Ibid.*, p. 143.
24 *Ibid.*, p. 184.
25 *Ibid.*, p. 186.
26 The population was divided into four main classes of working age wherein 'Housewives, that is married women of working age', was named category III. Housewives were stipulated to have their 'contributions made by the husband' (Sir William Beveridge, 'Social Insurance and Allied Services' (London: HMSO, 1942), *Bulletin of the World Health Organization* 78.6 (2000), pp. 847–55, 848).
27 'The Model Family: Women and the Welfare State'. Poster collection 1975–1985. LSE Finding Aid. TWL.2004.1014, archives.lse.ac.uk/Record.aspx?src=CalmView.Catalog&pos=1

28 Reassessments of the war's mythology include Elizabeth Wilson, *Only Halfway to Paradise: Women in Postwar Britain 1945–1968* (London: Tavistock Press, 1980); Angus Calder, *The People's War: Britain 1939–1945* (London: Pimlico, 1992); Jenny Hartley, *Millions Like Us: British Women's Fiction of the Second World War* (London: Virago Press, 1997); and Rose, *Which People's War?*
29 Rose, *Which People's War?*, pp. 131–4.
30 *Ibid.*, p. 133.
31 *Ibid.*, p. 140.
32 *Ibid.*, pp. 142–4.
33 Beveridge, 'Social Insurance', p. 847.
34 Rose, *Which People's War?*, p. 148.
35 Laski, *The Village*, p. 7.
36 For expansive academic studies on austerity, see Ina Zweiniger-Bargielowska, *Austerity in Britain: Rationing, Controls, and Consumption, 1939–1955* (Oxford: Oxford University Press, 2000); and Christopher Sladen, *The Conscription of Fashion: Utility Cloth, Clothing and Footwear, 1941–1952* (Farnham: Scolar Press, 1995). See also David Kynaston, *Austerity Britain, 1945–51* (London: Bloomsbury, 2007) for a history of the period under study through the lens of austerity.
37 Laski, *The Village*, p. 12.
38 *Ibid.*, p. 15.
39 *Ibid.*
40 *Ibid.*
41 *Ibid.*, p. 26.
42 *Ibid.*, p. 75.
43 *Ibid.*, p. 77.
44 *Ibid.*, p. 76.
45 *Ibid.*, p. 77.
46 *Ibid.*, p. 201.
47 *Ibid.*
48 *Ibid.*, p. 202.
49 *Ibid.*, p. 204. Here, Laski uses Jill's comment to point back to the British wartime fascination with Russia. On Russia, see Rose, *Which People's War?*, pp. 44–56.
50 Kynaston, *Austerity Britain*, p. 133.
51 *Ibid.*
52 The Anglo-American loan agreement made the Welfare State possible, and without it, Morgan asserts, 'Labour Britain would have faced extremes of austerity and impoverishment, worse than [...] confronted in 1931' (Morgan, *Labour in Power*, p. 151).
53 Isabelle Mallet, 'It Simply Isn't Done', BR5, *New York Times* (1 June 1952).
54 Laski, *The Village*, p. 95.
55 *Ibid.*, p. 94.
56 *Ibid.*, p. 145.
57 *Ibid.*, p. 114.

58 *Ibid.*, pp. 114–15.
59 *Ibid.*, pp. 117–18.
60 Kynaston, *Austerity Britain*, p. 135.
61 Laski, *The Village*, p. 163.
62 *Ibid.*, p. 164.
63 *Ibid.*, p. 254.
64 The Ministry of Information's famous 1939 trio, held at the Imperial War Museum, includes 'Your Courage Your Cheerfulness Your Resolution WILL BRING US VICTORY', 'FREEDOM IS IN PERIL DEFEND IT WITH ALL YOUR MIGHT' (original capitalization), and the unused 'Keep Calm and Carry On'.
65 Laski, *The Village*, pp. 265–6.
66 *Ibid.*, p. 26.
67 It should be noted that the Tilbury Docks is also where the *Empire Windrush* arrived carrying hundreds of West Indian travellers on 21 June 1948, a highly charged moment in the history of a changing post-war Britain and the end of Empire.

6

Beyond 'companionate marriage': Elizabeth Taylor's gendered critique of post-war consensus in *A View of the Harbour* and *A Wreath of Roses*

Geneviève Brassard

> A healthy family life must be fully ensured and parenthood must not be penalized if the population of Britain is to be prevented from dwindling.
> *Labour Party 1945 pamphlet* Let Us Face the Future[1]

English society was not exactly rejoicing in 1946, as Britain's political efforts to achieve a post-war consensus after years of loss, deprivation, and 'carry on' ethos were met with a grim reality on the ground.[2] As David Kynaston writes in his study of post-Second World War Britain,

> It is not fanciful to argue that within a year of VE Day there had set in not only a widespread sense of disenchantment – with peace, perhaps even with the Labour government – but also a certain sense of malaise, a feeling that society, which broadly speaking had held together during the war, was no longer working so well, was even starting to come apart.[3]

Even before the war's end, the widespread perception that wartime social dislocation had 'destroyed family bonds', with the 'decline of the birth rate' and increased juvenile delinquency as supposed proof, led to cultural and political pressures to re-centre marriage and motherhood as essential roles for the female citizen.[4] The rise of 'companionate marriage' – marriage based on affection, friendship, and partnership – as an ideal to anchor women in the home coincided with the peak of national preoccupation with the falling birth rate in the years 1945 to 1947, the same period when English novelist Elizabeth Taylor conceived her novels *A View of the Harbour* (1947) and *A Wreath of Roses* (1949).[5] As I show in this chapter, both novels not only directly address the mood of malaise and disillusionment Kynaston delineates, but also feature female characters at odds with the prevailing matrimonial ethos at the core of post-war reconstruction efforts.

As has already been discussed by other authors in this volume, the 1942 Beveridge Report anticipated that gender roles would resume along traditional lines post-war, as plans for the future welfare state positioned 'women within the home through taxation and social policy'.[6] Contradictory messaging around women and work further complicated matters post-war, when 'women found themselves subject to conflicting pressures – both to leave and to stay in the labour market',[7] while cultural products reinforced the centrality of homemaking: 'On the radio, in films, in women's magazines, femininity was almost exclusively identified with the home and the nurturing of children.'[8] Taylor's post-war fiction confronts these cultural pressures to centre domesticity as women's proper work. *A View of the Harbour* and *A Wreath of Roses* both suggest important continuities in Taylor's development as a novelist in her focus on the ways public and political issues can reverberate within domestic spaces and the private conflicts they harbour. Taylor, a 'lifelong and unquestioning atheist', joined the British Communist Party in her twenties and remained active within its ranks for a decade. Her views on communism, as described in a letter, provide a useful backdrop to her preoccupations around gender: 'I thought men and women might have an equal chance, brought up together from childhood, and a woman respected first as a person, not as a machine for reproduction.'[9] This desire to transcend a woman's reproductive role certainly plays out in Taylor's work, and her own struggles with reconciling creativity and domesticity inspired the tensions her female characters experience.[10]

A View of the Harbour and *A Wreath of Roses* reflect the fluid and transitory feeling of their post-war time, a time Gill Plain describes as 'not only a temporal space, but also a cultural sensibility', and they register the continuing impact of the conflict, the 'gradual emergence of grief and post-traumatic symptoms'.[11] My analysis of Taylor's work extends Plain's claim that 'The Second World War really does change everything' and joins recent scholarly efforts to centre the war experience and its impact on civilians as crucial to examinations of post-war fiction.[12] Taylor's work exemplifies 'mid-century fiction', defined by Marina MacKay and Lyndsey Stonebridge by its 'complex and under-thought relation to its own history – both to its historical and literary legacies and to the history of which it was such an uneasy part'.[13] Paula Derdiger's conceptual framework, 'Reconstruction Fiction', also provides a useful lens through which to read Taylor's post-war novels, especially their focus on 'vision' as a 'powerful humanistic social tool'. Taylor's work demonstrates Derdiger's argument that 'the realist mode of reconstruction fiction can be interpreted productively not as stylistically reactionary but as an imaginative necessity for reestablishing and reevaluating British society at key moments of transition throughout post-war history'.[14] I find Derdiger's claim of realism as 'imaginative necessity' especially useful to illuminate Taylor's layered representation of post-war gender roles. Post-war expectations for women centred on the 'resumption of heteronormativity: the family was to be reconstituted, relocated and encouraged to reproduce'.[15] As I show, both *A View of the Harbour* and *A Wreath of Roses* critique these heteronormative pressures through characters marginalized by the companionate marriage ethos and its emphasis on motherhood.

The plot of *A View of the Harbour* is set in motion by the intrusion of a stranger, would-be painter Bertram Hemingway, in a small coastal town still marked by the war. This outsider proves most disruptive to vulnerable women marginalized by class, age, or marital status (specifically Lilly Wilson, the war widow, and the invalid gossip Mrs Bracey), while his careless actions expose hidden tensions within marriages and friendships. Similarly, *A Wreath of Roses* opens with an unlikely meeting between a potentially dangerous con man, Richard Elton, and a shy spinster, Camilla Hill, at a train station where they witness a stranger's death by suicide. Camilla's vulnerability to Elton's advances is intensified by her sense of isolation now that her best friend Liz Nicholson is married with an infant son. Another of the novel's characters, Frances Rutherford, also deals with loneliness, as she struggles to find meaning in her art and entertains the possibility of companionship with a longtime admirer. Both novels foreground female characters who exist on the margins of the traditional marriage plot, or who strive for artistic expression despite domestic responsibilities. To various degrees, each of these female characters fails to meet the gender expectations of a unified post-war nation anchored by the domestic home.

Writer, mother, painter, spinster: women's fraught relationship to creativity

Taylor centres the struggles of female writers and artists to expose the limited powers of creativity to repair a fractured post-war society. Characters like the novelist Beth Cazabon in *A View of the Harbour* and the painter Frances Rutherford in *A Wreath of Roses* are especially constrained by gender expectations.[16] Both characters negotiate their desire to create against domestic expectations, aspirations, or regrets. For example, in *A View of the Harbour*, Beth feels conflicted between writing her novel and tending to her children, but this conflict appears more externally imposed than internally felt, whereas in *A Wreath of Roses*, Frances's conflict with her changing creative process is mainly internal and provoked by a rejection of her previous artistic style as derivative and sentimental.

Critics have commented on the similarities between Taylor and her fictional novelist in *A View of the Harbour*, Beth, whose creative energies are criticized by those around her and are frequently thwarted. While Taylor's portrayal has been dismissed as either satirical or unsympathetic, my analysis contextualizes Beth's struggles within cultural messages prioritizing domestic duties over possible creative pursuits for women.[17] For Beth, a doctor's wife, writing is a pleasure worthy of neglecting housekeeping and parenting, but this pleasure involves a degree of internalized guilt, as well as overt criticism from her loved ones. Taylor suggests that the burden of bad parenting falls squarely on the mother's shoulders. This guilt is exacerbated by Beth's husband, who unfairly blames her parental neglect on her writing despite the fact that he is pursuing an adulterous affair with his wife's oldest friend. For Beth, the healing powers of the creative process are restricted by real and perceived limitations placed on her endeavours, and yet the novel ends with Beth completing her book, despite her own misgivings, disparagement from her husband, a critical diatribe from her best friend, and her daughters' demands for attention. Through Beth, Taylor expresses ambivalence around women and creativity in the post-war setting and offers a nuanced critique of social pressures that centre motherhood at the expense of creativity.

An early scene cleverly stages the battle between mothering and writing for Beth. While immersed in imagining a fictional scene where a child dies, Beth reflects: 'This was how God might have felt, called upon to watch His children suffer, whom He might have saved but would not. Beth, however, was an atheist.'[18] At that precise moment, one of her daughters, five-year-old Stevie, appears: 'Her own child stood in the doorway ... But with the dying child still on her mind, Beth could not bring herself to welcome the living one.'[19] The multi-layered ironies of this moment capture Taylor's light perspective on a still tense situation: Stevie is merely back from school, she has no urgent need of her mother's attention, so Beth could be reasonably justified in focusing on the imaginary child for a moment longer. The fact that Beth is killing off children in her fiction could additionally be read as a bit tongue-in-cheek, as if Beth subconsciously wishes to be freed from parenting duties and dispatches fictional children instead of real-life ones. The comparison to God, while often ascribed to writers, is humorously undercut by the atheist comment and adds an extra layer of (possibly autobiographical) irony to the scene.

More serious criticism of Beth's creative process issues from characters who one might expect to be most supportive: her husband Robert and her oldest friend and next-door neighbour, Tory. Robert and Tory attack Beth's neglect and lack of focus on the real world around her while they pursue an emotionally messy affair. In a rare moment of anger, Tory lashes out at Beth:

> 'You've no idea of what is real, and how real people think', [...] 'Writers are ruined people. As a person, you're done for. Everywhere you go, all you see

and do, you are working up something unreal, something to go on to paper ... I've watched you for years and I've seen you gradually becoming inhuman, outside life, a machine.'[20]

Tory's verbal assault suggests a limited and limiting view of the creative process in general, and of fiction writing more specifically, a view Taylor herself laboured throughout her career to combat.[21] Unlike Tory's dim view of life and creation as distinct and separate entities, the goal of realist fiction such as Taylor's is arguably to capture what real life feels like, how actual humans experience it, and to achieve this goal, writers cannot exist or persist without merging real and imagined worlds on the page. Tory's diatribe extends to almost a full page, and the scene resolves with Tory's tears and contrition. However, Taylor still hints that Beth neglects her husband and children (perhaps suggesting that Tory justifies her own betrayal by indirectly blaming her friend as the underlying cause of the affair). Beth's dismayed response underscores the unfairness of the accusation: '"I should have to be a monster not to love my own children. And Robert? Why, I love him so well I don't even think about it any longer." She had never been so embarrassed in her life.'[22] Taylor may hint at her own bouts of writerly self-doubt in this passage, but she also presents Beth's creative pursuits as less damaging to her family life than her husband's affair and suggests that Robert and Tory's criticism stems more from their own guilt, and from their traditional views of domesticity, than from genuine concern for the well-being of Beth and Robert's two daughters. Tory's attack seems especially flavoured with a sense that Beth's creative pursuits are monstrous or unfeminine, because they presumably detract from her traditional domestic duties as wife and mother.[23]

This critical thread resurfaces later in the novel in a scene between Tory and Robert, where the latter laments the space that writing has taken in their household:

> 'I didn't count on it going on so long – not having books published, for instance. I thought when she had children ... but even then she used to sit up in bed scribbling. A confinement is a fine chance to finish off a novel, she thinks. When she was feeding poor Prue she wasn't thinking about her. It's a disease, a madness.'[24]

Like the earlier scene of Beth's living child interrupting the death of her fictional one, this criticism emphasizes the perceived unnaturalness of writing in contrast with the presumably natural womanly roles of birth and breastfeeding. Robert's critical view of writing as a hobby taken too far is especially striking, as it echoes public discourse lamenting the falling birth rate and the widespread influence of John Bowlby's core belief that 'natural motherhood also meant full-time motherhood'.[25] What Robert conveniently ignores here and elsewhere in the novel is that his culpability in his daughters' emotional distress due to his affair is much greater than Beth's supposed maternal neglect while writing her novel. Tory's response to Robert's complaint expresses greater perceptiveness toward Beth than her previous outburst: 'Perhaps in the end it is what she was intended for ... perhaps her writing is the Beth-ish thing. Not the children [...] She is about the only happy person I know. Don't you see how she is to be envied? Nothing people do can ever break her.'[26] Here Tory directly confronts the myth of the maternal instinct as primary and exclusionary, and she posits a view of female creativity at odds with prevailing cultural scripts, allowing Taylor to advance a not-so-subtle critique of domesticity as the sole purveyor of female contentment and fulfilment.

This critique, however, comes from a place of genuine tension, for Beth and presumably for Taylor as well. In a later scene, when Beth boards a train for an overnight trip to London to meet her publisher, she is wracked with guilt from the tantrum Stevie threw at her departure:

'I am a bad mother', she once more told herself and fought back the feelings of shame and oppression which assailed her at this admission. 'When I have finished this book I will never write another word. I'll devote myself to Stevie, get Prue married somehow, turn Robert's shirtcuffs, have the hall re-papered.'[27]

This reflection captures Beth's sense of guilt, but also her frustration for feeling guilty, and the underlying tone is a bit wry, especially for the way Beth imagines a life freed from creative distractions. The mix of earnest aspirations and tedious tasks feels like a poor substitute for the satisfactions of conjuring an entire world through language. In this scene, Taylor both acknowledges the genuine guilt Beth feels and targets the gendered nature of this guilt through Beth's shifting thought process:

'A man', she thought suddenly, 'would consider this a business outing. But then, a man would not have to cook the meals for the day overnight, nor consign his child to a friend, nor leave half-done the ironing, nor forget the grocery order as I now discover I have forgotten it. The artfulness of men', she thought. 'They implant in us, foster in us, instincts which it is to their advantage for us to have, and which, in the end, we feel shame at not possessing.'[28]

Here, Taylor comes closest to a feminist indictment of social and cultural pressures to reinforce domesticity as women's primary post-war role. The passage's potent language, with its mixture of quotidian chores and its larger commentary on the supposed maternal instinct, raises a timeless question: if this supposed 'instinct' can be implanted but also be lacking in some women, how genuine or natural is it really?

By contrast, Frances in *A Wreath of Roses* represents a more conflicted creative process, through a personal crisis of faith in one's talent and purpose. Previous analyses of this novel and its preoccupation with the artistic process have overlooked the war as a possible reason behind Frances's rejection of her previous, conventional style, and her embrace of darkness as both subject and mode of representation. Taylor points to the war experience as pivotal to Frances's artistic shift through descriptive and reflective moments focused on her paintings. Taylor also suggests that, like Beth, who feels the tension between fiction writing and the cultural expectations around motherhood, Frances, an ageing spinster, confronts possible regrets for her choice to live a single life focused on art, especially as her longtime supporter Morland Beddoes's visit reignites buried desires for companionship.

Taylor devotes important narrative space to Frances's paintings and characters' differing reactions to them. Liz's negative assessment of Frances's attempts at a new style suggests how difficult it can be for an artist to depart from one's established methods and perspectives: '"Frightening!"' Liz tells Camilla in response to her question about the new work.

> 'Great black and grey and purple and sulphurous pictures. All nonsense. So *different*. When you think ... All those flowers she used to paint ... And now these awful rocky pictures ... It is all part of the general ferocity – the sun wheeling round, violent cliffs and rocks, figures with black lines round them. And all amounting to – just nothing at all.'[29]

Liz's description highlights her personal aesthetic biases and her discomfort toward the violent sentiments being expressed in the new work, while the contrast between 'flowers' and 'violent cliffs and rocks' suggestively highlights the ability of the natural world to evoke beauty and horror in equal measures, depending on the sensibility at work observing it. Liz praises Frances's previous work for its reassuring representational quality: '"that was what I *call* a picture. Perhaps we always want paintings to be like novels."'[30] This comment seems subtly self-referential, a meta-commentary from Taylor about the novel we are reading. It also comments on the possibilities and limitations of each media: paintings can't be novels, and wishing that one art could substitute for another only diminishes the distinctive powers of each.[31]

Frances's own assessment of the shift in her work underscores the difficulty inherent in achieving one's true vision. First, Frances criticizes herself for the placidity, inauthenticity, and attendant popularity of her previous work: 'For was I not guilty of making ugliness charming? An English sadness like a veil over all I painted, until it became ladylike and nostalgic [and] utterly lacking in ferocity, brutality, violence.'[32] The language here is highly gendered, with 'charming' and 'ladylike' sounding like a performance of femininity projected onto a canvas.[33] For Frances, her previous paintings represent a lie of the soul, a secular sin committed against the truth-telling power of art in the name of an expected feminine propriety. 'Whereas in the centre of the earth', she goes on, 'in the heart of life, in the core of even everyday things is there not violence, with flames wheeling, turmoil, pain, chaos?'[34] The violence Frances perceives, the ferocity she wishes to render, the chaos she sees permeating everything, must surely be related to the war not long ended. Frances's attempts to express these newfound perceptions do not match what she seeks to capture through a new form: 'Her paintings this year, she knew, were four utter failures to express her new feelings, her rejection of prettiness, her tearing-down of the veils of sadness, of charm. She had become abstract, incoherent, lost.'[35] While Frances's reflections suggest an artistic defeat, they can also be read more positively as the progression of an artist coming into her own. Her inability to capture her 'new feelings' also suggests the limited power of art to process traumatic experiences such as war. The rupture between Frances's reliance on charm and her embrace of chaos could represent the impossibility of seeking reassuring pre-war tools to represent post-war reality.[36] Taylor's depiction of Frances's reckoning captures an 'anxiety' Gill Plain finds prevalent in post-war fiction 'precisely because it attempts to assimilate the fractured subjectivities and changed consciousnesses of wartime into templates of social and psychic organization based on an outmoded "normality" that ... was felt by few'.[37]

Taylor suggests through an exchange between Frances and Beddoes that an artist's assessment of her work might not hold the whole truth of its value, and opens up the possibility of believing in the limited but real healing powers of art. Beddoes, for whom Frances's paintings mattered to the point that he considered his memories of them a 'treasure' while in a prisoner-of-war camp, recalls 'trying to print on his closed eyelids the pictures he had seen'.[38] When Frances tells Beddoes that she 'committed a grave sin against the suffering of the world by ignoring it' in her pre-war paintings, Beddoes gently rebukes her using his own positive response to her painting of a young Liz as representative of her art's potentially transformative impact. Beddoes tells Frances, 'she was a woman alone in a room; as only God, I should have thought, could ever possibly have seen her. It was the truth ... That *is* life. It's loving-kindness and simplicity, and it lay there all the time in your pictures.'[39] Beddoes insists that however she finishes her incomplete painting, he will embrace her choice: 'Because I love you. Whatever you choose to say, I shall hold dear. I have always cherished you and promoted you, and now I only want you to be yourself.'[40] This unwavering show of support for her artistic choices emphasizes the power of a work of art to elude even its creator, and although Frances abandons her last painting depicting a wreath of roses, Taylor arguably offers a meta-commentary of her novel's truthful attempt to capture life as Frances describes it: 'it's darkness, and the terrible things we do to one another, and to ourselves'.[41]

'All separate yet without identity': isolation and loneliness in a fractured post-war consensus

Taylor's gendered assessment of post-war malaise coalesces in her exploration of pervasive isolation and loneliness as exemplary symptoms of failed social cohesion. *A View of the Harbour* and *A Wreath of Roses* both shed light on female characters struggling with a sense of disconnection and even dislocation within their community. Taylor centres her critique of enforced domesticity on two female characters in *A View of the Harbour*, in which a self-absorbed failed painter, Bertram Hemingway, ingratiates himself into both Lily Wilson's and Mrs Bracey's isolated lives, but with sharply different consequences. Taylor draws a connection between the two widows (one still young, the other ill and near death) as vulnerable victims of Bertram's superficial attention. Of the two, the consequences of his callous involvement are most devastating for Lily, whose status as a war widow has left her not only personally grieving but has also led to casual social ostracism.

Taylor introduces Lily as a war victim whose husband died in battle and left her, still young, alone and in charge of a derelict waxworks museum. The symbolic nature of Lily's dwelling (upstairs from the display galleries), perhaps obvious but still potent, represents Lily's inability to move on from her loss. Before meeting Bertram, Lily's routine involves short walks to the library, where a censorious old librarian terrorizes her into choosing morally appropriate reading material, and upon returning home, turning 'away from the sight of the place which only love had made tolerable'.[42] She starts visiting the pub where the single Bertram is staying, and dreads walking through the ghost-like figures in the museum after her evenings out. Initially, Bertram's offers to escort her home from the pub appear gallant and kind, and Lily briefly blossoms from the male attention. But Bertram's intentions stem more from performative self-regard than genuine interest in Lily, whose hopes that the older man's kindness will turn into romantic interest are dashed when he becomes intrigued by Tory. When Bertram admits to Tory his capacity to inflict harm, Taylor centres the pain he caused Lily as especially grievous: '"There are so many cruelties of omission." He thought at once of Lily Wilson, of how in the beginning he had inferred perhaps that he would do much for her. And had done nothing. (He did not know that he had done worse than nothing).'⁴³ This passage suggests the extent of Bertram's wilful blindness to the impact of his carelessness on Lily, and the sharp parenthetical statement aligns the narrator's sympathies with his innocent victim.

Taylor sensitively delineates the ways even haphazard attention from an eligible man might impact a vulnerable and lonely woman eager for companionship. She describes how

> it seemed to Lily Wilson that her very happiness was staked upon Bertram. The pattern of her life was reversed and all her days bent towards the evening. No longer did she fear the light failing and all those wretched thoughts about the future, about loneliness and old age ... In the warmth of Bertram's kindness her personality seemed to unfurl; she became, she thought, someone different, someone she would always have liked to have been.⁴⁴

These reflections underscore the profound impact of Bertram's attention on Lily, to the extent that she ascribes to him powers of transformation out of step with the mostly casual acquaintance they have developed. When he walks her home, he stays for a bit of tea and conversation before leaving, and 'since she had no reason to be ashamed of their relationship she innocently believed she would not be gossiped about, especially as he was old enough to be her father'.⁴⁵ But Taylor shows how cold and condemning a small community can be to its marginalized members, as Lily develops an alcohol dependency when Bertram drops her for Tory, and experiences a painful humiliation when she mistakes the intentions of a young French sailor in the pub. Afterwards, her thoughts turn to her dead husband: '"Why did you leave me?" She blamed the dead, feeling herself exposed to danger and humiliation. As she put her hand up to her eyes her scented skin made her shudder. Her shame seemed to be a real thing, following her upstairs and into her room.'⁴⁶ This moment captures the tension between loneliness and its potential remedy, companionship, when efforts to break one's isolation are rebuffed and one is left lamenting its original causes. As a war widow, Lily represents an important group of civilians left behind by combat casualties, a population for whom the war lingers and continues to impact domestic spaces at a time of increased cultural and political pressures to 'consolidate family life'.⁴⁷

The gendered expectations surrounding Lily's status and behaviour only compound her distress, as Taylor also explores the negative consequences of gossip as a means of connection for another lonely widow, Mrs Bracey. Taylor's portrayal of this bored, vindictive, but also inquisitive and imaginative working-class character is equally sensitive to the isolation of women as they age out of their procreative function. Unlike the youthful Lily, who might still find a companion to ease her continued grief, Mrs Bracey is not only older but immobilized by illness and forced to rely on her adult daughters for her most basic needs. For Mrs Bracey, gossip means connection to the community from her room; she mines her bartending daughter Iris for stories and demands to be moved upstairs so she can observe the view of the harbour as a means of entertainment and information, and a source for her overactive imagination.[48] Mrs Bracey portrays the gendered impact of social fragmentation through the way gossip can weaponize isolation even further, for the perpetrator as well as the victim, as she observes Lily walking out of the pub with the French sailor:

> Lily had not known she was being watched, nor that at that moment her reputation was slipping into that no man's land from which one can fall, with so little warning, from respectable widowhood to being the local harlot: and, as it was in Mrs Bracey's imagination that the first move towards that decline was made, the descent, no doubt, would be swift as well as untraceable (for gossip is a fluid, intangible thing). Scandals must have their beginnings somewhere, and the soil of Mrs Bracey's imagination was so fertile that often there seed and flower were one and the same thing.[49]

Taylor presents Lily as the innocent victim of the older woman's malice, and clearly condemns Mrs Bracey's judgement of Lily, as it is based on little more than a glimpse of two people walking together. The notion that Lily can slip so easily from 'respectable widowhood' to 'local harlot' illustrates the continued rigidity of traditional gender roles in post-war England, as well as the reactionary backlash against wartime relaxation of sexual mores.

Like Lily, Mrs Bracey is lonely and lacks the power to change her situation, and her imaginative powers are restricted to the limited field of vision a small window allows, instead of being put to more productive use. Taylor's complex portrayal of Mrs Bracey's isolation allows for sympathy as well as judgement, as she describes the limited but real satisfactions the old woman gets from actively combating her isolation through her limited means. When the visiting curate suggests bringing her library books for distraction, she replies: '"*That's* my book!" Mrs Bracey would tell the curate, pointing out of the window.'[50] Yet for her, modern life leaves much to be desired, and her reflections brim with a curious nostalgia for harder times: 'Distinctions were smoothed out, no curtsies were dropped, no coins thrown. Even the sea was smoothed out, for it no longer seemed to wash in wreckage, no longer deposited corpses at the cliff-foot.'[51] Mrs Bracey's lament suggests a longing for a past when she was young and mobile, but references to class hierarchies and their attendant customs also point to a critique of the post-war welfare state, where social distinctions are meant to be erased for the good of the majority.

Mrs Bracey's deathbed reflections bring Taylor's theme of female isolation to a close with generosity and sympathy as they invoke a universal fear of dying alone: 'Utterly alone, she lay and awaited death, cut off, discarded, like a man in a condemned cell … No one could reach her, she knew, and in that knowledge lay all her helplessness and terror.'[52] Isolation remains the constant of the human condition, Taylor reminds her reader, and she uses a troubled and troubling character to convey this painful lesson: 'All else had gone: her childhood, her married life, the triumphs of birth, the sorrows of death, good, evil, ambition, love; nothing remained but the little centre of fear in her amorphous body, floating on its bed, without weight, without pain, without anchorage.'[53] Mrs Bracey's dying reflections align with Taylor's own and suggest that post-war England remains atomized despite governmental efforts to invoke a communal spirit and implement community-based policies to achieve political consensus.

Whereas *A View of the Harbour* ends with a supporting character's demise, *A Wreath of Roses* opens with an arresting scene, the suicide of a stranger at a small train station, his 'sprawling jump'[54] witnessed by two strangers, Camilla and Elton, brought together by the unsettling experience. The man's identity and motivations remain unknown, but his fatal act suggests unresolved wartime trauma, and it affects Camilla irrevocably: 'This happening broke the afternoon in two.'[55] This anonymous, isolated, and unexplained death evokes the war experience of civilians who witnessed untimely and random death throughout the Blitz and other attacks. The scene resonates through the rest of the novel, as it sets the bleak tone Taylor lamented in a letter during its composition:

> I am worried about my book. I have turned my back on all that people liked in my other novels … there is nothing funny, no wit, no warmth, no children, no irony, no *perceptiveness*. It is *deadly serious*. Horribly sad. Cold. Everyone will hate it. It is also about people's bodies. They will feel insulted. The people in it are not pleasant consistently. The unpleasant are often *right*, and I have come out of my range – a great mistake – and have swept in violence, brutality, passion, religion, all the things that had been better left out.[56]

Taylor's misgivings about the novel's darkness, while obviously candid and legitimate, also suggest the anxiety of an author attempting to break an existing mould and doubting her own instincts as she strives to stretch her creative powers. (This is a struggle the painter Frances also faces, as discussed above.)

Like Lily in *A View of the Harbour*, Camilla in *A Wreath of Roses* is a single woman vulnerable to the attentions of an unlikely stranger. Thus, the opening scene not only serves to throw two strangers into an unlikely intimacy, it also uses the fatal despair of one nameless character as a conduit to draw two characters out of their own isolation to attempt a connection doomed to failure. Camilla's loneliness, like Lily's, is rooted in her exclusion from the companionate marriage ideal, and in her partially acknowledged longing for the intimacy that ideal might provide. Her close friendship with Liz has been disrupted by the latter's marriage and new motherhood, and Camilla feels more isolated than usual:

> [T]he only thing to make life worth living: human relationships. For our lives run into a loneliness which is like a dark ghetto. Fearing to be solitary, we hold aloft a wavering light to tempt our friends into the darkness. 'Look! It is thus!' we cry. The light falls not impartially, but directed by us, often unskillfully, so that cracks and fissures and grotesque shadows are inadvertently displayed. And in this clumsy illumination 'It is thus! It is thus!' We plead, and 'Thus is thus', the echoes go flying back over our shoulders. Our friends assent, but with their eyes perhaps on those uncovered cracks and fissures. They are never at our sides for long. And the wonder is that they should follow us at all.[57]

This extended meditation on human solitude and intimate companionship as fleeting remedy comes at an especially vulnerable time for Camilla, whose friendship with Liz has been destabilized. She finds herself drawn to Richard Elton's attractive but toxic persona and envious of the potential intimacy between their host and friend Frances and her would-be suitor Morland Beddoes.[58]

Camilla's reflections underscore the gendered nature of isolation and loneliness in the novel, and Taylor offers glimpses of ingrained differences in the ways men and women confront solitude. As Camilla sharply explains to Elton:

> 'You don't understand what my life has been. No man would understand what life is like for so many women. How can we take any of the things we want, that you expect to have – freedom, adventure, experience – without being taxed intolerably, or making ourselves ridiculous in other people's eyes, or in our own?'[59]

Camilla expresses frustrations connected, but not limited to, her exclusion from the traditional marriage plot here, and more broadly about the enforcing power of the concept. She may be drawn to Elton as an unlikely partner despite her friends' and her own misgivings, but she also laments restrictions still imposed on most women's lives, restrictions so pervasive and internalized that the idea of breaching them evokes certain shame. Soon after, Camilla reflects on Elton's power over her: '"It is true", she thought. "I hate him and desire him. I mock him, I chide him, I despise him, but all my body shakes at his touch, and when he goes away I shall despair."'[60] Camilla's reflections point to the causes of her vulnerability. As a spinster witnessing her closest friend's absorption into matrimony and remembering her past failures to join its expected path and potential rewards, Camilla represents countless single women urged toward marriage and motherhood in post-war England. Camilla's attraction to Elton might be 'irrational', considering their differences and the aura of danger surrounding him, but her impulse toward romantic involvement makes sense in light of persistent cultural pressures to uphold heteronormativity as women's central post-war duty.[61]

Near the novel's close, Taylor affirms her bleak outlook on human relations through Beddoes's perspective. An outsider to the community, he has been observing his host Frances and her young guests at close range, drawn to their sensitivity and vulnerability and eager to support and comfort them at a time of crisis in their friendship. During a group picnic on a hill above town, Beddoes describes the town as an entity, with 'a life of its own [...] a corporate thing, with its own atmosphere, its own set of characters', and compares it to Madame Bovary's town.[62] When he returns to his room alone, his perspective has shifted:

> Perhaps the changed weather, this withdrawal of brightness from the air, had discouraged him, but the market square, flat and shadowless, had a depressing look, presaging disaster. The drifting people suggested only dark lives spent in the back-rooms of little shops, in the coils of what is sometimes encouragingly called private enterprise; dragged down by daily worries, no vision elated them, no intimacy delighted. 'So we trail from birth to death', he thought ... 'From day to day, we drift along, glance at headlines, dully hope for the best, menaced chiefly by one another, all separate yet without identity.'[63]

The contrast between Beddoes's two perspectives within the same afternoon, the first expressed while part of a group and the second in a moment of isolation, suggests Taylor's multi-layered view on the atomization of post-war society; the picnic evokes a brief moment of social cohesion, with Camilla's hopeful belief that '"We shall look back on today and say: 'little did we know that it was the end of our anxieties, our last day of uncertainty.'"'[64] This point of view, combined with Beddoes's sense of the town as a fictional set, emphasizes the idealism and belief in a unified national identity very much in the spirit of the People's War ethos and the post-war consensus it inspired.[65]

But Beddoes's solitary reflections – his sense that despite deliberate efforts to bridge individual differences and cohere as a group, the town residents remain 'all separate yet without identity' – reinforce Taylor's sustained commentary about the rending of the post-war social fabric. That *A Wreath of Roses* ends the way it started, with another man (Elton) killing himself at a train station, can be read as confirming the individual and collective bleakness and despair the novel has excavated. The circular structure of the plot does not imply meaninglessness or nihilism, however. Between the two suicides, Camilla has faced private fears and learned to value her friendship with Liz; Frances has confronted the limitations of artistic expression but has responded favourably to Beddoes's attachment; and Elton's destabilizing masculine force has been neutralized and expelled through his suicide.[66]

A View of the Harbour and *A Wreath of Roses* stand apart from the lighter touch and often comedic tone of much of Taylor's work, and their publication dates suggest a pressing need on their author's part to register the continuing impact of the war beyond 1945. Taylor's sombre handling of tensions within domestic arrangements confronts real social issues with the perceptive tools of realist fiction to offer a nuanced and gendered 'Condition of England' portrayal. These novels function as snapshots of a still-struggling nation eager for cohesion, through sensitive attention to emotional fracture within and between marginalized female characters. And yet, amidst the 'unpleasantness'[67] Taylor feared would alienate readers, she also offers female friendship as a quietly resilient force, a 'frail but enduring shelter' against post-war fragmentation.[68] Lifelong friendships centre both novels, and despite threats from male intrusions or disruptions, as well as from post-war pressures to resume heteronormative arrangements, Taylor affirms the centrality and resilience of emotional bonds between women. In *A View of the Harbour,* Tory despairs of her divorced status and potentially damages her lifelong friendship with Beth, but ultimately chooses her tie to Beth over her misguided affair with Robert. In *A Wreath of Roses,* Liz's marriage and new baby open up a chasm between her and Camilla, whose potentially deadly attraction to Elton stems from her vulnerable position as the displaced partner in their friendship, which nevertheless survives at the novel's close.

Taylor's novels attest to the gendered nature of pressures to achieve social cohesion in austerity Britain and reconceive cohesion around female bonds as an alternative to expected heteronormative ties. Taylor's fiction exposes the genuine complexities and limitations of consensus and suggests that the 'wavering light' friends extend to each other provides an imperfect but genuine means of repair and healing in post-war domestic spaces.[69]

Notes

1 Quoted in Denise Riley, *War in the Nursery: Theories of the Child and Mother* (London: Virago, 1983), p. 140.
2 The debate among historians surrounding definitions of 'consensus' and the extent of the term's usefulness to describe post-war Britain is too complex to rehearse here, but the following definition is especially apt: 'a synonym for a historically unusual degree of agreement', consensus describes 'the full range of social and economic policies by which postwar government sought to fulfil its positive commitment to promote the welfare of all its citizen'. Rodney Lowe, 'The Second World War, Consensus, and the Foundation of the Welfare State', *Twentieth Century British History* 1.2 (1990), pp. 152–82. See also Kenneth O. Morgan for an overview of the aims of post-war consensus as an extension of perceived wartime social cohesion: 'The most fashionable interpretation [of the war] was that of "consensus", a somewhat ambiguous and deceptive concept, which broadly saw the war as enshrining welfare democracy as the dominant national creed.' Kenneth O. Morgan, *Britain Since 1945: The People's Peace* (Oxford: Oxford University Press, 2001), p. 5.
3 David Kynaston, *Austerity Britain, 1945–51* (New York: Walker & Co., 2008), p. 109.
4 Jane Lewis, *Women in Britain Since 1945, Women, Family, Work and the State in the Post-War Years* (Oxford: Blackwell, 1992), p. 14. Denise Riley further argues that 'Both during the war and most strikingly just after it, the reproductive woman at the heart of family policy was surrounded by the language of pronatalism', which she defines as 'alarm over the low birth rate, both past and as anticipated by demographers', to be remedied by encouraging women to have around four children (p. 151).
5 Janet Finch and Penny Summerfield, 'Social Reconstruction and the Emergence of Companionate Marriage, 1945–59', in *The Sociology of the Family: A Reader*, ed. Graham Allan (Malden, MA: Blackwell, 1999), pp. 12–13. Finch and Summerfield explain that even though the phrase 'companionate marriage' predated the war, 'it is in the postwar period that it appears more widely, being used to summarize a set of ideas about marriage which ranged from the notion that there should be greater companionship between partners whose roles essentially were different, through the idea of marriage as "teamwork", to the concept of marriages based on "sharing", implying the breakdown of clearly demarcated roles' (p. 12).
6 Lucy Noakes, *War and the British: Gender, Memory and National Identity* (London: I.B. Tauris, 1998), p. 16.
7 Lewis, *Women in Britain Since 1945*, p. 70.
8 Kynaston, *Austerity Britain, 1945–51*, p. 416. Feminist historian Ruth Adam stresses that the 'role that really mattered ... during the post-war period turned out to be neither nymph nor Amazon, but housewife'. See Adam, *A Woman's Place: 1910–1975* (London: Persephone Books, 2000), p. 229.

9 Nicola Beauman, *The Other Elizabeth Taylor* (London: Persephone Books, 2009), pp. 18, 70.
10 Taylor remains constantly on the verge of scholarly recovery, or rediscovery, 'best known for not being better known', as Benjamin Schwarz claimed in 2007, in part because her body of work resists easy classification. Better known in the United States for a thirty-year association with *The New Yorker*, where she published most of her short stories, Taylor has received scant scholarly attention, with the main focus remaining on her first book, *At Mrs. Lippincote's* (1945), set during the war, and on the highly satirical historical novel *Angel* (1957). See Benjamin Schwarz, 'The Other Elizabeth Taylor', *Atlantic Monthly* (September 2007), p. 109.
11 Gill Plain, *British Literature in Transition, 1940–1960: Postwar* (Cambridge: Cambridge University Press, 2019), pp. 4, 6.
12 Gill Plain, *Literature of the 1940s, Literature of the 1940s: War, Postwar and 'Peace'* (Edinburgh: Edinburgh University Press, 2013), p. 5. For instance, see Kristin Bluemel's 'The Aftermath of War', which advocates for women's postwar writing as a 'distinct literary period, one that is defined by the ambiguous intimacy of peacetime to wartime'. See Kristin Bluemel, 'The Aftermath of War', in *The History of British Women's Writing, 1945–1975*, ed. Claire Hanson and Susan Watkins (Basingstoke: Palgrave Macmillan, 2017), p. 142.
13 Marina McKay and Lyndsey Stonebridge (eds), *British Fiction after Modernism: The Novel at Mid-Century* (New York: Palgrave Macmillan, 2007), p. 2.
14 Paula Derdiger, *Reconstruction Fiction: Housing and Realist Literature in Postwar Britain* (Columbus, OH: Ohio State University Press, 2020), pp. 12, 13.
15 Plain, *British Literature in Transition*, p. 6.
16 Florence Leclercq also compares the function of artists in both novels, but without the gendered lens I find most pertinent to the post-war context: 'Taylor also acknowledges her debt to Virginia Woolf', according to Leclerq: 'both novels deal with perception and the vision of the artist, and attempt to give permanence to special "moments of being"'. See Florence Leclercq, *Elizabeth Taylor* (Boston, MA: Twayne, 1985), p. 26.
17 Leclercq, for instance, claims that Taylor 'mercilessly mocks both Bertram and Beth' (Leclercq, *Elizabeth Taylor*, p. 27), while Roxana Robinson's take is more nuanced; Taylor's 'treatment of Beth Cazabon is satirical, but it's also compassionate and truthful'. See Roxana Robinson, 'Introduction', in *A View of the Harbour* (New York: New York Review Books, 2015), p. viii.
18 Elizabeth Taylor, *A View of the Harbour* (London: Virago, 2006), p. 40.
19 *Ibid.*
20 *Ibid.*, p. 80.
21 In a letter to her longtime friend and sometime lover, Taylor wrote that 'Writers shouldn't be mothers, for they cannot be ruthless ... I feel instinctively that women who have children can't write. A certain single-mindedness is denied to them. In the end, children and writing suffer. Guilt is bound up with this' (Beauman, *The Other Elizabeth Taylor*, p. 153).

22 *Ibid.*, p. 82.
23 The rare professions considered legitimate for post-war women remained tied to traditional notions of femininity, such as domestic service or teaching, and typically excluded married women. Tory's criticism of Beth's supposed neglect of her wifely and maternal duties captures the flavour of widespread debates around women's paid work in the post-war period as threatening the companionate marriage ideal, as historian Helen McCarthy describes them: 'Working wives could imperil marital harmony because of the challenge they posed to men's "traditional" identity as providers and to the legitimacy and modernity of the full-time housewife-worker in the home.' See Helen McCarthy, 'Women, Marriage and Paid Work in Post-War Britain', *Women's History Review* 26.1 (2017), p. 48.
24 *Ibid.*, pp. 129–30.
25 Lewis, *Women in Britain Since 1945*, p. 18.
26 Taylor, *A View of the Harbour*, p. 130.
27 *Ibid.*, p. 186.
28 *Ibid.*
29 Elizabeth Taylor, *A Wreath of Roses* (London: Peter Davies, 1949), pp. 29–30.
30 *Ibid.*, p. 30.
31 In her introduction to the Virago edition of *A View of the Harbour*, Sarah Waters provides illuminating commentary on this subject: 'Taylor was interested in painting … But fiction … gave her opportunities to explore the roundness of personality, the nuances of human exchange, in a way that painting never could have.' See Sarah Waters, 'Introduction', in *A View of the Harbour* (London: Virago, 2006), p. 3.
32 Taylor, *A Wreath of Roses*, p. 42.
33 N.H. Reeve notes that Frances 'sounds more and more like an elderly, dismayed Lily Briscoe from Virginia Woolf's *To the Lighthouse*, coming to feel, contrary to her earlier beliefs, that in the midst of shape there was chaos'. See N.H. Reeve, *Elizabeth Taylor* (Liverpool: Liverpool University Press, Northcote House Publishers, 2008), p. 14.
34 Taylor, *A Wreath of Roses*, p. 42.
35 *Ibid.*
36 I disagree here with Robin Grove, who correlates Frances's failed paintings with *A Wreath of Roses* as Taylor's 'least original of her work'. See Robin Grove, 'From the Island: Elizabeth Taylor's Novels', *Studies in the Literary Imagination* 11.2 (1978), p. 83.
37 Plain, *Literature of the 1940s*, p. 180.
38 Taylor, *A Wreath of Roses*, p. 148.
39 *Ibid.*, p. 170. Clare Hanson also notes Beddoes's influential role here: 'Frances' sense of inadequacy of her art is strongly challenged in the novel.' See Clare Hanson, *Hysterical Fictions: The 'Woman's Novel' in the Twentieth Century* (Basingstoke: Palgrave, 2000), p. 81.
40 Taylor, *A Wreath of Roses*, p. 171.
41 *Ibid.*, p. 170.

42　Taylor, *A View of the Harbour*, p. 39.
43　Ibid., p. 224.
44　Ibid., p. 96.
45　Ibid., p. 98.
46　Ibid., p. 205.
47　Finch and Summerfield, 'Social Reconstruction and the Emergence of Companionate Marriage', p. 12.
48　Taylor's attention to the complex nature and function of gossip would remind her 1940s readers of the government's efforts to curb and harness 'careless talk' during the war. For a detailed exploration of this topic, see Jo Fox, 'Careless Talk: Tensions within British Domestic Propaganda during the Second World War', *Journal of British Studies* 51.4 (October 2012), pp. 936–66.
49　Taylor, *A View of the Harbour*, pp. 209–10.
50　Ibid., p. 218.
51　Ibid., pp. 217–18.
52　Ibid., p. 281.
53　Ibid., pp. 281–2.
54　Taylor, *A Wreath of Roses*, p. 3.
55　Ibid.
56　Beauman, *The Other Elizabeth Taylor*, p. 202.
57　Taylor, *A Wreath of Roses*, pp. 118–19.
58　In her review, Elizabeth Bowen also singles out Camilla's isolation as a major factor in her unlikely attraction to Richard Elton: 'But something more accounts for the hold Richard gains on Camilla's fancy, and on everything that that comprehends. Exclusion, desperateness, jealousy of Liz's baby drive Camilla, more and more, into Richard's orbit.' See Elizabeth Bowen, 'Review of *A Wreath of Roses*', in *The Weight of a World of Feeling: Reviews and Essays by Elizabeth Bowen*, ed. Alan Hepburn (Evanston, IL: Northwestern University Press, 2017), p. 238.
59　Taylor, *A Wreath of Roses*, p. 156.
60　Ibid., p. 193.
61　Bowen, 'Review of *A Wreath of Roses*', p. 237.
62　Taylor, *A Wreath of Roses*, p. 219.
63　Ibid., p. 224.
64　Ibid., p. 221.
65　See Morgan: 'Socially, the war consensus was taken to mean common citizenship and newly framed social rights' (Morgan, *Britain Since 1945*, p. 6). Lowe notes that this idealized view has been contested: 'A general feeling of "social solidarity" would also appear to have been an "artificially manufactured myth" [...] Ultimately, however, increased contact between the classes often intensified rather than alleviated prejudice' (Lowe, 'The Second World War', pp. 175–6).
66　See Lucy Hall for a perceptive analysis of authoritarian masculinity in domestic spaces, focused on the characters of Elton and of Liz's controlling husband Arthur in *A Wreath of Roses*. See Lucy Hall, 'Men of the House: Oppressive

Husbands and Displaced Wives in Interwar, War and Postwar Women's Fiction', in *British Women's Writing, 1930 to 1960: Between the Waves*, ed. Sue Kennedy and Jane Thomas (Liverpool: Liverpool University Press, 2020), pp. 161–78.
67 Beauman, *The Other Elizabeth Taylor*, p. 202.
68 Reeve, *Elizabeth Taylor*, p. 17.
69 Taylor, *A Wreath of Roses*, p. 118.

7

Dissident friendship and revolutionary love in the novels of Sabitri Roy and Sulekha Sanyal

Sabujkoli Bandopadhyay

The region of Bengal was central to the economy, trade, and politics of the British Empire, as Calcutta (now Kolkata) remained the capital of the British Raj until 1905. The area not only served as a location of cultural interface between the foreign occupier and the local population, but also played a significant role in the cultural transformation of the concepts of home, domesticity, political agency, and the public sphere. Bengali literature and cultural artefacts, in particular, shaped the subcontinental nationalist ideology in the nineteenth and twentieth centuries and spoke to the collective anxieties and desires of postcolonial citizens in the immediate aftermath of the partition and independence of India in 1947. Focusing on two Bengali novels from the 1950s, namely *Nabankur* or *The Seedling's Tale* (1956) by Sulekha Sanyal and *Paka Dhaner Gaan* or *Harvest Songs* (1956–8) by Sabitri Roy, this chapter explores how mid-century Bengali women's writing addressed issues of nationalism, citizenship identity, and gender politics. Sanyal's and Roy's novels not only reflect the complex modalities of politics and identity formation during the last decade of British colonial rule in the subcontinent, but also interrupt the patriarchal discourses on Indian nationalism that connected woman and motherland.[1] Through their female protagonists, who fight for reforms of the feudal system, participate in anti-colonial activities, and resist patriarchal violence that denies their subjecthood, both Sanyal and Roy represent the Bengali woman's struggle for agency and human rights. Read together, these novels offer a rare glimpse of the evolution of gender subjectivity in relation to anti-colonial struggles, peasant movements, the famine of 1943, and the subaltern uprising in 1950s Bengali literature.

In order to contextualize the significance of Sanyal's and Roy's novels, this chapter is split into four sections. The first section provides an overview of how the issue of female subjectivity and human rights for women were addressed in the Bengali public sphere. The second section provides context for the lives of the novelists, who transcended the expectations and limitations imposed on women at the time by questioning the imposition of gender norms and inequality. The chapter then turns to *The Seedling's Tale* and

Harvest Songs, both of which demonstrate how Sanyal and Roy introduce gender as an analytic lens to educate their readers about the ongoing and systemic issues of inequality and oppression. The final section reviews the politics and ethics associated with the translation and publication of these novels in the twenty-first century. Engaging with these 1950s Bengali novels, this chapter argues that while vertical rage against the colonizers and feudal landlords ignited a resistance movement that ultimately resulted in the independence of the country, women's writings of the mid-century focus intentionally on issues of gender equality, which was essential for the possibility of creating a just society in the postcolonial era. Both Sanyal's and Roy's novels show how dissident friendship and revolutionary love were the guiding forces that allowed middle-class women to form alliances. These often socialist-inspired coalitions with other women and community members strengthened their struggle against patriarchy and colonialism in the 1930s and 1940s and inspired the progressive movements in postcolonial India.

Women and the Bengali literary public sphere

Throughout the nineteenth century, colonial ideology proclaimed sexist and racist views that presented women as universally inferior beings, while the emerging nationalist ideology reduced the subcontinental middle-class woman to a custodian of traditions and cultures and thus constricted them within the sphere of domesticity.[2] Many legal reforms, such as the ban on Sati of 1829, the Widow Remarriage Act of 1856, the Resolution of Native Female Education of 1868, the criminalization of female infanticide of 1870, and the 1892 Age of Consent Bill, attempted to address the intense gender inequality in Bengali society.[3] This legislative and legal activism influenced the direction of fictional literature, as 'the reformers examined the consequences of these laws through fictional accounts that featured female protagonists who grappled with the injustices of a patriarchal society'.[4] It is important to note that women were mostly silenced and excluded from the political and legal debates regarding the status of women in the nineteenth century; however, the legal and social reforms prompted an atmosphere where women's writing began appearing sporadically in periodicals and journals by the mid-nineteenth century. As Sumanta Bannerjee observes:

> It is estimated that 190 odd women authors from 1856 to 1910 produced about 400 works, including poems, novels, plays, essays and auto-biographies. During the same period, 21 periodicals with which women were associated editorially, and which were primarily devoted to women's issues were in circulation in Bengal.[5]

By the early twentieth century, print culture and periodicals played a quintessential role in shaping and representing middle-class Bengali identity, which also included questions of gender inequality and women's oppression in the late-colonial period.[6] Essays like 'A Brief Description of the Present State of Women's Education in Bengal' (1931) by educator Nirajbasini Som and 'Women's Movement and Educated Women' (1938) by Arati Mukhopadhyay drew attention to the significance of women's education in progressive social transformations. Alongside issues of education, questions of political power and the social rights of women were explored in essays like 'Women's Right to Vote' (1933), 'Political Rights of Women' (1935), and 'The Issue of Freedom and The Women's Movement' (1938). By the 1940s, women's participation in the independence movement, as well as social reform movements focusing on issues of women's labour and employment, became prominent topics of discussion in literature.

In the 1940 essay 'Indian Women's Movement', published in the literary journal *Sankhya*, Renuka Mandal writes, 'the foreign rulers stood in the way of all social reform movements … [and] our nationalist movement in 1905 did not accommodate women … Hence women themselves needed to lead the women's movement.'[7] From this, it is evident that women understood how they were ignored by both the colonizing patriarchy as well as the nationalist patriarchy. In another essay, 'India's Women Workers', published in the literary journal *Choitra* in 1942, Supriti Majumder points out that '[a]ccording to the 1931 census … 31 percent of the total female population [was] engaged in earning their livelihood' and the 'majority of Indian female workers came from lower strata … and worked in mines, factories and tea gardens'.[8] These statements not only prove that colonized Indian women were an important part of the profits made from the colonies but also demonstrate that upper-class and literate women were cognizant of, and paying attention to, issues of labour rights for women.

These articles and essays published in the Bengali literary journals of the time demonstrate that by the 1940s, the 'woman question' had evolved to become a question of self-determination, labour and human rights, and emancipation for middle-class women. There is no denying that the subcontinent was still widely divided along class, caste, religion, and ethnic lines, but these women's literary activism had started to outline a commonality for women across the country: namely, they were excluded from the conversations on independence and justice. In their novels, Sanyal and Roy incorporate these observations about women's issues in the last decades of colonial rule and transform them into fictional worlds where women's life experiences are framed within the anti-colonial movement and class struggle. Working from within systems of patriarchy, Sanyal and Roy connect their literate middle-class audience with the struggles of women who are socially constructed as an 'other'. By doing so, they expose the potential of literature to represent the challenges of a significantly larger group of the population who were disenfranchised due to their gender identities.

Transcending gender roles: the personal, literary, and political lives of Sanyal and Roy

Before turning to their novels, a brief discussion of the backgrounds of Sulekha Sanyal and Sabitri Roy will help demonstrate how the authors simultaneously worked within and transcended socialist, political, and literary traditions. In their literary works, Sanyal and Roy demonstrate how women lived with, struggled within, and resisted domestic violence, the imposition of marriage, and widowhood, and how women sought emancipation through collective political struggle, education, and employment. Through their literary imaginations, both authors opened up the category of 'woman' to include those from rural-agrarian economy and peasantry, from middle-class and feudal backgrounds, as well as from other disenfranchised groups.

Sanyal was born in 1928 in a village called Korkandi, located in what is now the independent nation of Bangladesh. Like her protagonist Chhobi in *The Seedling's Tale*, Sanyal was born into a decaying *zamindar* or landholding feudal family. After receiving an informal education at home, Sanyal went to live with an aunt in the city of Chittagong, where she received a formal education. She grew up in a climate of political activism, as her brother and his associates were involved in anti-colonial resistance against British rule. In her foreword to the translation of the novel, Susie Tharu notes how Sanyal was influenced by the progressive humanist philosophies of Ramtanu Lahiri, a leading figure of the Bengal Renaissance in the nineteenth century, to whom Sanyal was related through her mother's lineage.[9] These experiences influenced her political beliefs, but she also expanded upon them and drew attention to the lesser-discussed issue of gender inequality within domestic and economic spheres.

During the Second World War, Chittagong, being a part of the British Empire, was bombed by Japanese forces.[10] When the residents of Chittagong were evacuated, Sanyal returned to her village and completed her high school education. Sanyal subsequently received her BA in Bengali from Scottish Church College under Calcutta University and her MA from Burdwan University. At the end of the war and prior to the independence of India, her family, along with millions of other displaced people, relocated to Calcutta, India. By 1948, Sanyal was an active member of the then-underground Communist Party of India and was imprisoned for a brief period in 1949 for her political activities. Sanyal remains one of only a handful of women whose socialist activism can be traced and acknowledged, as the political leadership of the left in Bengal has been dominated by men since its inception.

Thus, both in her personal life and her social activism, Sanyal broke gender barriers. As a result of this gender-based activism, however, she remained marginalized within her political circle. According to Tharu, Sanyal and her literary works were 'too political and too feminist for the mood of the 1950s and 1960s', which resulted in her works being hidden in obscurity until they were rediscovered in the 1980s.[11] While the genre of the Bengali novel has been a domain where discussions of gender and domesticity were welcome, historian Tanika Sarkar has pointed out that Bengali women writers like Sanyal and Roy are exemplary for focusing on the world of politics, which had been erstwhile a male domain.[12]

Roy was, like Sanyal, also from a village now located in Bangladesh. Born in 1918 in Palang in East-Bengal, she received her primary education through a boy's school in a nearby village as there was no girls' school available in the area. She subsequently received a Bachelor of Arts and a Bachelor of Teaching from Calcutta University and worked as a schoolteacher. Like Sanyal, Roy also devoted most of her life to socialism and the de-colonial movement, and these politics influenced her literary works. Unfortunately, very little academic or popular attention has been paid to Roy's complex political thought and literary trajectory, which demonstrates the apathy towards gender consciousness amongst the literary audience. It also points to a deliberate rejection of any debate around the intersection of class and gender within leftist intellectual tradition. The lack of biographical information on Roy demonstrates how she has been marginalized and excluded from discussions of mid-century women writers due to her progressive ideas and intersectional understanding of oppression.

Despite her dedication to bringing attention to the socialist cause, the Communist Party did not support Roy's work and creativity. Like her protagonist Lata in *Harvest Song*, Roy was also a comrade wife whose husband was a full-time revolutionary absorbed in the political responsibilities for creating a socialist world. Throughout her life and career, Roy addressed the issue of the authoritarianism that decimated communist politics across the globe and drew attention to the significance of the domestic sphere in the political and social transformation of society. *Harvest Song* is the only Bengali novel of the decade that draws attention to the role of comrade women and 'reveal[s] the marginalization of the politically committed housewife, the exploitation of her domestic skills and the domestication in a cruel and conservative family environment that the Party enforced in the late 1940s to enable male comrades to undertake dangerous underground activities without worries about the children'.[13] The novel offers a detailed exploration of the nature of patriarchy within the Communist Party and its unjust demands on women.

Dissident friendship and revolutionary love in the making of female subjectivities

In her seminal essay 'The Personal is Political' (1970), Carol Hanisch identifies the need to frame individual experiences of gender-based inequalities within a collective structure by addressing how the existing social-political-economic systems benefit from the continual devaluation of women's labour. For the citizens of the newly formed state of India, gender-based inequality remained a social and economic issue, even though women were given full electoral rights in 1947, when the country gained independence from British rule. Writing in Bengali during the 1950s, Sanyal and Roy focused on the everydayness of social inequality which was fostered through gendered and sexualized labour. Their fiction also registers how women challenged the reproduction of such exploitation through both direct, visible action and indirect, invisible moments of nonaction. For example, Sanyal's *The Seedling's Tale* is a *Bildungsroman* wherein a young woman grows up within extraordinary contexts of historical and national formations and transcends the gendered space of domesticity and public–private dualism, weaving together political and personal causes by using education as a tool of emancipation. In contrast, Roy's *Harvest Song* demonstrates the politicization of ordinary Bengali women during the 1940s and reconstructs the figure of the revolutionary into women who are driven by love and supported by friendship. Both *The Seedling's Tale* and *Harvest Song* suggest that one possible means of resistance to colonial rule and traditional patriarchal values can be achieved through social alliance amongst women of different castes, classes, religions, and ethnicities.

The predominantly provincial settings of *The Seedling's Tale* and *Harvest Song* facilitate a focus on social alliance. The novels explore the village world and its rural social structure – its morals, hierarchies, and exploitations, which are guided by a feudal worldview – through a feminist lens and bring attention to the living conditions of rural people, especially women. Sanyal and Roy also depict the world of the urban poor, living in city slums and fighting to survive in sub-human living conditions. The contexts of Tebhaga Movement and the Famine of Bengal of 1943, two events that left a lasting impact on the historical and cultural identities of the Bengali community, provide the socio-economic framing of Roy's and Sanyal's novels respectively. In both, the figure of the revolutionary is cultivated from within ordinary middle-class women subjects. This stands in contrast with the other examples of the male-centric genre where the revolutionary has been represented by the heterosexual male, often from an upper-caste background. Sanyal and Roy demonstrate that the class-based inequities in a feudal colonial society cannot produce a just world until gender inequality is addressed. Ultimately, both authors argue that friendship and revolutionary love are the tools of social transformation that can produce anti-oppressive societies.

Both *Harvest Song* and *A Seedling's Tale* address the need for connection amongst women who were separated not only by the walls that confined them within domestic spaces, but also by their inherited caste, class, and religious coordinates that held them captive. These novels demonstrate how connections and bridges become the necessary tools for women's emancipation within such contexts. These connections appear in the form of what Leela Gandhi theorizes as dissident friendship and what Sachelle Ford develops as revolutionary love.[14] When women from conflicting class and caste interests cross boundaries and connect with one another to demonstrate that power relations cannot be the only determining force for intimate human relations, they participate in dissident friendship which can present the 'possibility' of 'resistance to the divisive and fragmenting lies of structural power'.[15]

Sanyal's novel *Nabankur*, first published in 1956 and translated into English in 2001 as *The Seedling's Tale*, presents the story of a young girl, Chhobi, who grows up during the 1930s and 1940s. Partly autobiographical in nature, Chhobi is representative of middle-class, upper-caste (Bramhin) women in Hindu families who witnessed the anti-colonial nationalist movements, lived with the consequences of the Second World War and the Famine of Bengal, and demanded access to human rights, resulting in social and political equality in women's public and private lives. Born in a declining feudal landlord family that followed a patriarchal structure, Chhobi's experience of the gender relationships and power hierarchies (practised within the intimate sphere of her intergenerational living space) formulates her earliest conceptions of power and subordination. Through Chhobi, readers witness how education provided an opportunity for Bengali women to step outside the domestic sphere and participate in the public world – political, social, and economic activities – which in turn allowed these women to have an identity beyond those inherited through birth and marriage.

Throughout her childhood, Chhobi resists the patriarchal norms within the household as she 'quarrel[ed] over the size of her piece of fish',[16] promised that '[she] shall not cry' when she agreed to leave her village for a chance to get an education, protested against the marriage of her aunt Binti, and proclaimed that 'marriage is not a good thing at all'.[17] While Chhobi's kinship ties – specifically to mother Mamata, aunt Sukumari, and grandmother

Purnashashi – influence her life, it is friendship rather than familial or communal ties that allows Chhobi to form connections with characters from impoverished backgrounds, whose class, caste, religious, and ethnic identities are drastically different from her own.

For example, while living in Chittagong, Chhobi meets Nilu and Pilu, two destitute children who live with their family on her aunt and uncle's property. Chhobi's friendship with these two girls allows her to empathize with and humanize their pain and suffering. Chhobi also befriends Minu, a Christian girl in school, and Paribanu, a brilliant Pathan girl who lives in a shantytown with her mother.[18] Since children of the landholding, upper-caste families were forbidden to socialize with working-class children, Chhobi's cross-economic friendships offer an insight into the power of such relationships as acts of dissidence against feudalism, classism, and castism. Chhobi's dissident friendship is punished as her aunt: 'slapped her ... [because she believed that] Nilu was a thief, Minu a Christian, Paribanu and her mother were Muslims. They were not to be touched.'[19] Thus, Chhobi learned from a young age that women are to remain separated along class and religious lines through the use of violence – both physical and ideological. Friendships with children from Christian and Muslim backgrounds, like that between Chhobi and her classmates, also present a performative resistance against religious patriarchy which directed the organization of society into in-group and out-group categories. These friendships offer Chhobi a social identity which is earned, not inherited.

Chhobi's aunt and uncle, however, decide to leave the city of Chittagong after the outbreak of the Second World War and the subsequent bombing by the Japanese. As a result, Chhobi is sent back to her village, where she is again exposed to the patriarchal domestic sphere of her feudal family. When one of her aunts commits suicide, the family grieves in secrecy and silence as the death of '[a] dumb, dark, ugly woman, who had been thrown out of her parents-in-law's house' was not to be marked by the family as a collective loss.[20] In their lives and deaths, the daughters and wives of Chhobi's family remained undesirable and expendable within the domestic sphere. But while Chhobi is unable to change the hierarchy within her own family, she is able to step outside of the household to build social relationships through friendship and solidarity, which upended the role of kinship ties in predetermining women's social status and relationships. Although Chhobi is not successful in forming a meaningful resistance movement through these friendships, she 'comes to see [her]self as constructed in ... the Other's reality'; through this process, this 'pluralist friendship enhances [her] self knowledge'.[21] As a result, she forms meaningful relationships with characters from diverse backgrounds, and this empathy catalyses her political action after she returns to her village.

Chhobi's friendships evolve from social to direct political action when she joins the local efforts of the then-banned Communist Party to run soup kitchens for the peasantry impacted by the Famine of Bengal in 1943. While the peasantry was largely seen as an exploitable and dispensable labour force by the landholding classes like Chhobi's family, Chhobi abandons her inherited vertical relationship of oppressor and oppressed and instead forms a revolutionary solidarity with the starving masses by joining relief efforts in rural communities, administered by the underground Communist Party. By doing so, Chhobi defies the family's patriarchal rules that prevent women of her background from partaking in political action. Chhobi's decision to distribute food and advocate for the welfare of the famine-ridden population challenges the patriarchy of her household, which assumes women's labour is the property of the family and not the choice of the individual. When the family patriarch, her grandfather Dakshinaranjan, declares that 'A woman's work is to tend to the household, she has no business with scholarship nor with politics', Chhobi's defiance represents not only a feminist resistance but also a caste and class-based resistance.[22] By working side-by-side with men and serving people of lower caste-class backgrounds, Chhobi transcends the dominant gender divisions observed within leftist politics of the time. In addition, through her activism, she challenges the British imperial government behind the Famine of Bengal and demonstrates that women of the colony were not going to sit by while their fellow community members died. Her caregiving work, an extension of her friendship with her comrades as well as with the larger village community, becomes a symbol of protest against feudal patriarchy and imperial capitalism.

Chhobi's care work is also a representation of a feminist nationalism that is founded on an affective alliance that allows her to resist colonial oppression and class exploitation. Driven by a love of her extended community, she challenges patriarchal, feudal, and imperial authority. By caring for the exploited peasantry of rural Bengal, Chhobi carries out collective action, demonstrating that members of the lower strata of society have a right to demand care from the rest of society. As with her political action within the public space, Chhobi also relies on affective alliances within the domestic space. Her personal goals of independence and education are supported by women like her mother, her aunt, and finally even her grandmother. Their actions are outcomes of their love for and towards Chhobi, but their acts of support also strengthen the goals of gender equality and women's emancipation. Thus, through Chhobi's actions and those of her female family members, Sanyal argues that revolutionary action is dependent on empathy, and that revolutionary love is a crucial tool of feminist, class-based, and anti-colonial resistance.

Education is key in facilitating both Chhobi's participation in the public sphere and the friendships that become the foundation of her political activism. Other women from Chhobi's household were denied an education and therefore restricted to the domestic sphere, severely controlled by patriarchal rules. Education is thus presented in *The Seedling's Tale* as a significant road to emancipation. As Chhobi's aunt Sukumari states, 'I thought we would have an educated girl in our family ... to see if all that learning could help her avoid the fate of women.'[23] The novel ends with Chhobi taking the train to go to the city of Calcutta to start college. Chhobi, however, frames her desire to pursue education and activism as an act of love.[24]

Chhobi's trajectory in *The Seedling's Tale* comments on the evolving nature of family relationships and patriarchy during the late-colonial period in Bengal. It is important to note that the author chooses to direct the reader's attention to the power relations within the domestic space in the context of changing political and public spheres. In writing for newly independent citizen-readers, Sanyal asks for conscious attention to the domestic sphere and demonstrates ways to eliminate the oppression and subjugation of women that continued from the colonial to the postcolonial era. Likewise, Roy's *Harvest Song* also focuses on the struggles of women through a gendered analysis of the social, political, and economic structures during the late-colonial period. But where Sanyal's *The Seedling's Tale* follows the journey of a single protagonist, Roy's *Harvest Song* focuses on several women. Roy's novel also illustrates how the political struggle for independence during the last decade of British rule coexisted with active resistance movements against feudal repression and gender-based violence.

Harvest Song revolves around the life trajectories of several women, including Debaki, Lata, Bhadra, Meghi, and Saraswati, all of whom challenge the public–private divide on matters of politics and ideas of equality during a time of significant political transformation. Although Roy sets her novel during the Tebhaga movement,[25] this politically significant historical moment is squared up against women who survive systemic, physical, and epistemic violence through religious, social, and legal infrastructures. For example, the rural-to-urban migration of women fleeing gender-based violence in feudal communities is depicted in the journeys of Debaki, a young wife rejected by her husband, which results in her losing her infant son, and Meghi, a young widow who endures abuse and threats of sexual violence in her village. The stories of Lata and Debaki represent how educated, middle-class women navigated their personal and political commitments during a time of nation building, while Saraswati's narrative represents the rural, illiterate, lower-caste, poor women of the peasantry.

Despite facing hardships, the women in *Harvest Song* are not motivated by rage against the exploitative system, but rather by an acute sense of love for their community. According to Sachelle M. Ford, 'It is the love of humanity and community that inspires revolutionaries to risk their lives for the chance of creating a more egalitarian society.'[26] Women like Debaki, Lata, Meghi, Bhadra, and Saraswati come together in their revolutionary activism from the vantage point of love as political action. The romantic love that inspires these women to transgress social expectations ultimately becomes the source of their revolutionary love that initiates social and political activism, through which questions of justice and equality and addressed and demanded. These women are not simply satisfied by their own escapes from abuse and exploitation but rather dedicate their lives to creating systemic solutions so that the communities learn to value the rights and lives of the women of future generations. These women's revolutionary love is also an embodiment of the kind of self-love that June Jordon theorizes as 'the sociopsychic strength needed ... to be able and willing to love and respect ... [a diverse body of] women' across cultural, social, and economic boundaries.[27]

While the characters are connected by their curation of dissident friendships, their political action emerges from their desire to practice a revolutionary love that transcends patriarchal, feudal, and colonial control over their bodies and minds. When her parents terminated her studies after she completed the seventh grade and arranged for her marriage against her will, Debaki resisted (in vain) and expressed her first declaration of revolutionary love as she asked Partha to 'please marry me'.[28] Partha, a revolutionary leader organizing villagers to fight against the exploits of feudalism and colonialism, was from a lower caste, and thus such a relationship would challenge the social order of their village. As a younger child, Debaki perceived Partha as a vehicle of kindness and justice, both of which were rare in her life. As she learns about Partha's political activism, Debaki sees him as the embodiment of a revolution that promised a life of dignity and justice for all.

While Partha remains an active revolutionary throughout the novel, Debaki builds her revolutionary identity within the domestic sphere, questioning the multi-prong oppressions of a colonial society. Right before Debaki's wedding to Rajen, Partha gifts her a copy of *Pather Dabi*, a popular and well-known Bengali novel by Sarat Chandra Chattapadhyay, a narrative of anti-colonial activism that explores the figure of the revolutionary. Later, the book is burnt by Rajen, Debaki's abusive husband, who falsely accuses her of carrying out an extramarital affair with Partha. This conscious insertion of *Pather Dabi* as a catalyst for the forward momentum of the plot demonstrates that Roy was carving out a location for ordinary rural women like Debaki within the narrative of revolutionary subjectivity. Debaki directly compares her abuse at the hands of her husband for speaking out against his misogyny, classism, and imperialism with the torture

Partha endures at the hands of the British police for his activism as an anti-colonial revolutionary.[29] Nikhil Govind argues that 'there has been a persistent fascination with the figure of the revolutionary over a period of several decades in the Bengali novelist tradition', and Roy establishes ordinary Bengali women as the embodiment of the revolutionary whose subjectivity is ignited through their actions of love which, in the case of Debaki, remains her unrequited love for Partha.[30]

Debaki's life trajectory demonstrates that a revolutionary change in the social and cultural perceptions of gender identity was crucial if the late-colonial period was to transcend into an independent and just society. When Debaki refuses to return to her husband and in-laws' house after childbirth because of her ongoing abuse, her mother Subala rebukes her, saying, 'it's your fault. You haven't learned to please your husband … You are being selfish looking at your own interests. Some other daughter would have gone through much more so that her parents would have a better life.'[31] The role of mothers in upholding patriarchal violence and abuse is evident in this statement, which demonstrates how women are controlled through guilt and shame in normalizing intimate partner violence and submitting to such practice. Subsequently, when Debaki comes to retrieve her infant son Joydeb from Rajen, who had previously kidnapped and taken the child away, she is told, 'We can't let a loose woman touch him.'[32] Rajen further added, 'He is my son, and only I have the right to decide what to do with him.'[33] Here Rajen denies Debaki her parental rights by using two sets of patriarchal logic. First, he resorts to evoking the issue of chastity as a qualifier of a 'good' woman and, because of her alleged affair with Partha, Debaki is found guilty of being a loose woman and thus denied her parental rights. Secondly, Rajen evokes his ownership relationship with his child and claims that he has absolute control over him as the child's father. Incidentally, this patriarchal logic did not align with the legal code which acknowledged a mother's right to parent, as Lakshman points out: '"Why don't you go to court? Even the female inmates in jail are allowed to keep their children with them."'[34] Devaki, however, is never reunited with her child in the novel, which presents the dichotomy of right and justice; despite having the right to parent her child, Devaki never receives the institutional support necessary to pursue her wealthy in-laws and husband to return her child to her. So, while *Harvest Song* focuses on the second-class status assigned to women from birth within the domestic sphere, it also points out that education and employment were crucial tools for women if they were to claim human dignity and status within domestic as well as public spheres.

Other characters in *Harvest Song* also illustrate the value of revolutionary love for social activism. For the widow Meghi, revolutionary love allows her to resist the everyday brutal repression she received as a widow of an upper-caste Hindu family. By eloping with a Muslim man, she claims her sexual agency and revolutionary subjectivity as she ruptures the social mechanisms that controlled the lives of widows and other marginalized people in colonial, feudal, Hindu society. Following their unique trajectories, both Debaki and Meghi travel to Kolkata, the metropolis and regional capital, where they find work as nursing assistants at a tuberculosis hospital. This is an instance where offering care to the sick, needy, and marginalized becomes a way of resisting the oppressive axes of society for these women. Here, paid care work becomes the first step towards emancipation for women who were otherwise marginalized and exploited.

Debaki's childhood friend Lata also turns to revolutionary love as a means of political activism. Lata elopes with Sulakshan, severing all ties with her upper-middle-class family, and embraces a rural life of isolation and sacrifice to support her husband, who continues his organization and resistance activities as a member of the then-banned Communist Party. Lata ultimately establishes a homeschool for impoverished girls from the Badgi community, where she gives lessons in literacy, numeracy, and sewing. Lata's confinement to the domestic sphere does not go unnoticed by Sukhomoy, another revolutionary activist and a comrade of Sulakshan, who presents the questions: 'A comrade's wife spending all [their] time like an old-fashioned wife in kitchen? ... Why on earth did you marry a comrade?'[35] But despite such observations, Lata continues to sacrifice her own public activism to ensure her husband can carry out the important work. However, Lata's endeavours to sell baskets and other artefacts made by the poor, lower-caste women are acknowledged as a revolutionary step by the socialist leadership, as Partha agrees that 'it can become a livelihood. A woman who earns gains confidence. She can even stand up against her in-laws.'[36] Lata's contribution to the slow revolution of the domestic sphere ensures that women's financial liberation and equal status within the household are complementary and fundamental for a truly liberated society.

While the main driving force in Roy's *Harvest Song* remains revolutionary love, the friendships that transcend class and caste barriers allow the protagonists to evolve into revolutionary subjects. Throughout the novel, Bhadra and Lata exchange letters sharing their experiences in upholding the resistance movements against imperialism and feudalism. Similarly, Debaki and Lata support each other in their quests toward aiding the revolution that Partha has been leading for years. Finally, when Partha is murdered by the landlord's hired goons, his death becomes the catalyst that connects his love interest, Bhadra (representative of middle-class, upper-caste, urban-educated women) with Saraswati (representative of rural, illiterate, lower-caste, poor women of the peasantry). This connection becomes the basis of a dissident friendship as Bhadra comes from a landholding upper-caste background against whom Saraswati's community, the peasants of Hajong ethnicity, were fighting.

Harvest Song therefore demonstrates that women's activism and struggle for agency constitutes a vital project of self-determination of the postcolonial nation. By integrating questions of consent, contrasting laws regarding marriage and divorce, and the exploitative nature of unpaid domestic work, alongside questions of decolonization, resistance against feudalism, and class struggle, Roy demonstrates that true emancipation of the population can come about only when the issue of women's oppression is addressed through an intersectional lens. The disparate and diverging life stories of Debaki, Lata, Meghi, Bhadra, and Saraswati are threaded together with the dream of justice and equality. These women come from different classes and castes, but they are connected through solidarity. They have all been victims of gender-based discrimination within domestic spaces and unacknowledged as equal human beings with access to agency and rights. The multi-layered world of the novel demonstrates that the colonized-feudal-patriarchal society of Bengal needed to address the issue of gender-based discrimination and oppression if its communities were to achieve true emancipation.

Ultimately, *The Seedling's Tale* and *Harvest Song* frame individual experiences of living within a patriarchal system and an evolving political infrastructure in relation to a collective intersectional positionality embodied by middle-class Bengali women of the time. The novels allude to the promise of socialization of women's labour within collective settings by references to the 1930s and 1940s socialist and communist political movements on the subcontinent, where women actively participated in resisting both colonial and feudal systems of oppression. In doing so, the women activists of these movements punctured the patriarchal assumptions about gender inequality, which were foundational to both feudalism and colonialism.

The ethics and politics of revisiting
The Seedling's Tale and *Harvest Song*

Both Roy's and Sanyal's novels have found new lives in English translation. Roy's Bengali works, for example, have only recently been reprinted by publishers like Granthalay, but it is far easier to find translations of her works in English. According to Paulomi Chakraborty, 'Sabitri Roy had all but disappeared from the book shelves of libraries and book shops and, indeed, from the literary memory of the reading public excepting a small, select group.'[37] Similarly, Sanyal's works also seemed destined to be forgotten until their reprint and eventual translation into English in the twenty-first century. While not much is known about each author's biography, and there is little scholarship on their literary works even after their rediscovery and circulation in translation, Sanyal's and Roy's novels are ripe for exploration and analysis as their work pays witness to Bengali women's involvement in mid-century politics.

This study has attempted to do just that by tracing how domesticity and public life were conceptualized by women who lived through the late-colonial period, witnessed the independence of India from British rule in 1947, and reflected on the everyday social practices that fostered gender hierarchy.

But revisiting these novels in the twenty-first century within the academic space of the global north presents ethical and practical questions. The revival and translation of these two novels, the process which brought these literary works into circulation, and their consumption by an Anglophone literary audience deserve attention and analysis. Since neither of the authors or their works in the original Bengali gained significant popularity or academic attention at the time of their original publication and were mostly shelved in the following decades until their rediscovery in the 1980s and eventual translation in the 2000s, it is necessary to think about the ethics and purpose of reconnecting with these texts.

In this context, the significance of Stree as a publishing house in the works' recovery, translation, and circulation needs to be addressed. Both *The Seedling's Tale* and *Harvest Song* were published in the early twenty-first century by Stree, an Indian feminist publisher, which 'is a professional publishing company committed to bringing out high quality books in women's studies'.[38] Stree's establishment in 1990 added an avenue for publishing scholarly texts in Women's and Gender Studies in Kolkata. Mandira Sen points out that the academic and scholarly presses located in the global north enjoy a monopoly on all academic research, including those that focus on South Asian women. In such a context, a regional publisher like Stree has focused on supporting the 'local and regional concerns and initiatives' and resisted agendas that are determined by outsider perspectives.[39]

With this mandate of prioritizing the local over the global, Stree's decision to publish the English translations of these novels becomes a conscious act of archival and retrieval of a tradition of women's writing in Bengali. The process was also transnational; Gouranga Chattopadhyay writes in his 'Translator's Note' that the long and arduous process of the 2001 English translation of Sanyal's *Nabankur* into *The Seedling's Tale* began in the 1980s in Montreal. Similarly, the translation of Roy's *Paka Dhaner Gaan* into *Harvest Song* was the product of a successful transnational collaboration between Chandrima Bhattacharya and Adrita Mukherjee, who were based in India and New Zealand, respectively. Any understanding of this production process of the translations not only requires historical and linguistic sensitivity, but also demands an attention to spatial coordinates, as the original works and their authors remained alienated from the translated works through national and geographical borders. Thus, this effort of translation and circulation of the works are outcomes of a transnational feminist solidarity which allowed for these mid-century writers to be rediscovered and introduced to a global audience.

Sanyal and Roy were anti-colonial thinkers and activists influenced by socialist politics and ideologies. However, neither of them wrote socialist literature per se, and instead focused on women, whose emancipation was not prioritized in either the nationalist or socialist politics of the time. Before intersectionality had been theorized, these authors demonstrated that structural power relations work in multiplicity. The novels portray how and why 'an intersectional way of thinking about the problem of sameness and difference and its relation to power' is required to analyse the multiple axes of oppression that were directed at colonized women of caste-divided India/Bengal.[40] These fictions fall within the tradition where 'transcription of reality and literary imagination form one indivisible structure of experience'.[41] As voices of subcontinental women, who were constructed by their relational existence in global geopolitics and gendered conditioning within the historical context, *The Seedling's Tale* and *Harvest Song* offer unique points of view which address women's emancipation as a human right and gender as an intersectional category interlocked with class, caste, ethnicity, and religion. The rediscovery, translation, and circulation of these novels in the twenty-first century, therefore, continues to influence the construction of postcolonial subjectivities today.

Notes

1 In the nineteenth century, early nationalist imagination, represented through the genre of the novel, deprived women of any agency to become anti-colonial activists and instead posited all responsibility of embodying traditions of Hinduism (and Islam) to ensure that the colonized society retained its pre-colonial values and practices. Bengali novelist Bankim Chandra Chattopadhyay played a significant role in promoting the idea of the mother–land–goddess triad through his novel *Anandamath*, which was serialized in a periodical titled *Bangadarshan* from mid 1880 to December 1882 (Bhattacharya, pp. 201–2). Thus, the novel became an early cultural site that constructed an arbitrary position for women as an embodied site of conflict where both colonial ideology and nationalist discourse participated in the systemic erasure of women's agency and gender equality. See Sumangala Bhattacharya, 'Gender, Power, and Nation: The Promethean Heroine in Bankimchandra Chatterjee's Rajmohan's Wife, Debi Chaudhurani, and Anandamath', *Clio* 41.2 (2012), pp. 197–220.

2 For more on the nineteenth-century history of India, see Barbara Metcalf and Thomas Metcalf, *A Concise History of India* (Cambridge: Cambridge University Press, 2001).

3 For more information on these legislations and their social impact, read Lata Mani, 'Contentious Traditions: The Debate on Sati in Colonial India', *Cultural Critique* 7 (1987), pp. 119–56; Tanika Sarkar, 'A Prehistory of Rights: The Age of Consent Debate in Colonial Bengal', *Feminist Studies* 26.3 (2000), pp. 601–22; Tanika Sarkar, *Hindu Wife, Hindu Nation, Community, Religion, and Cultural Nationalism* (Bloomington, IN: Indiana University Press, 2001).

4 Krupa Shandilya, 'The Widow, the Wife, and the Courtesan: A Comparative Study of Social Reform in Premchand's *Sevasadan* and the Late Nineteenth-Century Bengali and Urdu Novel', *Comparative Literature Studies* 53.2 (2016), p. 273.

5 Kumkum Sangari and Sudesh Vaid, *Recasting Women: Essays in Indian Colonial History* (New Brunswick, NJ: Rutgers University Press, 1990), p. 160.

6 A comprehensive account of these publications can be found in Ipshita Chanda and Jayeeta Bagchi (eds), *Shaping the Discourse: Women's Writing in Bengali Periodical 1865–1947* (Kolkata: Stree, 2014).

7 Renuka Mandal, 'Indian Women's Movement', in *Shaping the Discourse*, p. 282.

8 Supriti Majumder, 'India's Women Workers', in *Shaping the Discourse*, p. 367.

9 Susie Tharu, 'Foreword', in *Nabankur: The Seedling's Tale* (Kolkata: Stree, 2001), p. vii.

10 Sudheshna Bhattacharya, 'The Making of a Popular Base for the Quit India Movement: The Impact of the Pacific War on the People and the Colonial State in India (1941–42)', *Proceedings of the Indian History Congress* 63 (2002), p. 685.

11 Tharu, 'Foreword', p. vii.

12 Tanika Sarkar, 'Foreword', in *Harvest Song: A Novel on the Tebhaga Movement* (Kolkata: Stree, 2006), p. vi.

13 *Ibid.*, pp. viii–ix.

14 See Leela Gandhi, *Affective Communities: Anticolonial Thought, Fin-de-Siècle Radicalism, and the Politics of Friendship* (Durham, NC: Duke University Press, 2006); and Sachelle M. Ford, 'Revolution', in *Gender: Love*, ed. Jennifer C. Nash (New York: Macmillan, 2016), pp. vii–x.

15 Elora Halim Chowdhury and Liz Philipose (eds), 'Introduction', in *Dissident Friendships: Feminism, Imperialism, and Transnational Solidarity* (Champaign, IL: University of Illinois Press, 2016), p. 12.

16 As a girl child, she would be offered a smaller portion compared to the male members.

17 Sulekha Sanyal, *Nabankur: The Seedling's Tale* (Kolkata: Stree, 2001), pp. 24, 47, 53.

18 Pastho-speaking population groups are found in Afghanistan, Pakistan, and Kashmir.

19 Sanyal, *Nabankur*, p. 107.

20 *Ibid.*, p. 197.
21 Maria Lugones, 'Heterosexualism and the Colonial/Modern Gender System', *Hypatia* 22.1 (2007), p. 143.
22 Sanyal, *Nabankur*, p. 204.
23 *Ibid.*, p. 148.
24 *Ibid.*, p. 214.
25 The Tebhaga movement was a grassroots-level peasant revolution where the landless peasantry demanded that the tax laws allow them to keep a third of their produce while they pay a third of their crops to the British government and another third to the feudal landlords. For more on the movement, read Krishnakanta Sarkar, *Colonial Rule, Rural Transformation and Tebhaga Movement in Bengal*, Jan. 2001, pp. 320–42; David Taylor, 'Peasant Movements in Bengal: A Critique of the "Moral Economy" Approach', *Flinders Journal of History & Politics* 10 (Jan. 1984), pp. 85–98.
26 Ford, 'Revolution', p. 167.
27 June Jordan, 'Where Is the Love?', in *In Civil Wars* (Boston, MA: Beacon Press, 1981), p. 144.
28 Sabitri Roy, *Harvest Song: A Novel on the Tebhaga Movement* (Kolkata: Stree, 2006), p. 29.
29 *Ibid.*, p. 61.
30 Nikhil Govind, 'Pluralizing Nationalism: Narrative, Politics and the Figure of the Revolutionary in the Hindi Novel from the 1930s to the 1950s' (PhD thesis, University of California Berkeley, 2011), p. 28. https://escholarship.org/content/qt2hm2q00n/qt2hm2q00n_noSplash_7cf02c2ebff9c587041b0968c15db29a.pdf
31 Roy, *Harvest Song*, p. 102.
32 *Ibid.*, p. 103.
33 *Ibid.*, p. 104.
34 *Ibid.*, p. 108.
35 *Ibid.*, pp. 260–1.
36 *Ibid.*, p. 264.
37 Paulomi Chakraborty, *The Refugee Woman: Partition of Bengal, Women, and the Everyday of the Nation* (Edmonton: University of Alberta, 2009), p. 279.
38 Mandira Sen and Mausumi Bhowmik, 'Publishing Women's Studies in India: Stree's Experience', *Women's Studies International Forum* 25.2 (2022), p. 186.
39 *Ibid.*
40 Sumi Cho, Kimberlé Williams, and Leslie McCall, 'Intersectionality: Theorizing Power, Empowering Theory', *Signs* 38.4 (2013), p. 795.
41 Jasodhara Bagchi and Subhoranjan Dasgupta, *The Trauma and the Triumph: Gender and Partition in Eastern India* (Kolkata, Bhatkal & Son, 2003), p. 10.

8

'The political theory of heaven': religious nationalism, mystical anarchism, and the Spanish Civil War in Sylvia Townsend Warner's *After the Death of Don Juan*

Charles Andrews

Speaking with the *PN Review* in 1975, Sylvia Townsend Warner reflected on her political awakening in the 1930s during the rise of fascism in Europe and her participation in resistance movements. The Reichstag Fire trial of 1933, the arrest of Comintern head Georgi Dimitrov, and the activities of the British Union of Fascists precipitated her involvement with the newly founded *Left Review*. She befriended its editor Edgell Rickword and forged a fraught but longstanding relationship with the British Communist Party. But the war in Spain that began with a military coup in July of 1936 became an especially significant site of political activism for Warner and her partner Valentine Ackland. They travelled to Spain in September of 1936 to work with a Red Cross unit giving material aid to victims of the civil war, encountered anarchist resistance groups, and witnessed the devastations of right-wing nationalism supported by the Spanish Catholic Church.[1] As Warner's biographer Claire Harman describes their trip, 'the work was clerical as much as medical, and lasted only three weeks, but in that time Sylvia developed a passion for Spain to match her passion for politics, seeing embodied in the spirit of Republican Spain the principles she held most dear'.[2] Activism and aesthetics united for both Warner and Ackland as they worked in Spain and wrote journalism, poetry, and fiction for the Republican cause and Spanish war victims.[3]

Warner promoted humanitarian anti-fascism while broadly accepting the many Spanish groups on the political left. In a series of articles for the *Left Review*, she denounced the fascist insurrection and reported on the suffering of Spanish people to generate support and material aid. She also spoke out against what Richard Baxell has called the essential 'elements of the Spanish right' – 'the powerful troika of landowners, army and Catholic Church'.[4] This 'troika' had long held sway in Spain, threatening the Liberal monarchy that formed in 1916 after the First World War, supporting the military dictatorship that held power from 1923 until the creation of the democratic Republican government in 1931, and ultimately contributing to what Francisco J. Romero Salvadó describes as 'the demise of Liberal Spain' that 'resulted in an unprecedented spiral of violence' and 'an authoritarian formula of social control'.[5] During the brief and fragile period of the Second Republic from 1931 until the outbreak of civil war in 1936, there was much division on the Spanish left, which weakened support for the government and manifested in the many groups allied against Franco but divided about ultimate political and social objectives. In the *Left Review*, Warner described vendors' stalls in Barcelona that offered trinkets from a few of these leftist organizations, and her report succinctly catalogues the major groups, their acronyms, and their political valences. Along with other wares, customers could find 'rings and badges and brooches carrying the initials of the anarchist F.A.I. and C.N.T., the Trotskyist P.O.U.M., the Communist P.S.U.C. and U.G.T.'.[6] But Warner refused to align herself exclusively with any of these groups or their political dogmas. Harman notes that Warner and Ackland 'bought a selection' of political materials from these vendors and in England 'donated them to the *Daily Worker* to auction for the Spanish Fund'.[7] Working for the Spanish people but not taking sides in the internecine conflicts on the left was Warner's consistent mode, and her uncompromising anti-fascism was matched by an openness to the political diversity of the left.

This refusal to choose among the competing forces on the Spanish left in favour of a more generalized humanitarianism risks the appearance of a stereotypically gendered response to the war, where women were less involved in party politics and organizational machinations. Angela Jackson has noted that 'nowhere in the writings of either [Warner or Ackland] on Spain is there any real attempt "to engage" with issues relating to the Communist Party's involvement in the suppression of [the anti-Stalinist] POUM' and concludes: 'in their omission of such matters from their writing, they are reflecting the common tendency of women to focus their attention on aspects of the war other than the political divisions within the Left'.[8] But Warner's reticence should not be viewed as disengagement from or ignorance of these divisions. Her relationship with the British Communist Party was committed but contentious; the party had denied Ackland and Warner's initial request to go to Spain as official representatives, making their activist labours adjacent to rather than sanctioned by the Party.[9] Both women were well aware of the dangers of in-fighting among leftist groups, and their position was radical because they stayed connected to their official party affiliations while struggling to achieve their own political and material goals.

Rather than a lack of interest in party politics, Warner exhibits through her activism and writing a capacity for creatively and imaginatively building bridges across divisions, retaining her orientation toward the Communist

Party but tenderly and thoughtfully engaging with Spanish anarchism. Paul Preston has shown how the battle for Madrid in 1936 during the first months of the war encapsulated divisions between Spanish communism and anarchism, where 'the anarchists accused the Communists of imposing the authoritarian rigidity of Soviet communism over the spontaneity of the libertarian social revolution' and 'the Communists responded with severe criticisms of the way anarchist inefficiency impeded the job of feeding the refugees crammed into the besieged city'.[10] That dispute between the ideals of collectivist centralization and individual liberty would persist throughout the war, and its problems were not lost on Warner. Her response, however, was to look for the potential value in these ideologies, and her affection was particularly stirred by Spanish anarchism. National character was crucial to her political disposition, as she told the *PN Review*: 'if the English turn to the left at all, they are natural anarchists. They are not orderly enough to be good Communists.'[11] Her official commitment to communism, she claimed, was 'simply because I was agin [sic] the Government but that of course is not a suitable frame of mind for a Communist for very long'.[12] It is possible, she speculated, that 'you can go on being an anarchist for the rest of your life' because 'you've always got something to be anarchic about – your life is one long excitement'.[13] 'Anarchists', she remarked, 'are the most *charming* people!'[14]

Essential to the 'charm' of anarchism was its rare combination of frankness and idealism – a politics Warner affirmed and incorporated into her fiction that responded to the civil war. In a letter to Elizabeth Wade White from 1936, Warner wrote, 'you cannot imagine after this mealy-mouthed country, the pleasure of seeing an office with a large painted sign, Organisation for the Persecution of Fascists. [...] That beautiful directness is typical of anarchism, a most engaging type of thought, though I do not want to be an anarchist myself.'[15] Warner's comments betray her worries about anarchism's practicality but also show her lingering attraction to idealistic and utopian politics. Gillian Beer observes that this ambivalence characterizes much of Warner's fiction in the 1930s, which is 'at once skeptical about belief and wholehearted in its relish of the possible' and where the novels' 'Utopian reach [...] is, over and over again, undermined sardonically from within'.[16] This sardonic scepticism does not, however, reject all hope for alternative political visions, but rather insists that a better world is still worth imagining. In a final gesture of support for anarchism, Warner asserted to White that 'the world is not yet worthy of it, but it ought to be the political theory of heaven'.[17] This mention of 'heaven' is a rhetorical flourish rather than a theological claim, but it exemplifies Warner's ambivalent relationship with both anarchism and religious faith. She is attracted to the liberating potential of anti-fascist, anti-nationalist ideologies such as anarchism without fully accepting their practical viability. Her language remains inflected with religious speech patterns residual from her upbringing in and cultural context of Christianity. Though held lightly and ambivalently, she endorses a political theology of anarchism that rivals the oppressive and destructive powers of church and state that plagued Spain, and alongside her journalism of the period that she described 'simply as propaganda [...] in favour of the Republic', her fiction richly displayed her theopolitical imagination.[18]

After the Death of Don Juan (1938) was the novel Warner wrote most directly from her experiences in Spain and, as I argue here, out of deep admiration for anarchism as a secular political theology that rivals the fusion of Catholicism, nationalism, and fascism that inflamed the Spanish Civil War. Her investigation of Catholic Christianity as a social force (rather than a private, devotional, or 'spiritual' faith) emerges through the experimental style of the novel, which Maud Ellmann describes as a 'hybrid form, interweaving history and myth, realism and allegory, farce and tragedy' that 'along with its feline sangfroid, represents a revolution in the genre, too radical to be enjoyed without discomfort'.[19] In an often-quoted letter to Nancy Cunard, Warner said that her book was 'a parable, if you like the word, or an allegory or what you will, of the political chemistry of the Spanish War, with the Don Juan – more of Molière than of Mozart – developing as the Fascist of the piece'.[20] By calling the novel a 'parable or an allegory', Warner signals her distance from realism, though many of its elements conform to the genre of historical fiction that she often embraced.[21] But her description also reveals her borrowing Christian generic forms emptied of specifically religious content and repurposed for political uses. This experiment with a modern parable or allegory offers resources for resisting the places where Christianity and nationalism combined to produce some of the worst ideological forces during the Spanish Civil War and its aftermath. The Catholic, Franco-supporting Spanish writer José María Pemán, for instance, wrote with a chilling certainty that 'The smoke of incense and the smoke of cannon, rising to God in Heaven, denote a single vertical will to affirm a faith, to save a world and to restore a civilization.'[22] Though Pemán's comment is an especially straightforward and extreme presentation of religion combining with nationalist violence, it demonstrates the essential elements of civil religion – the use of myth and ritual to bind together a people united in sacrifice. In nations such as Spain where Catholicism predominated, the mythic structures borrow language and symbols from Christianity that fuse with national identity to enhance both religious and nationalist ideologies. Warner's engagement with religious nationalism in *After the Death of Don Juan* provides resources for thinking about how creative work can challenge the orthodoxies of civil religion and interfere with the urges toward sacrificial violence found in voices like Pemán's. Religious nationalism cannot be defeated by ignoring or avoiding it, and Warner imagines a secular political theology to counteract its destructive power.

Anarchist style and political theology

Warner's engagement with Christianity as a socio-political force rather than private, individual 'devotion' was a longstanding and consistent part of her literary output, frequently intertwining with the feminist and queer politics that critics have typically focused on in her writing.[23] Her first novel, *Lolly Willowes* (1926), depicts a woman resisting her family's expectations about heterosexual marriage and familial service by escaping into life in a witches' coven. The Willowes family's Anglicanism is crucial to their identity, daily practices, and beliefs about how an ageing, unmarried woman ought to behave, and the swerve into witchcraft and the company of Satan is, as critics have argued, coded as anti-patriarchal and queer.[24] Anglicanism in *Lolly Willowes* is also essential to the family's sense of national identity and their participation in the First World War, and the titular character's deviation from the family's religious beliefs and values is politically charged, linking feminism and queerness with resistance to nationalism and militarism.

After the Death of Don Juan continues this engagement with religion as political through its depiction of Spanish Catholicism. The novel's queer themes are more muted than in some of her other novels, such as *Lolly Willowes* or *Mr. Fortune's Maggot* (1927), but it focuses even more consistently on the detrimental social influence of institutional religion while subtly commenting on the gender dynamics of religious faith and practice. Rather than a single protagonist, the novel moves through an ensemble of characters who operate in various degrees within or against the power of the church. Most of the ensemble are men from the land-owning class who benefit from the church's powers of coercion or upper-class women whose religious displays flaunt their unjust wealth. Against these figures are a variety of labouring-class characters whose debates about political action form a tentative strain of resistant thought – an alternative political theology to rival the consolidated power of landowners, church, military, and state that were the fuel mixture for Spanish fascism. This political alternative enacts the anarchist values Warner admired during her visits to Spain, and it extends the feminist critique of Christian social values from her earlier novels into a panoramic, collectivist form.

To speak of anarchism as a 'political theology' may seem to run counter to the history of anarchist thought in which religion has been generally viewed as detrimental.[25] Among Spanish anarchists in the 1930s, provisions were made for individual religious belief that was not imposed on others, such as the resolution in the *Confederación Nacional del Trabajo* (CNT) from 1936 asserting that 'religion, a purely subjective facet of the human being, will be acknowledged as long as it remains a matter of individual conscience, but in no instance may it be regarded as a form of public display or moral or intellectual coercion'.[26] This resolution maintains the anarchist emphasis on individual freedom – personal faith cannot be coerced but also cannot be prevented – but retains the sense that public displays of religion are problematically allied with state power. *After the Death of Don Juan* critically portrays such public faith and private superstition, but against the matrix of church, state, and military, it supplies an alternative theology of inclusive human love and broad economic justice. This secular theology resonates with what Simon Critchley has called 'mystical anarchism', in which 'the condition of possibility for a life of cooperation and solidarity with others' is created through 'an act of inward colonization, the act of love that demands a transformation of the self'.[27] By reorienting ourselves away from self-preservation or violent Utopianism and toward selfless care for others, new anarchist possibilities emerge that counter the enchanted powers of the state. Warner's fiction imagines such politics in a speculative and tentative way, refusing simplistic portrayals of idealized peasantry or political victory in favour of a complex endorsement of anarchist collectivity.[28]

The novel is set 'in the seventh decade of the eighteenth century', and its first paragraphs rapidly summarize the highlights of Mozart's *Don Giovanni* as told by the unreliable witness of Don Juan's servant Leporello.[29] This eighteenth-century setting helps achieve Warner's goal of a fable-like quality by removing events from the present, but its specific timeframe also evokes the conflicts roiling in Spain during a period where Enlightenment challenges to religious belief were met with hostility and repression from church and governmental authorities.[30] In this prologue, Don Juan attempts to seduce Doña Ana, but when her father the Commander intervenes, he is killed by Juan. Juan later visits the Commander's grave and tauntingly invites the deceased to dinner. The Commander's statue on top of his tomb becomes animate – possibly with the spirit of the Commander – and arrives in Don Juan's dining room to 'tell Don Juan that the hour had come when he must either repent or render up his soul to hell'.[31] Juan refuses, and the narrator succinctly notes: 'The room grew dark, the floor opened, devils appeared, and Don Juan was dragged down into the pit. The Commander, meanwhile, had retired.'[32] Though many of Leporello's listeners are sceptical about the factuality of this story, they all seem fairly convinced that descent into hell is an appropriate outcome for Don Juan. The pious Doña Ana is shocked by the story and, though 'she constantly affirmed that heaven would avenge her father's death', 'this demonstration of heavenly efficiency was too much for her'.[33]

Warner's elaboration on Mozart uses several alternating narrative styles. The rapid retelling of Mozart is tragicomic but laced with the serious, and realistic, irony that Juan's wealth and power might make him unassailable, immune even to divine justice. And, indeed, two-thirds of the way through the novel, we learn that Leporello's story was a ruse that allowed Juan to escape only to return with more terrible political force. Doña Ana's reaction to Juan's death is a combination of grief, Christian piety, and unresolved desire that sends her on an extravagant and costly pilgrimage to see Juan's father in his hometown of Tenoria Viejo – a move that causes Don Ottavio, her betrothed, to assert: 'Your conscience is overheated [...] you have lost command of your theology.'[34] Barbara Brothers claims that through Doña Ana and the church leaders Don Gil and Don Tomas, 'Warner portrays the values of the patriarchal church' which is 'devoted to power' and 'perpetuates illiteracy and superstition, thus enslaving women and the poor'.[35] One of the few ways Doña Ana can exert her influence is through an extravagant mourning rite that mobilizes her family's wealth and the church's power, and through this depiction Warner supplies the feminist critique that is latent in the narrative. Women in the novel are excluded from central importance among the landowners and relegated to domestic spaces among the labouring classes, and the conflicted blend of patriarchy, ecclesial power, and personal longing that motivates Doña Ana later becomes the context for the battles among the ruling class characters that ultimately lead to Don Juan's fascist triumph.[36]

Doña Ana's pilgrimage merges personal piety with public liturgy, which, Warner shows, is inextricable from the social and economic realities of village life. In Tenorio Viejo, Don Juan's father Don Saturno mourns the recent death of his sister Doña Isabel, and discussion of funerals reveals the political implications of religious grief rites. Doña Isabel's burial requests were quite specific and loaded with nationalist and racialist connotations: 'I wish to be buried like a woman of Spain and not pickled like a woman of Egypt.'[37] Such a burial is thus regarded as 'properly' Spanish, and Don Saturno remarks that with a 'mere death', an entire social and economic 'mechanism, like some fine piece of clockwork, begins to revolve', whereby the various labourers making tombstones, digging graves, filling roles in church, and completing legal arrangements are all cogs in machinery while 'delicate impulses of industry circulate through the whole community'.[38] 'I never attend a funeral without reflecting', Don Saturno admits, 'what a large number of excellent persons are gaining their bread by it.'[39] These observations highlight the material conditions of public and communal mourning, how the church is an essential element in the social functioning of society – at least at the level of the elite and wealthy who can set so much economic machinery in motion through their grief rituals. Personal emotions expressed through corporate and public worship show how the church is a conduit for an intimate public space where emotion is never merely private but has social and even national connotations. Like Doña Ana's pilgrimage, Doña Isabel's funeral requests reveal how ruling-class women exert their power through religious rituals that turn private life into public action, an indication of how patriarchy stifles even the social elites. By exposing this dynamic, Warner supplies a feminist critique of masculinist power that persists as the narrative moves forward with its predominately male ensemble who grip the levers of power more directly.

Warner primarily focuses on upper-class characters whose various forms of self-absorption, callousness, and outright malice profoundly affect the peasants in their domain, and this focus enables her exploration of the ideological forces that produce social collapse and rising fascism. Warner's description of her book as a parable or allegory of Spanish politics gives a clue to her stylistic experiments, and the focus on problematic and villainous elites rather than the more heroic, revolutionary under-classes is part of that experimental form. The religious-mythical or magical realist story of Don Juan's dragging to hell that opens the novel is repeated several times by Leporello, often at the behest of sceptical listeners such as Don Saturno, who finds the mythos irrational and its social implications unlikely; he fully accepts his son's attempting rape and committing murder but doubts the 'breach of good taste' implied in Juan's supposedly inviting his murder victim to dinner.[40] Similarly doubtful, but for other reasons, are the peasants who struggle with Leporello's assurance that their most abusive landholder is truly dead and that they are truly free. In several key moments, Warner adopts a collectivist and pluralistic point of view where the narrator speaks the opinions of the village in general or in a flurry of voices, rendering the villagers more communally than the contentious and self-aggrandizing elites. This style occurs when Ramon Perez, one of the leading voices among the peasantry, invites Leporello to tell of Don Juan's death at a gathering in the local inn. Unlike Saturno, who balks at the story's social implausibility and religious mythology, the peasants wave away talk of devils and damnation, saying, 'if Don Juan is in hell, that is his business'.[41] Far more crucial to them is confirming eyewitness proof that he is dead and 'off our backs at least' because, as one unnamed man in the crowd poetically declares: 'must we still sweat out the wine he drinks [...] shear our sheep to make satin tails for his harlots instead of coats for our children. He drinks wine, and our land gasps for water.'[42] Moving between characters and groups through narrative point of view, Warner achieves an effect that Wendy Mulford has likened to Eisenstein's dialectical montage, a method for expressing radical politics through experimental form.[43] I would add that this formal experimentation complicates Warner's own description of the novel as a parable or allegory. The most parable-like sections of narration are the repeated accounts of Don Juan's death, but those are challenged and questioned in order to achieve a more complex and thornier political tableau where oppressed peasants debate possibilities of dissent and resistance while ruling class landowners align with church functionaries to squabble over how to maintain power.

Warner hints at her stylistic experiments and their satirical purpose through a seemingly incidental character detail where she describes one of Don Saturno's favourite hobbies: translating the plays of Aristophanes. While noodling at this hobby, he muses that his attraction to these classics comes from the way that they 'slyly' show how 'the lever could be inserted, and without a word of offence to church or throne the power of both might be shaken by this author whose plays included so many deities and no kings'.[44] Displacing the conflicts in Spain of the 1930s onto a version of the Don Juan story set in the 1760s, Warner similarly enacts a literary slyness to jab at church and throne without mentioning Franco or twentieth-century Spanish Catholicism. Warner's fiction has often been praised for its 'sly' qualities, and especially for how she smuggles queer themes and characters into novels such as *Lolly Willowes*, which found mainstream success despite its radical feminism and queerness.[45] But her slyness also manifests in her playing with historical fiction, classics, parables, and other alternatives to realism that enable her to give biting commentary on contemporary problems without heavy-handed propaganda. By showing the complicity of a patriarchal church and oligarchic state in creating unjust social conditions, Warner comments on the ideological matrix that enabled the fascist coup in Spain.

The church and fascism

Doña Ana is the novel's most prominent figure of Christian piety as social practice, but several others emerge in Tenorio Viejo as church leaders whose religiosity is mainly power-play and whose ministry acts only to deal spiritual opium to the masses. Don Gil, the head sacristan of the church where Doña Ana keeps her vigil, takes great pleasure in acquiring power through the church's muscle. The narrator explains that when Don Gil was an orphan child in choir school, he was bullied by a choirmaster until one of the Canons, a person higher in the church's pecking order, told the choirmaster that he should not bully the boy so much. We learn that 'more than money or position or security or crayfish with saffron or a cigar in the summer dusk, Don Gil loved the sense of power', and this love arose with this ideal from his childhood abuse where he gained 'a new conception of power'.[46] How to manipulate the structures of religious leadership toward his own ends 'burst on the child. The tyrant he knew was afraid of a greater tyrant; and the greater tyrant of a greater tyrant yet.'[47] Don Gil feels inspired as 'a hierarchy of bullying opened before him' wherein 'fear ran through the social order as blood flows through the man; and behind the social order was God, the source and support of all fear, God like a heart eternally pumping fear into the universe'.[48] Humans can draw from this wellspring of divine fear and dress in its authority; Don Gil 'saw, and adored, and dedicated himself to becoming powerful'.[49] Though Warner later explained that she saw Don Juan as the central fascist, the clearest expression of fascism distilled occurs through this sacristan whose strategic grasping of church power is a means for terror and domination. The abuse Don Gil endorses echoes Warner's contribution to Nancy Cunard's famous pamphlet *Authors Take Sides on the Spanish War*, where she asserted that she was against fascism because 'its tyranny is an expression of envy, its terrorism is an expression of fear'.[50] From bullied child to bullying oppressor, Don Gil manifests the dehumanizing of fascism. While Don Juan bears an obvious resemblance to Franco in that he steals power through a kind of military coup, it is Don Gil who exposes the deep ideological allures of fascism, its capacity to sway and envelope the masses, and its intrinsic relationship with the church. Don Juan, like his father before him, maintains power through clinging to wealth, stifling working-class advances in education and resources, and applying brute-force violence where required. Don Gil supplies another layer of domination by connecting earthly power with divine force and the robust structures of a wealthy, respected, and hierarchical church. As one aristocrat says in affirmation of Don Gil: 'you have reared up a virtuous family, you have sons in the army, daughters in religion [...] you are a prop to Church and State'.[51] With his combination of avarice, ambition, and sadism, all fused with the enchantments of religious mythology and ecclesial community, Don Gil subtly and deviously enacts the narrative's fascism.

When violence between landowners and peasants finally erupts in the novel's conclusion, Warner makes explicit the role of military power in this fusion of church and state. Trouble has been brewing in Tenorio Viejo for quite some time, and material resources are in short supply due to landowner mismanagement and acquisitiveness. Through a montage of voices, we hear labourers say that 'for generations they've oppressed us. Did not our forefathers build the castle with their own hands, hew the stone and carry it and set it up with forced labour?'[52] 'Yes', another voice says, 'and did they not fetch artisans from the town to build the church under the noses of those here who should have been paid for doing it?'[53] This generational oppression where landowners come 'each worse than the last' is 'a devil's rosary' where the centrality of the church contributes to dominion over workers.⁵⁴ When the militia arrives, called by Don Juan to quash the rebellion, the peasant children who see them marching fall to their knees and cross themselves, 'for they had no experience of a procession that was not a religious procession'.⁵⁵ This moment near the novel's ending parallels its beginning with Doña Ana's pious journey, and the narrative shows religious practices joining with military rule. The children only know the current social order where the church shapes all public life, and their reaction to the marching troops is Warner's implication that religious processions and military surges are differing guises for similar powers. Not just an 'ordinary' instance of religious violence, this moment shows ritualized displays of power and force plus military insurrection – hallmarks of Spanish fascism in the 1930s that built upon centuries-old oppression.

Much of the town and its castles and churches are depicted as crumbling, the decaying site of systemic failure made worse by selfish leaders who ultimately yield to fascist impulses. The overdetermined name Tenorio Viejo translates to 'old seducer' (or, perhaps even 'old Don Juan'), and the eighteenth-century present-day Don Juan is but one in a long lineage of seductive wastrels with that name. His fascist schemes, such as ruling through military power and giving the peasants 'free' irrigation so long as they submit to his will, are new instances of familiar problems in Spain. As one peasant remarks, 'there is more on our backs than the son of Don Saturno […] If Tenorio Viejo were to become a paradise, it would still be in Spain.'⁵⁶ From a hilltop above the town, Don Ottavio views Tenorio Viejo and realizes its resemblance to 'the tumbled bleached bones of an ossuary' where the poplars along the river look like ribs 'and the church, looking at him with its hollow socketed doorway, was the skull. A bad omen.'⁵⁷ This death imagery with the church as its head portends the ruin and violence to come, and the image echoes Warner's comments in a letter from 1936 about destruction she witnessed in Spain: 'There are a great many shells and skulls of churches. It seemed quite natural that churches should have been used as machine-gun nests, I have never seen churches so heavy and hulking and bullying, one can see at a glance that they have always been reactionary fortresses.'⁵⁸ The bad omen that Don Ottavio feels while looking down at the church's place in Tenorio Viejo has its modern version in Warner's comments about the 'hulking and bullying' that lends itself to military violence. The ecclesial history of Spain's past prepares it for the modern violence that emerges with Franco's coup and the rise of fascism.

By the novel's end, Juan has established himself as the central ruler of Tenorio Viejo, proclaiming that under him there will become a Tenorio Nuevo, and his brute force is supplemented and enabled by civil religion that fuses Christian ritual with state power. In the final pages, Juan is more of a shadowy figure than a character. He never speaks, and the final image of him occurs as he walks through the carnage wrought by soldiers firing on rioting villagers – groups of lower-class people whom Warner renders more fully and richly than the upper-class protagonists who have faded from narrative prominence by the novel's conclusion. The last glimpse of Juan finds him taking cover from gunfire and surrounded by soldiers who 'were grimed with smoke and bulgy with pillage. And walking a little apart from them, fastidious and secluded, was Don Juan. Presently he mounted the steps to the church, and stood on the platform before the west door, holding up an optic glass and looking.'[59] Silently watching the people he is conquering, Don Juan is speechless. His victory is imminent, but Warner displaces his voice to give the last words to the peasants. Mercedes Aguirre has perceptively argued that the violent conflict at the end of the novel is based on the siege of Alcázar, a site with symbolic value because 'it not only echoed a past time of class-privilege, a manifest rejection of the ideals of equality propagated by the Spanish Republic, but it also evoked a past national grandeur in which military achievement and religion were closely related'.[60] And so, in this last image of Juan surveying his wreckage, he is linked with the church while suppressing the villagers and establishing himself within the great chain of bullies that Don Gil fantasized.

Mystical anarchism and communal love

There is also a counterweight in the novel to the ruling powers and rising fascism. Several times we learn about the interior lives of the peasants and from them glimpse the 'political theory of heaven' that gives tentative, provisional hope despite overwhelming oppression. Although Warner is careful to depict the peasant labourers through a panoramic, collectivist style that resists unduly privileging any single character, Ramon Perez functions as a moral leader whose views cast a broader vision. With sorrow, resignation, and disappointment, Ramon joins the revolutionary uprising and acknowledges his role as a political instigator. Though he never intended an armed revolt, the brokenness of the world means that his thoughtful, sincere questions about Don Juan's supposed death and his insistence that the landowners provide irrigation lead the villagers into violent conflict. Ramon is 'a man of steadfast ideas' and 'what made him peculiar was the steadfastness by which he lived according to his creed'.[61] This 'creed' asserts that life is hard and that plagues and droughts are unavoidable, but there is goodness in the ways humanity can join together, that 'the world is not so bad as we make it', and 'there should be justice for the poor; for though Death is welcomed to the house of the oppressed and driven away from the door of the rich man, yet in the end he knocks on both doors'.[62] Above all, he believes that 'neighbor should stand by neighbor' – a faith in collective action against natural disaster and systemic injustice that focuses on the bonds among people without hierarchical rule.[63] Ramon's convictions echo some core Christian values, but the novel depicts his creed as separate from the actions of the church and aligns him more with anarchist thinkers like Pyotr Kropotkin, who found the essence of social functioning in neighbourliness born from 'the conscience – be it only at the stage of an instinct – of human solidarity' and 'the practice of mutual aid'.[64] Without specialized education or political indoctrination, Ramon has intuited a natural, mystical anarchism. In presenting him as such, Warner perhaps indulges in some stereotypical idealization of the peasant class being more 'naturally' inclined toward collective politics, but she also situates his voice as one of many in a chorus of peasants who do not fully share Ramon's convictions and who act rashly and violently rather than embracing his measured care for solidarity. Moreover, Warner presents Ramon's ideals as wistful longing and political failure. The outcome of his beliefs is not a utopian success; his anarchist reflections arise while he sits by a dying boy who was shot during the uprising. His attitude of mournful, pensive conviction about neighbourly togetherness versus the deceitful enchantments of church and state offers a modestly hopeful alternative for Spain – desirable but seemingly unachievable.

This anarchist conviction becomes even more mystical as Ramon lies fatally injured from combat, aware that he will never know the future lives of his wife and children. He is cheered by Diego, another revolutionary peasant, who experiences their fate not as despair but with 'unassailable happiness' because 'the mistrust, the unsatisfied egoism which had tormented him all his life long had shrivelled and vanished', replaced by 'love of his fellows' as 'brotherly affection laced them all, living and dead, into a harmony where there was no compulsion, no bending of the individual from its true intonation'.[65] A transcendent aura emerges from apparent political failure, and the anarchist sense of communal love exceeds material conditions, becoming more than just a creed or ideology by blossoming into a kind of mystical spirituality.

The ending of *After the Death of Don Juan* achieves the mixture of despair and loss, Utopianism and realism, revolution and defeat that characterizes many of Warner's novels. Heather K. Love has argued that Warner's previous novel *Summer Will Show* (1936), another historical fiction about failed revolution, presents 'despair [...] as a kind of resource: as much as hope, it is necessary to make change happen'.[66] Warner excels at exploring the fusion of emotion, sexuality, and politics that may enable our political activism today. As Love writes, 'linking revolutionary longing to this history of queer longing, Warner explores the dark affects that fuel social change'.[67] While the relationships at the conclusion of *After the Death of Don Juan* are not coded with the same level of homoeroticism as some of Warner's other works, there is still a deep connection between two men that supplants the novel's focus on heterosexual entanglements among the upper-class rulers. The last lines of the novel are a conversation between Ramon and Diego, who are looking at a map while awaiting the approach of soldiers. Diego asks, 'What are you looking at, Ramon? What do you see?' and Ramon answers: 'So large a country [...] and there in the middle of it, like a heart, is Madrid. But our Tenorio Viejo is not marked. I have often looked for it. It is not there, though. It is too small, I suppose. We have lived in a very small place, Diego.' 'We have lived in Spain', Diego replies, and then 'they looked at each other long and intently, as though they were pledged to meet again and would ensure a recognition'.[68] This tender and intimate moment reinforces their loving bond, possibly with erotic overtones but certainly with political communion that seems 'mystical'. They are both condemned but selflessly join together to imagine some unknown reunion, a glimmer of something 'heavenly' despite their material fate. This conclusion evokes crucial anarchist ideals – a group of people sharing a common vision, uniting with each other rather than around a single charismatic leader, and embracing a specific place and piece of land they love even though it does not appear on a map. Warner does not conclude the novel with a successful, stateless utopia – her realism and practicality prevent that – but she offers the yearning for a better Spanish society in which economic justice, sexual equality, and peace are possible, free from the grip of a centralized government and landowning class. This vision is a final aspiration, held in an in-between, imaginative space. Through the discomfiture of its ending, where incense and gunsmoke blend in the consolidation of fascist power, confirming the fusion of religion and nation, Warner supplies a narrative form that resists easy resolution and the devastations of civil religious ideology. The political theology of her fiction is anti-utopian, but it expresses a complex and emotionally rich desire for ways of life that could give sustenance and flourishing for the Spanish people – even if that desire cannot be fully realized this side of 'heaven'.

Notes

1 See Frances Lannon, *Privilege, Persecution, and Prophecy: The Catholic Church in Spain, 1875–1975* (Oxford: Clarendon, 1987).
2 Claire Harman, *Sylvia Townsend Warner: A Biography* (London: Penguin, 1989), p. 153.
3 See Wendy Mulford, *This Narrow Place: Sylvia Townsend Warner and Valentine Ackland: Life, Letters and Politics, 1930–1951* (London: Pandora,

1988), pp. 87–103. On their literary collaboration, see Janine Utell, *Literary Couples and 20th-Century Life Writing: Narrative and Intimacy* (London: Bloomsbury Academic, 2020), pp. 85–118.
4 Richard Baxell, *Unlikely Warriors: The British in the Spanish Civil War and the Struggle Against Fascism* (London: Aurum, 2012), p. 4.
5 Francisco J. Romero Salvadó, *The Foundations of Civil War: Revolution, Social Conflict and Reaction in Liberal Spain, 1916–1923* (New York: Routledge, 2008), p. xii.
6 Quoted in Harman, *Warner: A Biography*, p. 154.
7 Harman, *Warner: A Biography*, p. 154.
8 Angela Jackson, *British Women and the Spanish Civil War* (London: Routledge, 2002), p. 135. As an important exception to women's reticence about divisions on the left, Jackson cites Ethel Mannin's response to Cunard's *Authors Take Sides* pamphlet where Mannin announces her preference for the anarchist CNT-FAI over Soviet-style alternatives, *British Women*, p. 139.
9 Harman, *Warner: A Biography*, p. 153.
10 Paul Preston, *The Spanish Civil War: Reaction, Revolution and Revenge* (New York: Norton, 2006), pp. 176–7.
11 Michael Schmidt and Val Warner, 'Sylvia Townsend Warner in Conversation', *PN Review* 23 8.3 (January–February 1982), p. 36. See also Val Warner, *With the Hunted: Selected Writings*, ed. Peter Tolhurst (Norwich: Black Dog Books, 2012), pp. 399–407.
12 Ibid.
13 Ibid.
14 Ibid.
15 Sylvia Townsend Warner, *Letters*, ed. William Maxwell (London: Chatto & Windus, 1982), p. 42.
16 Gillian Beer, 'Sylvia Townsend Warner: The Centrifugal Kick', in *Women Writers of the 1930s: Gender, Power, Resistance*, ed. Maroula Joannou (Edinburgh: Edinburgh University Press, 1999), p. 76.
17 Warner, *Letters*, p. 42.
18 Schmidt and Warner, 'Warner in Conversation', p. 36. On Warner's other Spanish Civil War writing, see Barbara Brothers, 'Through the "Pantry Window": Sylvia Townsend Warner and the Spanish Civil War', in *Rewriting the Good Fight: Critical Essays on the Literature of the Spanish Civil War*, ed. Frieda S. Brown, Malcolm Alan Compitello, Victor M. Howard, and Robert A. Martin (East Lansing, MI: Michigan State University Press, 1989), pp. 161–74. See also Jake O'Leary, 'Propaganda, Pacifism and Periodicals: Conflicted Anti-Fascism in Sylvia Townsend Warner's Spanish Civil War Writing', *The Journal of the Sylvia Townsend Warner Society* 18.2 (2019), pp. 50–9.
19 Maud Ellmann, '*After the Death of Don Juan*: Sylvia Townsend Warner's Spanish Novel', *The Journal of the Sylvia Townsend Warner Society* 17.2 (2017), p. 23.
20 Warner, *Letters*, p. 51, n1.

21 On the novel's playfulness with historical fiction, see Chris Hopkins, 'Sylvia Townsend Warner and the Historical Novel, 1936–1948', in *Critical Essays on Sylvia Townsend Warner, English Novelist 1893–1978*, ed. Gill Davies, David Malcolm, and John Simons (Lewiston: Edwin Mellen, 2006), pp. 117–44.
22 Hilari Raguer, *Gunpowder and Incense: The Catholic Church and the Spanish Civil War*, trans. Gerald Howson (London: Routledge, 2007), p. xx.
23 See Gay Wachman, *Lesbian Empire: Radical Crosswriting in the Twenties* (New Brunswick, NJ: Rutgers University Press, 2001).
24 See Peter Swaab, 'The Queerness of *Lolly Willowes*', *The Journal of the Sylvia Townsend Warner Society* 11.1 (2010), pp. 29–52.
25 The classic work is Mikhail Bakunin, *God and the State* (1882).
26 Robert Graham (ed.), *Anarchism: A Documentary History of Libertarian Ideas, Volume One, From Anarchy to Anarchism (300 CE to 1939)* (Montreal: Black Rose Books, 2005), p. 473.
27 Simon Critchley, 'Mystical Anarchism', *Critical Horizons: A Journal of Philosophy and Social Theory* 10.2 (2009), pp. 299, 305.
28 Warner's political fiction is complex, but I do not share Harman's claim that *After the Death of Don Juan* is 'detached' and 'politically objective' – it criticizes the upper classes while unequivocally endorsing peasant collectivity (Harman, *Warner: A Biography*, p. 175).
29 Sylvia Townsend Warner, *After the Death of Don Juan*, 1938 (London: Penguin, 2021), p. 1.
30 See James Casey, *Early Modern Spain: A Social History* (London: Routledge, 1999), pp. 222–49.
31 *Ibid.*, p. 2.
32 *Ibid.*
33 *Ibid.*
34 *Ibid.*, p. 5.
35 Barbara Brothers, 'Writing against the Grain: Sylvia Townsend Warner and the Spanish Civil War', in *Women's Writing in Exile*, ed. Mary Lynn Broe and Angela Ingram (Chapel Hill, NC: University of North Carolina Press, 1989), p. 355. On the oppression of women under Franco, see Francisco Cobo Romero and Teresa María Ortega López, 'Francoist Antifeminism and the Violent Reversal of Women's Liberation, 1936–1951', in *Mass Killings and Violence in Spain, 1936–1952: Grappling with the Past*, ed. Peter Anderson and Miguel Ángel del Arco Blanco (New York: Routledge, 2015), pp. 59–71.
36 Wendy Mulford says Ana 'is the most unsympathetic character Sylvia ever created' since her piety and self-absorption injure everyone around her. Mulford, *This Narrow Place*, p. 130.
37 Warner, *After the Death of Don Juan*, p. 23.
38 *Ibid.*, p. 22.
39 *Ibid.*
40 *Ibid.*, p. 26.
41 *Ibid.*, p. 85.

42 Ibid.
43 Wendy Mulford, 'Introduction', in *After the Death of Don Juan*, by Sylvia Townsend Warner (London: Virago, 1989), p. xii.
44 Warner, *After the Death of Don Juan*, p. 58.
45 See Jane Garrity, *Step-Daughters of England: British Women Modernists and the National Imaginary* (Manchester: Manchester University Press, 2003), p. 151.
46 Warner, *After the Death of Don Juan*, p. 122.
47 Ibid.
48 Ibid.
49 Ibid.
50 Nancy Cunard (ed.), *Authors Take Sides on the Spanish War* (London: Left Review, 1936).
51 Warner, *After the Death of Don Juan*, p. 99.
52 Ibid., p. 91.
53 Ibid., pp. 91–2.
54 Ibid., p. 92.
55 Ibid., p. 226.
56 Ibid., p. 86.
57 Ibid., p. 199.
58 Warner, *Letters*, p. 42.
59 Warner, *After the Death of Don Juan*, p. 235.
60 Mercedes Aguirre, 'History and Myth in *After the Death of Don Juan*', *Sylvia Townsend Warner Journal* 15.1 (2014), p. 84.
61 Warner, *After the Death of Don Juan*, p. 195. Mulford notes that Warner identified with Ramon's political integrity and marked this passage in the copy of the novel she gave to Ackland. See Mulford, 'Introduction', pp. xii–xiv.
62 Warner, *After the Death of Don Juan*, p. 196.
63 Ibid.
64 Graham (ed.), *Anarchism: A Documentary History*, p. 184.
65 Ibid., p. 235.
66 Heather K. Love, *Feeling Backward: Loss and the Politics of Queer History* (Cambridge, MA: Harvard University Press, 2007), p. 131.
67 Ibid.
68 Warner, *After the Death of Don Juan*, p. 236.

Part III

Women beyond the nation

Introduction to Part III

Ravenel Richardson

The title of this part, 'Women Beyond the Nation', asks us what is revealed when we attend to the writing of British women that, while retaining intense focus on the domestic and the national, was simultaneously concerned with the larger global forces shaping even the most mundane individual experiences and personal relationships. Each of the lives of the writers in this part – Phyllis Bottome, Iris Murdoch, Anna Gmeyner, and Attia Hosain – were profoundly and directly shaped by historical events, namely war and genocide, which in many cases spurred or forced them to live and work in other countries. These women writers took to fiction, specifically to novels set in middle-class domestic settings, to examine how the political violence being wrought globally was impacting individual lives. Their fiction demonstrates how global and national traumas, and the ideological forces underpinning them, permeated the cultural and social fabric of the mid-century, from its literature to its drawing rooms. Collectively, the novels examined in this part do not paint a picture of women's progress or opportunity, but one of fraught and often compromised positions, subjectivities, and identities. As such, they serve as a sobering antidote to cultural narratives of feminist waves, the values of liberal democracy, and the general sense that women were entering an age of newfound freedoms in the mid-century.

This series of chapters follows from the prior part in its focus on the intersectionality of gender, class, and nationality in British women's mid-century writing, while also attending to how transnational British writing in the mid-century truly was. These chapters reveal the nuances and connections between subordinate positions of women and other subjugated populations in the class and gender-based systems of hierarchical power in Germany, India, and Britain. For example, in Chapter 9, '"A Woman is Always a Woman!": British Women Writers and Refugees', Katherine Cooper details how British women writers such as Phyllis Bottome and Iris Murdoch were shaped and inspired by their experiences working with First- and Second-World-War refugees in Austria and Switzerland. Ultimately, for Cooper, British women writers' examinations of the fraught refugee experience were an act of democratic responsibility and an acknowledgement that human rights, or the denial thereof, are connected. Phyllis Lassner also focuses on refugees in her chapter on Austrian Jewish writer Anna Gmeyner, who escaped death by the Nazis when she fled to Britain in the 1930s. In Chapter 10, 'Families in a Time of Catastrophe: Anna Gmeyner's *Manja*, 1920–33', Lassner offers a searing analysis of Gmeyner's dystopic family saga *Manja*, which portends the Nazi horrors that were to follow its publication. Finally, in Chapter 11, '"Some Other Land, Some Other Sea": Attia Hosain's Fiction and Nonfiction in *Distant Traveller*', Ambreen Hai details the diasporic writing of Attia Hosain, who migrated from India to Britain in 1947, just before the violent Partition. Hai's readings of Hosain suggest that what appear to be struggles in individual lives in fact reflect national and social politics of oppression. As Hai and Lassner note, the exilic and diasporic writings of British women authors demonstrate a poignant seeking of the meaning of home – both domestically and nationally – in ways that reveal how impossible it is to divorce the public notions of home (nation-state) from private ones (family).

But the refugee crisis and mass migration were symptoms of larger, more broad-scale, industrialized traumas of the mid-century, including the Second World War, the Holocaust, and Partition. These traumas, as writers in this part point out, may have originated in the public, political sphere, but their impacts penetrated every aspect of private life. It is well established that the First and Second World Wars resulted in scalar crises of masculinity (from the individual to the patriarchal), as broad socio-cultural, economic, and wartime upheavals coupled with dehumanizing technological advancements left both men and masculinist nation-states reeling. The novels of Bottome, Murdoch, and Gmeyner demonstrate the ways that these crises of masculinity, which originated on national and global levels, were mercilessly enacted on the familial level. Lassner and Cooper detail the rape, verbal abuse, and sexual assault of women and children by their lovers, fathers, husbands, and strangers across the novels in this part. Ranging from the mentally ill to women driven to abusive and exploitative behaviour, prostitution, and even suicide by the confines and brutality of patriarchal family and cultural systems, most of the women characters discussed in this part have been eviscerated by the societies and families they inhabit. The novels offer little in the way of feminist sisterhood or resistance (as we see in Cornish's or Bandopadhyay's chapters in Part II), instead providing an overarching narrative of cyclical and dehumanizing violence; in many instances, women's subjugation results in a collapse of empathy or their own abuse and subjugation of others over whom they can exert power. The comfort and trappings of British and German middle-class homes, purported to be a woman's domain and safe haven, are represented as either dissonantly opulent or in states of festering, claustrophobic decay. Rather than places of harmony, they are sites of torture, fighting, abuse, and rape that hauntingly mirror the global landscape of war and genocide. As each author in this part is at pains to point out, the bi-directional flow of masculinist violence between the home and nation-state shatters any notions of a public/private binary.

Such patriarchal abuse takes many forms, including that of institutional violence. Cooper is careful to note that while the disenfranchisement of British women is not comparable to that of refugees, women writers' experiences of patriarchal subordination made them particularly attuned to the indignities experienced by refugees in post-war Britain's competition for scarce resources. Cooper's readings of Bottome's *Within the Cup* (1943) and Murdoch's *The Flight from the Enchanter* (1956) explore how both women writers, shaped by feelings of shared precarity and alienation, related to stateless figures and recorded refugees' negotiations of statehood and citizenship in their writing. Murdoch, in particular, paints a dismal picture; her characters, who initially intend to help one another but inevitably end up enacting egregious harm, demonstrate how even when the stateless and disempowered 'attempt to band together, any impression of power or advantage of either side yields immediate violent subordination of one party'. Human connection in these novels is rendered impossible by systemic subjugation.

The lack of human connection can be seen in other chapters. For example, Lassner delineates how Gmeyner's novel *Manja* enacts the reverberating effects of the loss of empathy that was a hallmark of the 'psychological scars' of the early twentieth century, arguing that Gmeyner dramatizes how the 'corrosive effects of self-interest begin within families and extend outward to neighbours, communities, and an entire nation'. Lassner's analysis of *Manja* also highlights the bi-directional destruction of Nazism, as Gmeyner's portraits of five enmeshed German families show how each family is both 'subject to the emerging oppression of a crumbling society' and a political ideology that 'professes to value family cohesiveness while lacerating it'. Not one relationship in the wide-spanning novel survives the ideological violence that seeps into every crevice of family life.

In the final chapter of this collection, Hai introduces us to a previously unpublished work of Hosain, who was deeply attuned to women's oppression both by British colonialism and Indian patriarchal practices. Unlike the other writers in this chapter, however, Hai gestures towards a more hopeful future. Her readings of Hosain reveal the opportunities that Britain provided for 'cross-class affiliations in the diaspora' that were impossible in South Asia while at the same time examining the 'cost of settling in Britain and the tragic yearning for lost home'. Hai argues that Hosain was particularly attuned to how gender shaped the diasporic experience, with her women characters recognizing that the social democracy of the British state offered them freedoms that the postcolonial Indian state, which left them dependent on individual private solutions, did not. Yet despite the relative freedoms described, Hosain's writing is threaded with British racism, from the casual and interpersonal to the colonial and lethal. It was a racism that her women characters, in particular, were willing to withstand as the steep price of their independence.

British women writers in this collection, who, as Cooper elucidates, lacked full citizenship themselves until 1948, were keenly aware of the threats of fascism, imperialism, and authoritarianism that spread darkly across the globe in the mid-century. As Gmeyner and Hosain's lives attest, Britain, as a liberal democracy, offered safe haven and opportunity to a range of individuals in the mid-century period. Yet, as Hai incisively elucidates, we would do well to remember that Britain's ability to financially support the waves of refugees and immigrants that entered its borders following the Second World War and Partition was a direct result of centuries of rapacious imperialism and colonialism that subjugated many of the population who eventually arrived on British shores. Cooper and Hai also complicate the relative freedoms Britain offered immigrants and refugees by detailing British women writers' depictions of the antisemitism, fascism, nationalism, violent misogyny, and both structural and casual racism that punctured individuals' private lives. Whether it be through the home-grown activism of Hosain's 'Leader of Women' or Manja's rape by a member of the Hitler Youth, British women writers' depictions of the porous exchange of political ideology across the supposedly insular boundary of the domestic sphere forcefully disrupt any notion that public and private are useful categories for analysing women's lives or literature.

Many of the novels and stories discussed, not just in this part but also across this volume, either remained unpublished, were subject to fraught publication attempts, or receded into relative obscurity upon publication. We see their politically charged subject matter was a key component of their reception, and it is especially significant that several have only been re-introduced to the reading public and literary scholars in recent years by Persephone Books, Handheld Books, and other publishers. It is our hope that the more inclusive, diverse, and expansive category of mid-century literature will continue to provide a space for the examination and re-examination of British women writers who used their writing to face, and more importantly to implore their readers to face, the brutality and inhumanity wrought during this time period and the impact it had on women's and other vulnerable populations' lives.

9

'A woman is always a woman!': British women writers and refugees[1]

Katherine Cooper

In 1929, a full decade before war would be declared in Europe for the second time, Ellen Wilkinson, the influential female Labour MP, was serving as part of a four-member panel for the WILPF (the Women's International League for Peace and Freedom) on the subject of 'Nationality of Married Women and *Hermatlose* (the stateless)'.[2] The connection of these two issues was not as unusual as may first be supposed: not only had women's rights been brought into the spotlight as a result of the suffrage campaigns in the early decades of the century, but following the First World War, the rights of the stateless and those displaced by war and persecution were also beginning to be discussed at the highest levels, manifesting in such early legislation as the Minority Treaties and the Nansen passport scheme. Even before rights were discussed on a more international level following the Second World War, the first war had brought into sharp relief crucial questions concerning nationality and citizenship and of women's rights. While in 1918 women over the age of thirty, and in 1928 all men and women over twenty-one, were lawfully enfranchised in Britain, there remained another issue in need of scrutiny and one which has received significantly less scholarly attention, namely, the continued refusal to acknowledge women as full British citizens. This was epitomized by the British Nationality and Status of Aliens Act of 1914, which stipulated that 'the wife of a British subject shall be deemed to be a British subject, and the wife of an alien shall be deemed to be an alien'.[3] While this may seem innocuous or even obvious at first, this meant that women did not carry their citizenship as men did: their citizenship was inherited from a father and 'borrowed' from a husband; it was never really theirs. During the 1920s, this was a well-publicized issue and was regularly raised in Parliament by progressive MPs such as Wilkinson. Their arguments were ignored by the government of the time, as M. Page Baldwin describes, because of 'the imperial nature of the nationality laws and Dominion disagreement with [any] change'.[4] The British government was concerned that discussions of citizenship and rights in Britain might have a knock-on effect across the Empire.

This piece of legislation is not surprising in and of itself, coming in the months following the outbreak of the First World War, when all 'aliens' were subject to suspicion and persecution. However, what I argue here is that it exemplified something about the status of British women at this time – like their exclusion from the vote and the bar to owning property, working in professions, or earning money of their own – it placed women in a vulnerable position with regard to their citizenship and their sense of belonging.[5] Virginia Woolf herself, of course, had famously written in *Three Guineas* in 1938 that '[a]s a woman, I have no country. As a woman I want no country.'[6] She actually refers to the British Nationality and Status of Aliens Act earlier in the same passage, writing that '"Our" country still ceases to be mine if I marry a foreigner', demonstrating the high profile of the Act at the time; she did not even need to refer to it by name.[7] Women were subject to the claims of citizenship in that they paid taxes and contributed to the war effort (many in perilous positions even if not as frontline soldiers), but they were excluded from many of the boons or perks of this position. As Ruth Lister argues, women's exclusion from traditional forms of citizenship based around property and self-governance 'has not been accidental but integral' to its construction and still 'affects the terms on which women are today admitted to citizenship'.[8] From classical times, citizenship was predicated upon what Thomas Hobbes in 1651 came to refer to as a 'covenant': Women do not fulfil crucial aspects of this 'covenant', being historically barred from owning property, from serving in the armed forces, and from taking part in the democratic process.[9] As Rebecca Grant rightly points out, '[a]ll of Hobbes' analyses of rights, sovereign power and political responsibility appear to pertain only to men'[10] because, as Anna Yeatman explains, the pervasiveness of this classically rooted 'patrimonial citizenship' is predicated on the citizen who has 'propertied independence which is expressed as a relationship both of self-government and government of those who are one's dependents'.[11] Women are therefore excluded from the founding principles of citizenship because the concept was explicitly founded upon 'a definitely male citizen and [...] his interests and concerns have traditionally dictated the agenda'.[12] In this sense, women's citizenship has always been precarious, uncertain, and entirely dependent on the status of her relationship to a man, husband, father, or brother. The British Nationality and Status of Aliens Act highlighted this tension within women's citizenship; hence it attracted the attention of feminists like Wilkinson.

British women writers and refugees

What links the position of the rights of married women to those of the *Hermatlose*, or stateless, is not only a convergence of historical moment but, I suggest, a convergence of interests, as both groups sought to have their rights recognized in law. In the early twentieth century, British women (and indeed, combatants from elsewhere in the Empire, as many critics have discussed) were good enough to lay down their lives for Britain but not to vote for the government that asked them to do so. Similarly, the stateless or refugees were often asked to undertake war work and propaganda in Britain and yet were often vilified and distrusted and were even imprisoned in internment camps by the government of the time. For the women writers in this chapter, Phyllis Bottome and Iris Murdoch, and other British women writers who coalesced around this cause such as Vera Brittain, Phyllis Bentley, Storm Jameson, and Rebecca West, the newly won freedoms of women after the First World War brought exciting opportunities but they also highlighted continuing inequalities. The connection between these disparate writers – from different parts of the UK, from different backgrounds, across the generations even – is that all of these women writers worked significantly with refugees in their lives and depicted them in their writing. They did so with pride and compassion, for humanitarian reasons and in line with their internationalist views. They also, I argue here, recognized something which they saw in their own lives in these figures: While they did not share the experiences of violent persecution and could never have imagined the suffering endured when one is forcibly removed from one's home, one's life, and one's country, they could imagine just what it was like to be a second-class citizen, to be excluded from certain areas of public life, to be precarious or reliant in one's citizenship. Here, I explore the ways in which these women related to stateless figures, and the ways in which they record the negotiations of statehood and citizenship in their own works, which are underpinned by a feeling of shared precarity and alienation. I suggest that, in part, their efforts with refugees as well as their fictional representations of them helped these women writers to come to terms with their own feelings of powerlessness in the face of exclusion from a British state conceived in patriarchal terms, as all states are, were, and have always been.

Women writers became involved with the refugee cause – and many other causes, from Phyllis Bentley's work for the Ministry of Information to Rose Macaulay's ambulance driving – because, like men, they wanted to contribute to the war effort. They were also not permitted to fight, and often not considered for the high-level jobs in government offered to their male colleagues. This meant that women were – in some ways – more available for relief work. Many female writers of this period were extremely active in campaigning for, raising money for, and even providing personal and emotional support for refugees from Europe during the interwar years and into the Second World War. That is not to say that male writers were not: H.G. Wells, E.M. Forster, and J.B. Priestley all contributed to the PEN Refugee Fund, they wrote letters and sponsored visas, and they often addressed events for writers living in exile in the UK. However, there was a difference in male writers' interactions, which lacked some of the vigour and commitment of their female counterparts, and which were not as sustained as Storm Jameson's day-to-day work in the PEN offices drafting requests for money and coordinating finances, nor Bottome's fervent campaigning and badgering of public figures, nor Murdoch's desire to travel to refugee camps to see life for herself. For these women writers, the struggles of refugees became part of the fabric of their daily lives, colouring and underpinning their other experiences, inflecting how they experienced not only their own rights and exclusions but also those of others. This chapter focuses on two very different British women writers – Bottome and Murdoch – and the ways in which they became involved with refugees, before moving to consider how they represented refugees in their work, and finally the ways in which this may be inflected by their own feelings about their lives as women in Britain at this time.

For the purposes of this chapter, the focus falls on just two of these women; this is primarily because their novels prove especially illustrative of some of the reasons that I argue women became involved with and empathized with refugees but also because, in the interests of brevity, it is impractical to analyse more texts in detail. For Bottome, the refugee as a figure represents the means to explore the experience of hospitality, of reliance on others for recognition, for status, and for safety. This male refugee figure is ever mindful of what he owes and what that entails, but as a result of this, he is also uniquely alert to the sufferings of the female characters, what they sacrifice for safety in a male world and the sorts of daily compromises they make when living in a world in which they are, in many senses, guests in their masters' homes. In Murdoch's case, this identification is because she is young and unsure of her place in the world. This sense of placelessness allowed for an identification with the refugee, also placeless, unrooted, and uncertain, albeit for very different reasons. Her novel positions a woman in contest with refugees to see just how far one might get as a female citizen and what the particular impact of gender is on life experience, but also of how the rights and rules of women's citizenship might weaken her in some circumstances in which a woman is always vulnerable.[13] Each of these women explores a different part of refugee experience, expressing compassion and empathy for figures who have experienced extreme violence and the loss of statehood, but also navigating the ways in which these experiences intersect with the rival claims of gender. These become negotiations in which British female characters, refugees, and refugee female characters interact to illuminate the fine threads and invisible lines which govern rights and citizenship in an unstable and unequal world.

Although a generation apart, both Iris Murdoch and Phyllis Bottome engaged in work with refugees, and both represented them in their work. For

Phyllis Bottome, the engagement with refugees came easily and obviously: She had spent the 1920s in Vienna, Austria, as a result of her husband's job working as part of the British Legation. The pair had only just missed the *Anschluss* – leaving Vienna in 1933 – and they continued to be in touch with a great many close friends, many of whom were Jewish. She wrote to Frank Adams, 'we inadvertently escaped the avalanche in Vienna by three days. Had we known it was so near we should have stayed to try to get out friends out; now we are sitting in Paris trying to use a corkscrew on those we can lay our hands on.'[14] Bottome was heavily involved in refugee organizations from the early 1930s and was one of the first to warn of Hitler's true intentions in Europe. During this time, as her biographer Pam Hirsch describes, she and her husband used their diplomatic contacts, their friends in America and Britain, and their own money to get as many refugees as possible out of Europe.[15] Bottome travelled across America and Britain giving talks to highlight the issue of refugees and the importance of defeating Nazism. Her key concern, though, was to write a novel about refugees. This she viewed as part of her propaganda work, the need to change minds and to elicit empathy. She writes that 'I don't think [refugees'] mentality is understood by most people',[16] and this was something that she sought to address in her 1943 novel *Within the Cup* (published as *Survival* in the United States).[17]

Murdoch's representation of refugees is slightly more morally complex and seems more heavily based on making her own sense of the world than necessarily foregrounding a cause. Whilst Bottome and contemporaries like Jameson, West, and Macaulay were well into their fourth or even fifth decade by the time the Second World War broke out, Murdoch was barely twenty years old. Nonetheless, her engagement with refugees was significant, despite her youth. Not only do refugee characters pepper her novels but her first job after leaving university was working with UNRRA (United Nationals Relief and Rehabilitation Association). UNRRA – a precursor to the office of the United Nations High Commissioner for Refugees (UNHCR) – was designed, as Peter Gatrell has described, to 'cooperate with the military to arrange for [displaced people's] repatriation, initially by assembling DPs in holding centres'.[18] Murdoch began working there in 1944, less through a burning desire to alleviate suffering than through a fervent and increasing need to escape post-war England and acquire something amounting to a lived experience of the hardships of the war.[19] Although she spent a good deal of her time based at the London office, which provided the blueprint for *The Flight From the Enchanter*'s (1956) obscure and obscuring government department SELIB, she was able to escape Britain and served in both Switzerland and Austria. During this time, Murdoch lived an apparently charmed life – a young single woman with a good salary in London. Yet she feels frustrated, and not only with the ill-judged love affairs with which many critics and biographers are so preoccupied, but also with how little agency she appears to have in her own day to day living. She describes her work at UNRRA initially thus: 'there I wander, amid the chaos of what may one day be an organisation, trying to persuade myself and others that I am doing a job',[20] and her life in London seems to run in a similar vein and she is 'hellishly lonely in my great and beautiful and exciting London'.[21] It is only when she reaches the refugee camps in Graz that she writes, 'Why didn't I come here months ago instead of hanging around in HQs waiting to be promoted?'[22] For Murdoch, it was not the bureaucracy of UNRRA's London offices but the feeling of being in Europe and in a position to be of assistance to the displaced which allowed her to progress personally and professionally. These formative experiences would inform much of her later life and work, and the figure of the refugee would haunt her novels throughout her career.

'[A] disinherited, disenfranchised speck': displacement and the female experience in Phyllis Bottome's *Within the Cup*

Phyllis Bottome's novel *Within the Cup* (1943) owed much to her own experience in 1920s Vienna and to her concern with Jewish refugees. The novel centres around an Austrian Jewish doctor, Rudi von Ritterhaus, who flees to Britain and sanctuary in the home of his two close friends James and Eunice Wendover and their young daughter Rosemary. It describes von Ritterhaus's integration into British society but also the impact that he has on the lives of two central female characters in the novel: Lady Wendover (James's aunt) and Virginia Esdaile, an American woman married to the local clergyman. In her seminal 1998 study *British Women Writers of Second World War*, Phyllis Lassner makes the argument that all of these women are trapped in some way within the patriarchal hierarchy of mid-twentieth century Britain, confined by relations to husbands, fathers, brothers, and male lovers, and therefore unable to realize their full potential or live their own free and independent lives. She goes on to point out that 'the good doctor thus directs his energies towards the exploited and weakened Other as a way of building Britain's resolve to fight the Nazi order'.[23] The patriarchal hierarchy, as Lassner astutely argues, is part of precisely the same masculine will to power which actuates the Nazi cause and which places Europe in danger. As Lassner explains, von Ritterhaus's work with these women – as a psychologist in the Adlerian school which so beguiled Bottome herself – can free these women and thus, symbolically, Britain, from the cult of this patriarchal urge to dominate and to repress the Other, in this case women, but on a European level Jews, like von Ritterhaus himself.

Lassner's reading emphasizes another instance through which the experiences of being a woman map onto the sorts of subordinate positions inhabited by the refugee within patriarchal, nationalist culture. As Lassner – a leading scholar of Holocaust studies – is at pains to point out, 'the analogy here between this English family system and the system that produced death camps is neither gratuitous nor does it elide their differences', but the connection is illustrative, demonstrating a hierarchical and masculine culture which seeks to subordinate the Other, whether woman or Jew.[24] Von Ritterhaus's experiences and compelling narration in fact allow Bottome to allude to the suffering of all of those living under this hierarchy of humanity, making what is in many ways an almost anachronistic case for human rights, over and above the refugee 'mentality' that the author sought to reveal.[25] Whilst Lassner's initial extrapolation of this relationship between von Ritterhaus's work with female characters and his anti-fascism is compelling, I want to focus more specifically on the ways in which von Ritterhaus's feelings of disempowerment and dependence both echo and are echoed in the experiences of his female patients within British patriarchal society.

Lady Wendover is a flawed and highly privileged upper-class Englishwoman but one also forced to reckon with this patriarchal hierarchy for her livelihood. As von Ritterhaus describes, 'this woman was brought up in the wrong way, to think that she could achieve success by accepting her wishes as a standard, and her beauty and money as weapons to fight with in order to carry out these selfish standards'.[26] For Lady Wendover, her only marketable commodity had been her looks and the family wealth and influence with which she was able to adorn them. These functioned, of course, to attract a mate of sufficient wealth and standing to secure her financially and to ensure that her 'selfish standards' of material possessions, but also of power and influence, might be provided for. The loss of this, along with her husband's sexual attention to a younger woman, negate her power, forcing her to re-address her entire approach to life. Von Ritterhaus recognizes this, as a result not only of his psychological training but also of his own experiences. On moving to Britain, he is unable to practice as a doctor because 'the General Medical Council refused to open its doors' to refugee doctors and grant them licenses to practice.[27] He is then forced to rely financially on his friends, which he despises 'because you feel guilty when you have no work' and he has 'only twelve marks with [him], and as far as [he] could see, beyond selling [his] gold watch with cuff links, no particular way of getting more'.[28] This was a real concern during the early years of the war when British medics reacted angrily to fears that the foreigners would take their jobs or stymie their income. As Hirsch describes, both Bottome and her husband wrote to the General Medical Council to try to encourage a repeal of their ban on refugee doctors and dentists practising in Britain. Von

Ritterhaus only feels restored in both his self-worth and his personal agency when he is finally permitted to practise in Tom Wendover's hospital, where he immediately felt 'like a man when life has been too suddenly restored to him [...] for my life has always been my work'.[29] Later, when he receives a trust left by his friend, James – who is tragically killed in an air raid along with his family – it makes him feel finally 'independent and secure'.[30] Whilst he had previously been Tom Wendover's 'servant, rootless, with no certainties of time or place, no assets beyond my medical training', his profession and now the financial security provided by his friend will allows him to transcend his previous existence as 'a disinherited, disenfranchised speck of Austrian dust'.[31] Lady Wendover – though she will never be destitute in her husband's lifetime – will remain 'disenfranchised' and dependent but also unfulfilled, professionally and sexually.

The American woman Virginia Esdaile, who is unhappily married to the local curate, also finds herself entrapped within the patriarchal systems. She is both uniquely empowered and imprisoned by her good looks and her charm, and 'she knew exactly what weapons she possesses – and how to use them'.[32] Her unhappy marriage and jealous husband drive Virginia to do exactly as the man feared and embark on an affair with Tom Wendover, and even a dalliance with his son, Adrian. Von Ritterhaus is not immune to her charms, nor is he hostile to her predicament, because he recognizes Virginia's powerlessness and her desperation – like Lady Wendover – to wrest whatever skills and talents that she has to try to exercise power over her own life. Unfortunately, the very charm and beauty that Virginia had cultivated for this purpose destroy her marriage and cause her misery because 'her husband does not forgive her dreadful power to charm', in part as a result of his religious piety and in part through his desire to control and possess her.[33] As von Ritterhaus describes, 'I had not been half an hour in Virginia's house when I realised that her servants despised and disapproved of her; her children were estranged from her; and her husband was relentlessly destroying and undermining all her capacities for usefulness.'[34] Virginia's misery and her reliance on her husband for her living and her access to the world appeals to von Ritterhaus as reflecting his own dependence, as a foreigner, on his hosts, and his position as entirely subject to their pleasure and displeasure with both his demeanour and his person. Her precarity is due not to her American citizenship – *she* is just as British as any other British woman, because her husband is British – but to her gender and her position as wife and mother, and the expectations of these roles. For her husband, these include absolute and complete sacrifice of personality to the household and its duties and demands. Tellingly, Virginia is paralysed whilst delivering another woman's baby during an air raid, showing her eventual and enforced sacrifice of herself to these ideals. The fact that this sacrifice is finally violently inflicted by the Nazis – whose own gender policies sought even more explicitly to limit female experience to housekeeping and motherhood – is also notable. The eradication of self, against which Virginia had so vehemently and tragically rebelled, echoes some of fascism's worst excesses, yet her sacrifice in the closing pages of the novel is lauded as an act of unrivalled heroism which earns her local celebrity and returns her to the hallowed ground of her husband's affections.

While Bottome's professed intention with the novel was to reveal the 'mentality' of the refugee to the British public, and presumably to assuage fears about foreign others and difference, in making von Ritterhaus so engaged with these female characters as a psychologist, she achieves almost the opposite. Rather than signalling *his* sense of alienation, dependence, and disempowerment within British systems, her novel illustrates *their* experiences of these feelings and the ways in which they are rooted in British patriarchal culture. She also demonstrates the ways in which this patriarchal culture is tied, as Lassner attests, to Nazism and fascism. Specifically, Bottome's novel illuminates the double standard within a British society which seeks to fight and extinguish the hierarchical machismo of fascism but which is equally wedded to its own hierarchies and oppressive power relations, particularly when it comes to gender. Bottome makes a compelling point – that von Ritterhaus's feelings of alienation, of dependence, and of disempowerment allow him to empathize more closely with his female patients and their own predicaments within the patriarchal world order in a way that he may not have grasped so easily without his own experiences as a refugee. Of course, the reverse is also true – Bottome's revelations around von Ritterhaus's precarity in terms of his citizenship as a Jew in Austria and as a refugee in Britain become more sympathetic to a British readership when placed in the context of Britain's class and gender-based systems of power.

'[I]t's a freer world that you are in as a man than a woman': gender relations and female empowerment in Iris Murdoch's *The Flight from the Enchanter*

In her second novel, *The Flight from the Enchanter* (1956), Murdoch synthesizes her experiences working for UNRRA and as a young woman living alone in London, weaving together narratives of powerless and dehumanized refugees with powerless and dehumanized women to demonstrate the ways in which both are what Erich Maria Remarque once termed 'flotsam' on the endless tides of administrative violence and political indifference produced the British nation-state.[35] Gender itself is a little remarked and underdiscussed element of Murdoch's work. When questioned about her own decisions around gender, Murdoch was non-committal. However, in 1978, she observes that her choice of gender for her characters is

> kind of a comment on the unliberated role of women [...] I think I want to write about things on the whole where it doesn't matter whether you're male or female, in which case, you'd better be male, because a male represents ordinary human beings, whereas a woman is always a woman!

She goes on, 'I'm interested in them both as a citizen and as a free writer [...] it's a freer world that you are in as a man than a woman.'[36] This echoes the point made above that man is – to all intents and purposes – the ideal citizen. *The Flight from the Enchanter* uses subtle comparison and the undermining of a bellicose and outdated male protagonist to explore relations of power and powerlessness through both gender and through statelessness. As Lyndsey Stonebridge notes, 'Murdoch's earlier writings [...] are also an attempt to grasp the elusive figure that appears in between the withdrawal and the granting of rights: the refugee or displaced person, or as Murdoch would probably put it, the human individual.'[37] In fact, this novel explores precisely the assumption which, according to Miles Leeson, led to Murdoch's rejection of existentialism during this early period of her life, namely that '[t]he (male) individual is posited at the centre of the world, as both agent and subject in his own world'.[38] In this novel, Murdoch's characters serve to demonstrate the power dynamics of post-war Britain, in which those robbed of their agency and subjectivity by the British state scuffle and skirmish for power over each other, enacting a subtle and nuanced critique of this lauding of the British male citizen as 'both agent and subject in his own world'.

Leeson notes that '[a]lthough Murdoch often places male narrators at the centre of the text, the centre of narrative power can reside with a female' and this is true of Rosa in *The Flight From the Enchanter*.[39] Whilst seemingly, like Murdoch herself, Rosa is the recipient of English citizenship, education, and all of the privilege money provides, it is her gender which makes her vulnerable to both exploitation and isolation. Her position is, like the exiled characters, subject entirely to the approval and continued appraisal of others, those who truly wield the power here: whether it is her brother Hunter in letting her live as a guest in his house, the men at the factory where she works who grudgingly accept her presence, or the Luciewicz brothers who accept her help, Rosa is always accommodated in the world only through the discretion or indulgence of men. Even within the novel itself she is frequently displaced, nosed aside by the narrative dominance of the male protagonist John Rainborough and others. It is the fragility of her position, the lack of surety in her place and her standing, which leave her vulnerable to exploitation but also make Rosa a keen manipulator of power relations which may, even momentarily, place her in a position of dominance. Such is the situation when Rosa meets two refugee brothers from Poland at the factory. The Luciewiczes are in a precarious position, themselves pariahs at their workplace and in the English society they hope will accept them. Initially she wishes to be 'their protector' as '[t]hey spoke practically no English and would sit together upon a bench, looking up at Rosa with their blue eyes full of confusion and terror'.[40] Rosa enjoys her sense of power over these men, a power only available to her because of her relative advantage as a British citizen, and they treat her at first 'with an inarticulate deference which resembled religious awe'.[41] She is, from the start, their 'English lady'.[42] However, as time goes on, the brothers gain more power in the community, using 'their beauty, their awkward English'.[43] This, it turns out, 'commended them to the women [of the factory], touched by an appearance of helplessness which was now comprehensible enough to be charming'.[44] Perhaps this is rather an essentialism on Murdoch's part, that these women are attracted by wishing to care for these men, but their 'helplessness' also underlines the sense in which they are not seen to represent a threat: they appear safe, neutralized in the danger engendered by their masculinity by the disadvantages of their displacement.

However, as Rosa discovers to her cost, this is certainly not the case: Rosa may have indulged in a maternal coddling of the brothers, or even in a more opportunistic manipulation of their position for her own gratification, but she is, as Murdoch herself observes, 'always a woman'. Her awakening to this fact occurs at the same time as her first encounter with the boy's mother, and Rosa is 'shocked at the way in which the old woman was stored there in the corner of [their] room'.[45] This foreshadows later events in which Rosa encounters the full force of the brothers when they perceive that they are in a position of power. Her sexual encounters with the brothers are imbued from the start with an accepting passivity rather than an enthusiastic consent on Rosa's part: 'when she felt his weight upon her, all the will was drained out of her body'.[46] She sleeps with them, first one and then days later the other, because 'there was nothing else she could do'.[47] Later in the novel, they pass her from one to the other in a shocking scene with connotations of gang rape, as, when Rosa finishes with his brother, Jan demands '[f]or Stefan but not for me? No is *not*!' and Rosa concedes 'trembling between anger and despair'.[48] In these scenes, Rosa is no longer the exotic and untouchable 'English lady' but is treated with a sense of entitlement and derision. Their friendship with Rosa simply allowed the brothers to conceive of better ways of inhabiting Britain's class and gender structures to then turn them against her in increasingly violent and voyeuristic acts of sexual exploitation and even violence. Rosa's rape by the brothers signifies not just their move toward criminality but also the ease with which they re-establish and seek to exploit patriarchal power structures, structures which are all too familiar to them.

To look at this as a reassertion of the rights and violence of patriarchal authority allows us to read these events as an illustration not just of the horror of refugee experience but also of the inherent horror and violence of female experience. This is not to equate the two but to suggest that the greatest enchantment – to use Murdoch's term – of the patriarchal state is to engender such inescapable fear in the stateless and disempowered that even when they attempt to band together, any impression of power or advantage on either side yields immediate violent subordination of one party. Whilst the sequence of events may appear to play, at first, into British fears about refugee men violating British women and therefore British territory in precisely the ways envisioned by the 1914 Act, Rosa's lack of reaction, her quiet acceptance, her frightened reluctance to raise the alarm, belie far more about her knowledge of men and of male violence than her experience of refugees. She becomes afraid *because* they behave like men, and that is something with which she is familiar. Whilst the power dynamics of this relationship had once been relatively even, or had even actively favoured Rosa, by the end of the novel they have returned to mirror precisely those that she endures with the other men in the novel. Rosa is once again belittled, infantilized, and even brutalized because she is after all, 'always a woman'. Indeed, I would suggest that the 'Enchanter' of the novel's name – far from being a despot fled by the refugee characters – is actually Rosa's charismatic lifelong lover, Mischa, who lives overseas and maintains their abusive relationship with the charm and indifference of a man who is absolutely 'both agent and subject in his own world': the enchantment that Rosa flees is the thrall of patriarchy itself.

However, the clearest and most jarring example of the intersection of these two factors – gender and statelessness – in Murdoch's novel is in the character of Nina. Nina, a refugee, lacks both the advantages of gender and birth that so significantly ease the lives of characters such as Hunter and Rainborough and even Rosa herself. A talented dressmaker 'with a charming and quite undiagnosable foreign accent',[49] Nina induces in one English customer 'a mixture of possessiveness, nervousness and contempt'.[50] Nina is an ephemeral character in the novel, one who attempts to raise her increasingly desperate situation with its main characters but who is drowned out and pushed aside by the force of stronger currents within the story. Like Remarque's 'flotsam', Nina's fortunes are toyed with roughly by a number of characters with greater privilege than hers but eventually thoughtlessly discarded by all. Even following her suicide at the end of the novel, her death is dismissed by Rosa. Rosa, herself failing to acknowledge her own complicity in the situation – Nina had asked her repeatedly to help her – simply declares, '"who would have believed" said Rosa with a wail in her voice, wiping away the tears with the back of her hand, "that Nina would have been so foolish"'.[51] The 'wail' perhaps belies some sense of responsibility, but ultimately there is a failure in every character to adequately acknowledge or appreciate the realities of Nina's predicament at the mercy of SELIP and threatened with destitution, imprisonment, and even deportation. Rosa has only a faint and instinctive grasp of the potential she might have had to use her position as a British woman and her superior knowledge and contacts to alleviate Nina's suffering through the simple act of listening, just as the Polish brothers think little about assuming a dominant role over Rosa. Each character is oblivious to their own complicity in perpetuating the administrative violence of the British state. Again, the enchanter is so adept at veiling the apparatus of oppression that the oppressed fail to recognize it, both in themselves and in each other.

For both Bottome and Murdoch, their explorations of female characters alongside those of their refugee characters serve to illustrate shared ground and potentially a shared or mutually recognized precarity in terms of social, political, and even financial agency. It is this recognition which draws Rudi von Ritterhaus to Lady Wendover and Virginia and this which draws the Luciewicz brothers to Rosa, albeit for quite different reasons. Rudi empathically recognizes a powerlessness which he seeks to offer agency and understanding; the Luciewiczes, who we come to understand abused women at home in Poland, see only weakness and opportunity for exploitation. Each group recognizes in the other a disadvantage, one created by the state but sustained and compounded by political and social custom. For Bottome and Murdoch, these similarities offer points of compassion and perhaps empathy for the British reader, an opportunity to evaluate the meaning of citizenship and the inequalities and privileges which exist within it.

Conclusion

In 1948, women in the United Kingdom were finally granted the right to their own nationality, regardless of their marital status, when the 1914 British Nationality and Status of Aliens Act was finally abolished. Tellingly, it was in this year also that the Universal Declaration of Human Rights was created, a piece of legislation which, as Allan Hepburn has described, 'detaches rights from the prerogatives of citizenship and the sovereignty of nation-states' in a way that attempted to prevent individuals from slipping through the gaps of national laws and becoming vulnerable to persecution or mistreatment.[52] This chapter does not attempt to equate the lives of privileged British women with those of stateless and destitute refugees or with the victims of the greater horrors of the time, but rather to enact a reading of these women's interactions with refugees which demonstrates an exploration of rights and citizenship, a testing and scrutinizing of inequality, of hierarchy and of patriarchy, which these writers are uniquely placed to undertake because they are, as Murdoch explains, 'always women'. Whilst Murdoch's novel was published some eight years after the Act was repealed, laws excluding women from public and economic life remained and remain on the statute books. The overall sense of unease and precarity even for privileged, white, cis, British women remains in some sense, even whilst it is dwarfed by the experiences of women operating at other intersections of female identity in terms of race, disability, gender identity, and, certainly, displacement.

These women novelists were attracted to assisting refugees, it is certain, because of their own care for and desire to help fellow human beings. But I want to show that, beneath this, an unconscious or conscious desire to interact with, to understand, and to engage with their own feelings of statelessness and alienation also drove them towards this type of work. For Hilary Newitt, writing in *Women Must Choose: The Position of Women in Europe Today* (1937), her study of the changes in women's rights and in the feminist movement across Europe during the interwar period, the fight for women's rights is, like the WILPF, tied firmly to the struggle for rights and equality across the world. In the book – which is prefaced by Storm Jameson – she writes, '[t]hese countries [who have recently enfranchised women] stand themselves at the crossroads of social, economic and political decisions which will vitally affect all their citizens [...] a choice lies before women in these democracies'.[53] Newitt believed that women's apparent newfound power should come with similarly newfound responsibilities to contribute to the struggle for rights and for a better world. For British women writers like West and Jameson, Bottome and Murdoch, these struggles are not simply a question of democratic responsibility but of a recognition that all rights are connected, that inequalities for one group can often impact those of another, and that all are not always equal in the eyes of the law because, as Allan Hepburn writes, '[a]ll citizens have rights, but not all people are citizens'.[54]

Notes

1 Many thanks to Miles Leeson for gifting me a copy of *The Flight from the Enchanter*, for bringing my attention to Murdoch's activities with refugees, and for being a mine of information on all things Murdoch. Thanks also to Nonia Williams for frequent and crucial discussions of the subject of British women writers and refugees.

2 Laura Beers, *Red Ellen: The Life of Ellen Wilkinson, Socialist, Feminist, Internationalist* (Cambridge, MA: Harvard University Press, 2016), p. 215.
3 The National Status Archives, 'British Nationality and of Aliens Act 1914', Legislation.gov.uk, https://www.legislation.gov.uk/ukpga/Geo5/4-5/17/enacted (accessed 17 January 2023).
4 M. Page Baldwin, 'Subject to Empire: Married Women and the British Nationality and Status of Aliens Act', in *The Journal of British Studies* 40.4 (2001), pp. 522–56, 522.
5 A number of these issues were addressed during these years, from the Sex Discrimination (Removal) Act (1920), which notionally allowed women access to the professions, to the Law of Property Act (1922), which allowed a wife to inherit her husband's property for the first time. Indeed, in 1926, women were finally allowed to hold and dispose of property on the same terms as men. These piecemeal advances were largely thanks to the presence of female MPs such as Wilkinson, ensuring a female voice in Parliament for the first time.
6 Virginia Woolf, *Three Guineas* (Oxford: Oxford University Press 2015), p. 125.
7 *Ibid.*, p. 124.
8 Ruth Lister, *Citizenship: Feminist Perspectives* (Basingstoke: Macmillan, 1997), p. 197.
9 Thomas Hobbes, *Leviathan* (1651) (New York: Dover Publications, 2006), p. 80.
10 Rachel Grant, 'Sources of Gender Bias in International Relations Theory', in *Gender and International Relations*, ed. Rachel Grant and Kathleen Newland (Milton Keynes: Open University Press, 1991), pp. 8–26, 10.
11 Anna Yeatman, 'Feminism and Citizenship', in *Politics and Culture: A Theory, Culture & Society Series: Culture and Citizenship*, ed. N. Stevenson (London: SAGE, 2001), p. 140.
12 Lister, *Citizenship*, p. 3.
13 See Katherine Cooper, 'Figures on the Threshold: Refugees and the Politics of Hospitality, 1930–1951', *Literature and History* 27.2 (November 2018), pp. 189–204 and Katherine Cooper, '"His Dearest Property": Women, Nation and Displacement in Storm Jameson's *Cloudless May*', in *War and Displacement in the Twentieth Century*, ed. Angela K. Smith and Sandra Barkof (Abingdon: Routledge, 2014), pp. 168–82
14 Quoted in Pam Hirsch, *The Constant Liberal: The Life and Work of Phyllis Bottome* (London: Quartet, 2010), p. 228.
15 *Ibid.*, p. 229.
16 *Ibid.*, p. 277.
17 I will refer to this throughout by its US title, as mine is a US copy.
18 Peter Gatrell, *The Making of the Modern Refugee* (Oxford: Oxford University Press, 2013), p. 36.
19 Peter M. Conradi, *Iris Murdoch: A Writer at War, Letters and Diaries 1938–46* (London: Short Books, 2010), p. 206.
20 Iris Murdoch, 'Letter to Leo Pliatzky, 17 June 1944', in *Living on Paper: Letters from Iris Murdoch, 1934–1995*, ed. Avril Horner and Anne Rowe (London: Chatto and Windus, 2015), p. 37.

21 Iris Murdoch, 'Letter to Frank Thompson, 22 Jan 1943', in *Living on Paper*, p. 32.
22 Iris Murdoch, 'Letter to Raymond Queneau, 2 June 1946', in *Living on Paper*, p. 71.
23 Phyllis Lassner, *British Women Writers of the Second World War: Battlegrounds of Their Own* (Basingstoke: Palgrave Macmillan, 1998), p. 228.
24 *Ibid.*, p. 226.
25 Hirsch, *The Constant Liberal*, p. 277.
26 Phyllis Bottome, *Survival* (Boston, MA: Little Brown, 1943), p. 201.
27 *Ibid.*, p. 19.
28 *Ibid.*, p. 14.
29 *Ibid.*, p. 49.
30 *Ibid.*, p. 214.
31 *Ibid.*
32 *Ibid.*, p. 80.
33 *Ibid.*, p. 81.
34 *Ibid.*, p. 148.
35 Erich Maria Remarque, *Flotsam* (New York: Random House, 2017).
36 Chevalier cited in Miles Leeson, 'The Engendered and Dis-engendered Other in Iris Murdoch's Early Fiction', in *Cross-Gendered Literary Voices: Appropriating, Resisting, Embracing*, ed. Kim Rina and Claire Westall (London: Palgrave Macmillan, 2012), p. 114.
37 Lyndsey Stonebridge, *The Judicial Imagination: Writing After Nuremburg* (Edinburgh: Edinburgh University Press, 2011), p. 143.
38 Miles Leeson, *Iris Murdoch: Philosophical Novelist* (London: Continuum, 2011), p. 29.
39 *Ibid.*, p. 116.
40 Iris Murdoch, *The Flight from the Enchanter* (London: Triad/Panther, 1976), p. 40.
41 *Ibid.*, p. 43.
42 *Ibid.*
43 *Ibid.*, p. 41.
44 *Ibid.*
45 *Ibid.*, p. 45.
46 *Ibid.*, p. 49.
47 *Ibid.*
48 *Ibid.*, p. 52.
49 *Ibid.*, p. 72.
50 *Ibid.*, p. 73.
51 *Ibid.*, p. 275.
52 Allan Hepburn, *Around 1945: Literature, Citizenship, Rights* (Montreal: McGill-Queens University Press, 2009), p. 3.
53 Hilary Newitt, *Women Must Choose: The Position of Women in Europe Today* (London: Gollancz, 1937), p. 33.
54 Hepburn, *Around 1945*, p. 3.

10

Families in a time of catastrophe: Anna Gmeyner's *Manja*, 1920–33

Phyllis Lassner

The mid-twentieth century is now recognized as having produced a multifaceted and transnational literature and culture that reflects and responds to the period's political and social turbulence.[1] Hovering around the late 1930s and continuing to the height of the Cold War, the temporal boundaries of the mid-century are fluid, anticipating and responding to the apocalyptic destruction of the Second World War and its personal experiences of loss and to suspicions about the future. Once the war was over, revelations of Hitler's death camps provoked ethical questions about fictional and other artistic forms of representation.[2] Modernist experimental narratives of individual psychology, experience, and consciousness now had to contend with the global breadth of the war's realities. Among these unprecedented realities were the human efforts and costs of defeating the Axis powers and the traumatic effects of the Holocaust on survivors. The war's countless millions of civilian and combatant deaths and widespread suffering, Nazism's industrialized killings, and the uncertain future created for so many challenged the primacy of individual consciousness as it had been represented both in realist and experimental fiction. Instead, fiction writers were now inspired to grapple with narrative forms that attempted to grasp the moral, psychological, and cultural significance of individuals caught up in a boundless collective experience.

Many writers in the late 1930s, throughout the war, and in the aftermath confronted the ethical and mimetic challenges of representing the disorientating and tortuous experiences that led to and included mass deportation, incarceration, starvation, slave labour, gassing, and incineration. The aftermath of the war was a time of inconclusive reckoning, including homelessness, statelessness, and the mass migrations following the formation of new nation-states as well as the crumbling of empires. Overall, the mid-twentieth century, from the late 1930s through the 1960s, in the United States, Britain, and Europe, is marked by the rise of Fascism and Nazism, the war, exile, economic recovery, and the Cold War, each of which, and in tandem, provoked writers to reconsider what subjectivity meant when Fascism had almost succeeded in crushing it. Looking back in an attempt to understand the fears that led to confusion about an ethics of war with the Axis powers, Storm Jameson wrote:

> I told myself, and I believed, that to accept, as genuine pacifists do, anything rather than war, total disrespect for freedom, the systematic crushing or deformation of the spirit, is to accept a death as final as the death of the body. Even in hell, one could not give up fighting for freedom of mind.[3]

In her fiction of the 1930s through the Second World War and its aftermath, Jameson was joined by other writers who re-imagined the formation of individual subjectivity as driven by collective fear and courage in the face of the Fascist threat not only to themselves but also to others.

This chapter will consider a mid-century novel that was published in 1938 and that in its timeframe of 1920–33 represents a prelude or literary prophesy of the unrelenting Nazi-perpetrated horrors that Timothy Snyder identifies as 'the central event of modern European history'.[4] *Manja* was written by the Austrian Jewish writer Anna Gmeyner in London, where she had fled from Berlin in 1935 in response to the first signs of Nazi terror.[5] The career Gmeyner left behind, writing journalism and plays as well as working in the German film industry, had contributed to the efflorescence of German Expressionist culture.[6] She had been working with the film director Georg Wilhelm Pabst when Hitler became Chancellor in 1933 and decided to leave when the Gestapo started arresting her friends and colleagues. Following a brief stay in Vienna, she moved to Paris, where so many exiled artists had fled and which is the setting of her 1941 novel *Café du Dôme*.[7] The social and political insights of her writing emphasized a 'commitment to social justice'[8] that began in her youth and never wavered, even when her precarious status as a stateless refugee prevented her from activating her political beliefs.[9] Gmeyner originally published *Manja* under a pseudonym, Anna Reiner, to 'protect those of [her] mother's relatives who were still in Europe'.[10] Despite emotional, social, and political disorientations, Gmeyner's position and experience in exile inspired her to consider the subjectivity of fictional characters as they become enmeshed in the disintegration of German social relations that left so many of Nazism's victims vulnerable to the indifference of their neighbours.[11] With its panoramic dystopian narrative, *Manja* expresses Gmeyner's understanding of both the appeal and the fears Nazism inspired on the Continent and in Britain.

Manja depicts the myriad ways in which the psychological scars of the First World War and an unstable Weimar democracy and economy led to the loss of faith 'in humanity's enlightened progress'.[12] As interpreted by Rachel Brenner, the humanistic values that were abandoned included 'the capacity for empathy, which enables human beings to recognize each other's mental and emotional sameness'.[13] Becoming subject to the loss of empathy shapes the plotting of Gmeyner's *Manja*, which dramatizes how the corrosive effects of self-interest begin within families and extend outwards to neighbours, communities, and an entire nation. As *Manja* illustrates, all that was gained by abrogating collective responsibility was psychological, moral, and social isolation, and therefore more vulnerability.

Gmeyner was not alone in her fictional response to the devastating effects of Fascism and Nazism in particular on individual and collective ethical responses. Between the time she fled Nazi Germany's 1935 Nuremberg race laws and wrote *Manja*, the spread of Fascism across Europe did not escape the attention of other writers. In Britain, there were women writers whose fears that Fascism could take hold in their democratic society were expressed by creating dystopian novels in a variety of experimental forms. Naomi Mitchison's *We Have Been Warned* (1935) and Storm Jameson's *In the Second Year* (1936) dissected the corruption of political ambition.[14] Both writers were concerned that Oswald Mosley's British Union of Fascists portended the dissolution of British democracy in favour of a Fascist government that promised order in an unstable time. In her 1937 polemical novel *The Mortal Storm*, Phyllis Bottome warned British readers of the global dangers of Nazism by depicting the fate of a Jewish scientist and his family in Germany when comradeship and collegiality melt into ideological antipathy.[15] From the imagined vantage point of seven hundred years after Hitler's victory, Katherine Burdekin's 1937 dialogic novel *Swastika Night* offered an analysis of the appeals and dehumanizing effects of Nazism's triumphalist mythology.[16] The apprehensions of these British writers had been confirmed in their travels to Germany in the early 1930s where they witnessed Nazism's brutality, but in the cheers at Nazi rallies, they also recognized that its appeal did not stop at Germany's borders.

In *Manja*, a prologue titled 'Beginning with the End', printed in italics and dated late autumn 1933, announces Gmeyner's teleological vision of Germany's turn to Nazism as a chthonic force with primordial origins:

Every moment grows, like a plant with tangled, hidden roots, out of the soil of the past, and is invisibly shaped by it. What these children had suffered, uncomprehendingly, reached back further than their memories, back into the time before they existed and before their lives began.[17]

With this portentous beginning, in late autumn 1933, when Nazism is in the process of instituting the suffering of millions, the novel excavates Germany's recent First World War past to show how the unhealed wounds of that war fester in the nation's Fascist present. The following chapters then take us back to 1920, when the novel's five child protagonists are conceived on the same night and delivered in the same hospital, but in dramatically different family circumstances. This contrivance establishes the novel's baseline for tracing the origins of Nazism's appeal and terror from within the nation's already threatened family and social relations and economic structures.

Gmeyner's dystopian vision is represented by interrelating five children and their families in key incidents that criss-cross over the years of her narrative. Just as she offers a list of main characters and a chronology to guide readers through her complicated schema, so I begin with a summary of the *dramatis personae*. Heini Heidemann is raised with the progressive values of his parents, Hanna, a piano teacher, and Ernst, a medical doctor. Franz Meissner, the son of Frieda and Anton, cannot escape his father's turn to Nazism. In political contrast, the consequences of Eduard Müller's communist activism will be borne by his son Karl and wife Anna. That Nazism brings Jewish assimilation into German society to a brutal end is illustrated by Harry, the son of Max Hartung, a half-Jewish banker, and his Aryan German wife Hilde. Manja, the only girl and only fully identified Jew among the five friends, suffers the effects of her single mother's poverty and the Nazi legitimization of antisemitism. These family portraits are undergirded by a pre-determining narrative structure that is impelled by the trajectory of interwar German political history. As Gmeyner observed it from her exiled position in 1938 Britain and feared for the safety of European Jews, she foresaw, as Bernard Wasserstein proffers, that 'more and more Jews in Europe were being reduced to wandering refugees. They were being ground down into a camp people, without the right to a home anywhere and consequently with rights almost nowhere.'[18]

Gmeyner constructs an imaginative analysis of a multi-faceted nation united under a totalitarian regime that will transform impotent resentment into patriotic action against an imagined enemy. With a cumulative effect, the novel's alternation among its five children and their families shows how each family is subject to the emerging oppression of a crumbling society and the forces that deliver the final blow. Holistically, the novel becomes a self-fulfilling prophecy. As Nazi power builds momentum, asphyxiating what remains of German humanity, the novel moves inexorably in an irrevocable drive towards Germany's failure to defeat its own determination to fulfil Nazism's destructive promises.

The novel's prologue prepares readers to recognize that child characters and the presumption of childhood innocence constitute a myth of hopefulness that is doomed from the start. The first sentences position the children in a tableau in which 'The five bright stars of Cassiopeia' recall the mythical ancient Greek queen who brought disaster upon her land and death to her daughter Andromeda for proclaiming their superior beauty. Like Cassiopeia's self-inflation, Hitler's proclamation of a German Aryan master race will lead to the destruction of his empire and millions of those subject to his fantasy of racial supremacy. The five children and their families, reflected in the five bright stars, will not be nurtured by the light of Cassiopeia's stars but will fulfil the constellation's prophesy of self-immolation, set ablaze by the explosions stoked by hatred.

That the Nazi drive to power and destruction was cultivated by Germany's stagnant unrest and failure to heal its war wounds is revealed in the novel's characterization of its five families, who represent a range of political views and disjunctive economic and social positions. In one sense, this intranarrative structure, moving back and forth among its five families, resembles the European family and social epics of the first half of the twentieth century, including Thomas Mann's 1901 *Buddenbrooks* and I.J. Singer's 1943 *The Family Carnovsky*.[19] Like these novels, *Manja* charts and assesses the collective impact of fateful choices made by fully developed adult characters. Where Gmeyner's novel differs is its focus on five child characters who, even in their complexity, are prevented from developing into adults who make independent choices. *Manja* interprets the disintegration of Weimar social relations by compressing wide-ranging emotional and ethical effects into the five children's close but ill-fated relationship. Both focused and kaleidoscopic, the novel creates a sense of vertiginous oscillations, a textual equivalent to Germany's agitations.

Anchoring this panoramic perspective is Manja's fate as the iconic victim of Nazism. From birth until her death at the age of thirteen, Manja embodies the mass victimization produced by the nation's inexorable shattering of empathy. In turn, this collective experience is anatomized by dramatizing the responses of each of the four boys to Manja's inescapable jeopardy. Although the children are each subject to the emotional fallout from their families' declining economic and social fates, until the cataclysmic eruption of state-sponsored violence, they are held together by Manja's captivating and empathetic emotional imagination and her promise of humanistic optimism. Her iconic status in the novel consolidates the effects of the four boys' destabilized and threatening family histories. With political and social dissolution accelerating at the moment of the children's births in 1920, Manja's presence in the boys' lives can only provide a fleeting healing effect. Neither the narrator's nor Manja's deeply felt empathy for the boys can counter or ameliorate the disorientations and economic effects of the nation's cascading disasters as the Weimar Republic shatters.[20]

In Gmeyner's interpretation, as individual desperation leads to the unravelling of a social contract, for all too many, the divisive enmity of Fascist terror represents a remedy. It is this paradox that drives the historical foundation on which the fictional plotting of *Manja* finds its locus of meaning. An expressionist tableau halfway through the novel in Chapter 20 depicts the hopefulness of Weimar democracy burning along with the Reichstag fire on 27 February 1933, which, in turn, is cause for celebrating Germany's new cohesion: [21]

> Women and children lined the streets. Torchlight flickered on their excited faces. With open mouths they sang and shouted, their raised hands glowing red in the torchlight. The music – hard, shrill, rhythmical – hammered into them. Men marching four abreast [...] Youths with lean shining faces, in brown uniforms. And after them more figures, heads lifted to the light of torches, their faces scarred, rapt, red. Their black shadows marched beside them to the same music, monstrously magnified, silhouetted on the walls and over the crowd that stood as if bewitched. [...] The beating of drums, piercing yells, slogans in chorus, wind instruments, flags and boots, boots across the entire country. Had war broken out or were they celebrating some strange carnival? [...] The poor would be rich, the weak strong, dried-up women desirable, the blind would see, the lame walk. [...] now there was hope.[22]

The spectacle portrayed in this insistent description recalls Freud's oft-cited repetition compulsion, replaying an illusory hopefulness. Historically, this fantasy would only replay the 'monumental melancholy' that, as Modris Eksteins explains, was produced by post-First World War German realities: 'The homes promised its heroes remained fictional palaces, and the utopian social dreams evoked by wartime rhetoric were brutally erased by inflation, unemployment, and widespread deprivation [...] Disillusionment was the inevitable upshot of the peace.'[23] As Gmeyner sensed, if marching boots once again represented triumphant hope for Germany, even disillusionment would be an understatement for those deemed undesirable and within reach of the Reich.[24]

A Polish Jew living in Germany, already in exile as an unprotected refugee, Manja is born into and remains in a precarious state from start to finish. Her genealogy foretells her vulnerability. Her mother, Lea, whose family surname is never identified, and who has run away from her home and family in Poland, and Manja's father, David Goldstaub, a would-be composer, are strangers until they impulsively bond at a Mahler concert in a moment of 'strange enchantment'.[25] Redolent of the heightened emotionalism of German Romanticism, the spontaneous combustion of their passion portentously inspires David's thought that 'tonight's events were decided, pre-determined'.[26] The novel depicts the lovers' place in the tumultuous mid-twentieth century as though the historical present is a prison; there is no release from the traumatizing past and its persistent hatreds and helplessness. The narrator explains that David has never been able to escape from the haunting memory of the pogrom that destroyed his family and which leads inexorably to his suicide the night of his tryst with Lea.

In 1920, in the wake of a world war that produced global destruction and forced migrations, and in Germany political volatility instead of imperial triumph, there is no possibility of a romantically fulfilling relationship. In another example, what might have been a conventional seduction based on a fleeting mutual passion is narrated as a mordant twist of the oft-told fairy tale. As though Prince Charming has yielded to his alter ego, Edward Hyde, with 'no hesitation, no scruples', aristocrat Walter von Adrian allows 'Lunatic, breathtaking excitement [to] attack [...] him like a wild beast, clawing at his chest' and sexually overtakes the novel's sleeping beauty, the mentally vulnerable Hilde Hartung, described as 'a sleepwalker'.[27] So far apart in economic and social circumstances, yet Hilde's suffering is aligned with that of Lea who realizes 'for the first time how close the ecstasy of coupling is to the torment of death'.[28] Lea's conception of Manja on her one doomed night of ecstasy portends the tragic end of her story and her daughter's.

The abject domestic lives of Hilde and other women characters fare little better. From the perspective of 1938, Gmeyner constructs the precariousness of family life as endemic to the nation's failures, determined by and leading to the rise of Nazism in the 1920s and its consolidation of power by the end of 1933. That Nazi power extends from ideology to everyday life, through the streets and into German homes, is evident in the price it exacts on family life. Even mutually loving, capable, and stalwart family support is no match for institutionalized cruelty. Key examples are the stories of two families, the Heidemanns and the Müllers. Despite their humanitarian beliefs, neither of these families can withstand the invasion of an ideology that professes to value family cohesiveness while lacerating it. Heini will flourish in his parents' loving marriage, but his future is questioned by the fate of his father, whose humanitarian vision is stonewalled by the authoritarian forces of Nazism already present in hospital protocols. Karl's fate will be shaped by his father's incarceration for the crime of supporting downtrodden workers. Gmeyner imagines the other three families as deceived by their belief that the rise of Nazism is an opportunity for self-improvement.

If Manja and her mother cannot escape their intractable place as unwanted outsiders, the deeply entrenched but collapsing social-economic conditions of German society into which the four boys are born and bred undermine the possibility of their promising life trajectories. The Heidemanns' loving and stable relationship, signalling a more hopeful ordinary time, is already under threat, as suggested by the description of their 'third rate pension', filled with 'noises' that 'pierce the nerves like needles', that resonate with the tonalities of German Expressionist film and 'cling like poisonous arrows'.[29] In synch with the mordant expectations of Expressionist thrillers, each of the novel's 36 chapters begins with tense moments of women waiting for their men, moments that erupt into emotional or physical violence. As though anticipating such violence, the first chapter begins with a description that resembles a Freudian defence mechanism. With compulsively detailed repetition, the narrator fixates on the wallpaper in Hanna and Ernst's room, covered with 'purple roses repeated [...] six times – the parrots five and a half'.[30] The half-page description is narrated with excruciating arithmetical analysis: 'Thus, forty-eight times four (not quite) is one hundred and ninety-two roses and one hundred and seventy-six parrots.'[31] Whatever appeal the wall covering may have once had has been lost in impoverished decay, and the present-tense description suggests that there is no end in sight for the despair that has become the new quotidian. The lovers and their son are caught in 'the web of the years to come'.[32]

That the years to come and the fate of families are dominated by a compulsion to both revive and escape the past is the trope on which Gmeyner's interpretation of interwar German disequilibrium pivots. Max Hartung, the socially ambitious but self-hating Jewish banker, cannot refuse his Jewish father shelter, but hides him in a back room of his mansion which despite its opulence and social expansiveness, resembles the Heidemanns' third-rate pension, 'like a prison with many cells, where everyone lived walled in by impenetrable loneliness'.[33] Samuel Hamburger, representing his son's hidden Polish past, is 'a ghost from the ghetto and a reproach to his son's conscience'.[34] To make matters worse, although Hartung has acquired all the material trappings of assimilation, his son Harry's face and meek demeanour betray his efforts. The boy's stereotypical Jewish face, with 'large nose and spectacles', is an affront to his father's ambitions, an atavistic throwback to the origins from which wealth had promised escape.[35] Historically, Jewish self-hatred was no anomaly among those desperate for social and economic integration into German society. As George Mosse explains, 'It was the reaction of outsiders trying to get inside and finding the door locked for no conceivable fault of their own.[36] In Gmeyner's chain of historical and ideological references, her depiction of Hartung's genealogy suggests that the epigenetics of age-old antisemitism have shaped his son.[37] Hartung's emotional abuse of Harry can therefore be seen as the result of having internalized antisemitic claims of Jewish venality, physical and moral degeneracy, and sexual depravity. In effect, the Jewish banker expresses his self-hatred by despising his son.

With bitter irony, the narrator depicts father and son as already imprisoned by embodying Nazi racial persecution. Although Harry's mother Hilde is a non-Jewish German, 'her perfect, doll-like beauty' and 'coldness' evince the 'dread of him' Hartung detects in her 'evasive glance'.[38] The Hartung marriage recalls Sander Gilman's analysis of Jewish attempts to assimilate into German society through intermarriage as a mechanism of denial or cover-up of the Jew they once were.[39] To demonstrate the inevitable failure of such denial in a nation that will institute racial purity, Gmeyner creates a genetic backlash. Hilde's one and only sexual encounter with von Adrian, the German aristocrat, produces a beautiful blond boy whom Hartung believes is his. Compounding this irony is Hartung's belief that the boy resembles a fake portrait of his mother, painted as a blond Aryan beauty. Although he makes few appearances, the boy, Hans Peter, embodies overdetermined symbolic political meaning. His purely Aryan appearance fulfils the Nazis' self-deceiving self-image, 'an aestheticizing of existence [...] a beautiful lie, [...] an alternative to a daily reality that would otherwise be spiritual vacuum'.[40] But the boy also mirrors Hartung's self-deception. Given the anti-semitic policies that endangered millions of Jews at the time Gmeyner was writing *Manja*, her portrait of Hartung assumes an ethical risk. Layers of his self-loathing are judged by the novel's sardonic irony, mocking the Jew's fantasy of assimilation, as though money and social manipulations could produce a biological, ontological transfiguration.

Instead, however, the novel entangles Hartung in German–Jewish social and political relations at the time in which the German citizenship of prosperous, cultivated Jews encouraged them to think of themselves fully integrated. As Bernard Wasserstein reports, 'Under the Weimar Republic in Germany, Jews looked forward to the consolidation of more than a century of progress toward legal equality and social acceptance.'[41] Almost immediately following the first signs of the Great Depression in October 1929, however, German Jewry was toppled 'from its pedestal as the most proud, wealthy, creative, and forward-looking Jewish community in Europe'.[42] Regardless of his individual complexity as a fictional character, Hartung's fate is tethered to the collective history of European Jewry. Because his status as unwanted alien is irrevocable, he must be the loser in his mutually exploitative relationship with von Adrian, which began with 'mutual loathing' and ends with the Jew's defeat.[43]

In another odd coupling of symbiotic antipathy, the novel pits the assimilated, self-hating Jewish banker Hartung against his antisemitic employee, Anton Meissner, who transforms his failures into 'feverish, glittering, and unstable' hatred of the Jews.[44] Once a proud soldier in the Kaiser's army, Meissner now sports a porter's uniform, opening doors at Hartung's bank for the privileged. Antisemitism, for him, as Nietzsche is reported to have remarked, 'is the ideology of those who felt cheated'.[45] Meissner's revenge, like that of von Adrian, slashing the Jew's attempts at assimilation, is legitimized by Nazi power. His triumph will be to take over the Jew's bank and humiliate him by robbing him of his economic prowess and social ambitions. Nazism provides the ideological and political structures that enable Meissner to avenge his economic and social subservience and assume martial power:

> [C]onvinced that he spoke for universal justice and not just for himself, he freed himself in one bound from all the humiliations and degradations of offended vanity that had been bottled up in him for years. Everyone knew about the international Jewish conspiracy.[46]

In response to the defeat of Germany's First World War masculinist order, in which, as Modris Eksteins explains, 'the myth of inevitable victory fragmented',[47] Nazism offered its men a self-righteous defence, showing once again, as Meissner asserts, that 'Real men still exist in Germany.'[48] Nowhere was this German masculinist imperative more visible than in the continued presence and prestige of the military and its 'brutalization of politics', the result of which, George Mosse proffers, was to impel men 'into action against the political enemy, or to numb men and women in the face of human cruelty and the loss of life'.[49]

As the novel evinces in portraits of Meissner's and Hartung's wives, public compensation in the form of defeating the Jew, along with recognition of German manliness, are insufficient without reinforcement in the private sphere. Because women's subservience has already been intensified by post-war economic privation and children are born helpless, the private sphere offers men a comfortable if hostile space that invites their expression of unbridled, unrepentant, and unpunished rage. Moreover, in the novel's social relations, there is no language with which to create common cause or cross class boundaries with other women to express mutual understanding and compassion. In her pairing of Hartung and Meissner, Gmeyner extends her analysis of male perpetrated violence to elide distinctions between victim and perpetrator. The emotional brutality with which Hartung relates to his son and wife runs parallel to the physical abuse that defines Anton Meissner's treatment of his wife Frieda and children. Meissner's son Franz, conceived during marital rape, when the springtime hopefulness of his parents' love has already turned to brute force, is subject to his Nazi father's paranoid rages, which are projected onto his wife. In response, the narrator's empathetic voice merges with Frieda to lament, 'Now there is no more cherry blossom.'[50]

That women bear the brunt of men's prolonged winters of discontent is key to Gmeyner's analysis of gender roles as the disjunctions of Weimar Germany were yielding to Nazism's promises of economic recovery and political power. Andrea Hammell offers a social historical context to explain gender relations in *Manja:*

> What was hardly ever disputed [...] was that the first duty of married women was to look after the family and that being a mother was to be a woman's primary aim whereas men would take on most responsibilities outside the home.

This dualistic view of gender was still accepted by all but the most radical during the first third of the 20th century.[51]

Each of the mothers in *Manja*, regardless of her economic, social, or political position, suffers as a result of her husband's failure to fulfil his ambitions outside the home. Even Hanna Heidemann and Anna Müller have no recourse to social support when their husbands are defeated. Lea is abandoned by both her daughter's father and the man she marries for economic stability. With no supportive resources or skills with which to support herself and her three children, she is reduced to cleaning other people's homes and accepting abuse as a prostitute. As a result, in Hammell's analysis, Lea is 'demonized as a woman with questionable morals and an inadequate carer for her children. On a more symbolical level, she embodies the breakup of both Jewish and German society.'[52] Lea is characterized as responding to desperation founded on her economic and emotional destitution, a condition that reflects on the indifference and contempt of her non-Jewish neighbours and employers.

Despite the five mothers' emotional and economic deprivation, their mutual if only momentary support represents an ideological and political possibility for good. In a hospital where rules overwhelm Ernst Heidemann's humanitarian concern for his patients, Anna Müller offers her life-giving milk to save Lea's newborn daughter Manja. Anna's words, followed by the narrator's interpretation, orient the reader towards a feminist revisionist myth of regeneration:

> 'We're both the same, you and me', said Anna, holding her hands behind the little dark head just as if it was her own baby's. This simple sentence expressed the understanding between all the women, uniting the white islands of their beds like a branching stream.[53]

Andrea Hammell analyses the significance of this act as resistance: 'Because a woman is shown to feed a differently racialized baby, daughter of a complete stranger, a direct challenge is made to the racial ideology of National Socialism and to motherhood in the patriarchal nuclear family.'[54] Yet even as the women are united in this moment of mutual empathetic motherhood, a later encounter between Frieda Meissner and Anna Müller betrays their mythic unity and binds their nation with resentment. Frieda, who has no money to pay Anna for washing her family's laundry, reminds us of the reality of their economic and emotional impoverishment: 'For everything that Frieda had expected of love, of marriage, of motherhood, was as different from reality as bad-smelling, rancid war-fat was to real butter.'[55] If at some level Frieda understands that Anna is also a victim and blameless, she identifies another convenient villain – the inherently irredeemable alien. Like the response of her husband, Anton Meissner, hatred of 'blood-suckers, Jewish scum, [...] gave Anna a glorious feeling of strength so long denied her'.[56] That each family's response to their abject conditions has determining power is evinced in the development of their sons' characters.

Narrated as an escape from their families' escalating social, economic, and political turbulence, the four boys meet Manja every Wednesday and Saturday at a derelict wall above a river. The allusive dystopian images – 'the trees black and strange', Manja's torn, 'sodden' scarf – portend violent disenchantment: *'They had once been like kittens snuggling together for warmth. Now their childhood nest had been destroyed and they would never climb into it again.'*[57] Throughout the novel, Manja's near saintly character nurtures the boys' humanity. Her imagination transforms poverty into a celestial vision – 'one hundred and fifty thousand stars of pure, pure silver'.[58] With mythic resonance, she is portrayed as 'the delicate, large-eyed girl with the elfin, flower-like face [...] who could rejoice without shame, so that everything about her was filled with joy'.[59] Joy and nurture, however, are depicted as illusory sylvan myths and states of being, as the narrator alerts us; Manja is 'like a tiny plucked bird in a cage'.[60] Her father's memory of a pogrom and presentiments of doom echo in this image which then manifest as his legacy – an accretion of antisemitic indictments of his daughter. From birth to adolescence, the Jewish girl's development is not only truncated, but demonized.

As a stateless refugee with no right to self-determination, Manja's character embodies a rupture in literary history in which the genre of self-discovery, the *Bildungsroman*, has become obsolete. There is no coming-of-age story for Manja when instead of a Bat Mitzvah at the age of thirteen, she is driven to suicide. Self-discovery and open endings are no longer possible.[61] The signs of deadly persecution are already evident, as in the episode where Manja's teacher views the bloodstain from the girl's menstruation as a sign of Jewish depravity, 'mysteriously bound up with the cynical rapacity which was part of her race'.[62] Even the children's united front is subject to forces beyond their control. Manja explains why, already in 1933, two years before the passage of the Nuremberg race laws, the chants 'Death to the Jews!' signify her congenital guilt and eviction from the hopeful society their friendship has represented.[63] With ideological wisdom, she knows that however she identifies herself, she is condemned as 'a near-eastern, oriental, central-asiatic, Nordic-hamitic, negroid hybrid'.[64] Manja and her friends are helpless when history demolishes the joy only to be found in mythology. Martin, a Hitler youth, stalks and bullies them and climactically lays siege to their sanctuary, culminating in his rape of Manja, which is the final blow that drives her to suicide and the four boys asunder. Abandoned to state-incited brutality, the indifference of neighbours, and the helplessness of her friends, Manja has no recourse to life.

Martin's sexual brutality aligns him with both Anton Meissner and Walter von Adrian, who use women's bodies to affirm their masculinity, and in combination signify the ideological yearnings of the Third Reich. Nonetheless, the abuse of these women marks the men as failures, according to the Nazi ideal of manliness, including 'the practice of self-control, steeling the body in order to be best at sports and games, to be chivalrous toward girls while refusing to squander one's sexuality'.[65] If these men view themselves as heroes whose actions signify the restoration of Germany's power and glory, *Manja* suggests a contravening interpretation and outcome. From the perspective of 1938, when Gmeyner composed *Manja*, she foresaw that the racially supremacist hatred and domination of Jews and others eradicates the possibility for a nation's healing and regeneration. Ultimately, as her 'Beginning of the End' predicts, the effects of this hatred are intergenerational, infecting the children who cannot thrive in a future paved with self-destruction.

Gmeyner's iconic victim and protagonist, a Jewish woman character who generates no protest on her behalf, has no future except defeat, but her empathetic imagination haunts that of Anna Gmeyner and the collective historical consciousness she creates in her novel. Manja's short and brutal life inspires the narrator to address the four German boys at the end of the novel, warning them and readers of the dangers of believing that 'Nothing had happened', either as terror was taking hold or as part of their historical memory decades later.[66] In effect, she assumes the role of authorial moral responsibility that shapes her aesthetic. As Jaroslaw Anders notes of Central European culture, 'This is hardly unusual in a part of the world, where, at least since the Romantic era, literature has played an important part in public debates, and writers have often doubled as moral authorities and political guides of their nations.'[67] If the boys were to repeat their nation's withdrawal from collective responsibility and empathy, they would once again leave themselves 'on a reef against which the flood of events impotently dashed itself, and then was silent'.[68] Alongside other courageous British women writers, Gmeyner breaks the silence of her time and later.

Notes

1 This chapter is dedicated to Holocaust educators everywhere who continue the work of Anna Gmeyner by warning us of the dangers of ignoring or dismissing the lethal threat of antisemitism and forgetting the Holocaust.

2 For comprehensive discussion of the ethics of representing the Holocaust, see Simone Gigliotti, Jacob Golomb, and Caroline S. Gould (eds), *Ethics, Art, and Representations of the Holocaust* (Lanham, MD: Lexington Books, 2014).
3 Storm Jameson, *In the Second Year* (New York: Macmillan, 1936), p. 38.
4 Timothy Snyder, 'Commemorative Causality', *Modernism/Modernity* 20.1 (2013), pp. 77–94, 77.
5 Hilzinger observes that after 1933, around 30,000 political refugees, 5,500 creative artists, 2,500 writers and journalists, and those declared 'non-Aryans' fled Germany, with Jews comprising the largest number. Sonja Hilzinger, 'Writing in Exile', in *A History of Women's Writing in Germany, Austria, And Switzerland*, ed. Jo Catling (Cambridge: Cambridge University Press, 2000), p. 157. Brinson examines refugee conditions in Britain until 1938 as regulated by restrictive employment policies. Domestic work was approved for women. Charmian Brinson, 'A Woman's Place: German-Speaking Women in Exile in Britain, 1933–1945', *German Life and Letters* 51.2 (1998), pp. 204–24, 204.
6 J.M. Ritchie points out that the Nazis, after some hesitation, decided that Expressionism was 'undesirable', a judgement that 'could mean exile or death' to the movement's artists. J.M. Ritchie, 'Women in Exile in Great Britain', *German Life and Letters* 47.1 (1994), pp. 51–66, 57.
7 See Hammell and Ibbotson for Gmeyner's biographical details. Andrea Hammell, *Everyday Life as Alternative Space in Exile Writing: The Novels of Anna Gmeyner, Selma Kahn, Hilde Spiel, Martina Wied and Hermynia Zur Mühlen* (Oxford: Oxford University Press, 2008); Andrea Hammell, 'Negotiating the "I" and the "We": Aspects of Modernism in the Exile Novels of Anna Gmeyner and Martina Wied', *Leo Baeck Institute Year Book* 63.1 (2018), pp. 35–154; and Eva Ibbotson, 'Preface', in *Manja: The Story of Five Children*, by Anna Gmeyner (London: Persephone Books, 2003), pp. v–xiv.
8 Hammell, *Everyday Life*, p. 91.
9 Rachel Pistol notes that when war broke out, 'the immigrants became not just refugees but also enemy aliens'. Rachel Pistol, 'Heavy is the Responsibility for All the Lives that Might Have Been Saved in the Pre-War Years: British Perceptions of Refugees 1933–1940', *European Judaism* 50.2 (2017), pp. 42–9, 45.
10 Ibbotson, 'Preface', p. vii.
11 Dagmar Lorenz reports that women writers were marginalized within the study of exile with their biographies being of greater interest than their works, the quality of which was disputed. Dagmar Lorenz, 'Jewish Women Authors and the Exile Experience: Claire Goll, Veza Canetti, Else Lasker-Schüler, Nelly Sachs, Cordelia Edvardson', *German Life and Letters* 51.2 (April 1998), pp. 225–39, 226.
12 Rachel Brenner, *The Ethics of Witnessing: The Holocaust in Polish Writers' Diaries from Warsaw, 1939–1945* (Evanston, IL: Northwestern University Press, 2014), p. 3.
13 *Ibid.*, p. 4.
14 Naomi Mitchison, *We Have Been Warned* (London: Constable, 1935).

Families in a time of catastrophe 199

15 Phyllis Bottome, *The Mortal Storm* (London: Faber, 1937).
16 Katharine Burdekin, *Swastika Night* (London: Gollancz, 1985). For extensive study of these dystopias and other fictional responses to the rise of fascism and its consequences, see Phyllis Lassner, *British Women Writers of World War II: Battlegrounds of Their Own* (Basingstoke: Macmillan, 1998).
17 Original italics. Anna Gmeyner, *Manja: The Story of Five Children*, trans. Kate Phillips (London: Persephone Books, 2003), p. 2.
18 Bernard Wasserstein, *On the Eve: The Jews of Europe Before the Second World War* (New York: Simon and Schuster, 2012), p. xx.
19 Thomas Mann, *Buddenbrooks* (Berlin: S. Fischer Verlag, 1901). Singer's novel is also relevant to Gmeyner's biography in its characterization of an assimilated but threatened German-Jewish family that must emigrate after the Nazis come to power. I.J. Singer, *The Brothers Carnovsky* (New York: Schocken Books, 1943).
20 See Anthony Grenville for a comprehensive history of the Weimar Republic. Anthony Grenville, *Cockpit of Ideologies: The Literature and Political History of the Weimar Republic* (Bern: Peter Lang, 1995).
21 Nazi leaders and their coalition partners used the fire to institute emergency legislation to underscore the need to defend against a false claim that Communists planned a violent coup. The resulting Reichstag Fire Decree 'abolished a number of constitutional protections and paved the way for Nazi dictatorship'. United States Holocaust Memorial Museum (USHMM), 'Reichstag Fire', USHMM Website, https://encyclopedia.ushmm.org/content/en/article/the-reichstag-fire (accessed 9 June 2022).
22 Gmeyner, *Manja*, pp. 239, 241.
23 Modris Eksteins, *Rites of Spring: The Great War and the Birth of the Modern Age* (New York: Doubleday, 1989), p. 253.
24 Whereas I maintain that Gmeyner critiques Germany's wishful thinking, Pinfold argues that the novel 'is a piece of perfectly sincere wishful thinking that portrays the values Gmeyner hopes will prevail in Germany to avoid catastrophe'. Debbie Pinfold, 'The Fallen Child', in *The Child's View of the Third Reich in German Literature* (Oxford: Oxford University Press, 2001), pp. 33–90.
25 Gmeyner, *Manja*, p. 43. It's almost certain that Gmeyner chose Mahler (1860–1911) because of the historical context of his fame. In 1897, he converted to Catholicism because the position he sought, director of the Vienna Court Opera, was denied to Jews.
26 Gmeyner, *Manja*, p. 46.
27 *Ibid.*, pp. 159, 158, 163.
28 *Ibid.*, pp. 46, 48.
29 *Ibid.*, pp. 8, 7.
30 *Ibid.*, p. 6.
31 *Ibid.*
32 *Ibid.*, p. 10.
33 *Ibid.*, p. 185.
34 *Ibid.*, p. 184.

35 *Ibid.*, p. 1.
36 George L. Mosse, *Nationalism and Sexuality: Middle-Class Morality and Sexual Norms in Modern Europe* (Madison, WI: University of Wisconsin Press, 1985), p. 36.
37 Gmeyner, *Manja*, p. 191.
38 *Ibid.*, pp. 27, 29.
39 Sander Gilman, *Jewish Self-Hatred: Antisemitism and the Hidden Language of the Jews* (Baltimore, MD: Johns Hopkins University Press, 1986).
40 Eksteins, *Rites of Spring*, p. 304.
41 Wasserstein, *On the Eve*, p. 3.
42 *Ibid.*, p. 6.
43 Gmeyner, *Manja*, p. 207.
44 *Ibid.*, p. 134.
45 Neitzsche quoted in Eksteins, *Rites of Spring*, p. 318.
46 Gmeyner, *Manja*, p. 76.
47 Eksteins, *Rites of Spring*, p. 202.
48 Gmeyner, *Manja*, p. 76. Notably, Oswald Mosley wrote, fascism 'has produced not only a new system of government, but also a new type of man, who differs from politicians of the old world as men from another planet', quoted in Eksteins, *Rites of Spring*, p. 303.
49 George L. Mosse, *Fallen Soldiers: Reshaping the Memory of the World Wars* (Oxford: Oxford University Press, 1990), p. 159.
50 Gmeyner, *Manja*, p. 20.
51 Andrea Hammell, 'Idealized and Demonized: Representations of Jewish Motherhood by Anna Gmeyner and Selma Kahn', in *'Not an Essence But a Positioning': German-Jewish Women Writers*, ed. Andrea Hammell and Godela Weiss-Sussex (Munich: Martin Meidenbauer Verlagsbuchhandlung, 2009), pp. 95–112, 96.
52 *Ibid.*, p. 97.
53 Gmeyner, *Manja*, p. 109.
54 Hammell, 'Idealized and Demonized', p. 106.
55 *Ibid.*
56 Gmeyner, *Manja*, p. 123.
57 *Ibid.*, p. 1. Original italics.
58 *Ibid.*, p. 215.
59 *Ibid.*, pp. 140, 229.
60 *Ibid.*, p. 144.
61 Pinfold discusses the *Bildungsroman* in terms of 'a constant tension between the demands of institutions and the claims of the individual, and this prefigures the odd combination of conformity with instinctive revolt found in so many child narratives set in the Third Reich'. Pinfold, *The Child's View of the Third Reich in German Literature*, p. 46.
62 Gmeyner, *Manja*, p. 330.
63 *Ibid.*, p. 241.

64 *Ibid.*, p. 450.
65 Mosse, *Nationalism and Sexuality*, p. 46.
66 Gmeyner, *Manja*, p. 526.
67 Jaroslaw Anders, 'Hansel and Gretel in Belarus', *The New York Review of Books* LXVIII (10 June 2010), pp. 39–41, 39.
68 Gmeyner, *Manja*, p. 526.

11

'Some other land, some other sea': Attia Hosain's fiction and non-fiction in *Distant Traveller*

Ambreen Hai

Attia Hosain's work is well known among specialists in Anglophone South Asian literary studies, but almost unheard of among scholars of twentieth-century British literature. Yet as an Indian Muslim woman who migrated to England in 1947, just before Indian independence, who became a British citizen and lived in London until her death in 1998, and who wrote and published all her major fiction in England, Hosain deserves attention from scholars in a variety of fields. Born in 1913 to a wealthy aristocratic Indian Muslim family, Hosain attended a prestigious English girls' school in the cosmopolitan city of Lucknow, studied Urdu, Persian, and Arabic at home, and, in 1933, was the first girl from an Indian landowning (*taluqdari*) family to graduate from college.[1] Characteristically independent-minded, she married the man she chose for herself, despite family opposition, and, after the 1947 Partition of British India into modern India and Pakistan, decided to stay in Britain with her two children, instead of choosing either India or Pakistan, as her divided family wished. In London, Hosain worked as a broadcaster for the BBC, and wrote and published *Phoenix Fled* (1953), a collection of short stories, and her magnum opus, the semi-autobiographical novel *Sunlight on a Broken Column* (1961).[2] Hosain published no more fiction after 1961, but posthumously, in 2013, Hosain's daughter Shama Habibullah, and a family friend, the writer-scholar Aamer Hussein, co-edited *Distant Traveller*, a volume that includes excerpts from Hosain's unfinished novel titled 'No New Lands, No New Seas', selected short stories (some previously unpublished), and a memoir essay.

Many feminist and postcolonial scholars, including Anuradha Dingwaney Needham, Susheila Nasta, and Antoinette Burton, have hailed Hosain's novel *Sunlight* as a significant achievement.[3] Their approaches, however, view Hosain as looking backwards to a lost past (in India), rather than to the present or future. This is understandable, since scholars did not have access to her writing about South Asians living in postimperial, post-war England until the publication of *Distant Traveller* (2013). Yet even a decade later, there are no scholarly articles about this volume. This chapter breaks fresh ground by focusing on Hosain's unfinished novel 'No New Lands', and some other fiction and non-fiction in the collection. Approaching Hosain's work anew from the vantage point of questions central to *Mid-Century Women's Writing* (such as how women disrupt the public/private divide and how their work complicates earlier narratives of British women's experience of war), I suggest that reading *Distant Traveller* as the work of *both* a British and postcolonial Indian writer helps us see new aspects of Hosain's writing and complicates our understandings of Anglophone mid-century women writers' responses both to the Second World War and to post-war, postimperial Britain.

Hosain was a deeply intersectional writer. She understood that gender interacts with multiple other aspects of identity, such as race, class, and religion. She was at once anti-imperialist and feminist. After the Second World War and Indian independence, her diasporic location in Britain at mid-century gave her the expatriate vision and distance to look back critically at both imperialism and Indian patriarchal norms, to examine from a different vantage point how women in colonial India faced (and negotiated) the interlocking oppressions of colonization and sexism, or what Petersen and Rutherford famously termed 'double colonization'.[4] Hosain also had the migrant positionality to assess the difficulties of South Asians facing racial prejudice in Britain as intersected by their class or gender positions. *Distant Traveller* includes fiction and non-fiction that addresses Indian women's lives both under British colonialism and in postimperial Britain. In what follows, I look closely at some of her writings collected in *Distant Traveller* to show how she challenged the public/private divide, and argue that, in her writing – whether concerning war, colonialism, or diaspora and displacement – Hosain makes public and political what may seem to be private, and offers beautifully crafted, nuanced, intersectional analyses that invite complex understandings and resist a single-minded approach.

Writing about war and the public/private divide

Scholars do not usually think about Attia Hosain as writing about war. But Hosain was born in 1913, a year before the First World War began, lived in India during the interwar period, and moved to Britain right after the Second World War ended. In her essay 'Deep Roots', written just before her death, Hosain describes her excitement at arriving in England in 1947 and seeing the sites and places where she had 'travelled for so long in [her] thoughts and imagination'.[5] But 'London in the aftermath of war' presented a different reality:

streets were dark early … there were gaps in bomb-damaged buildings and strict rationing. Yet I enjoyed each simple encounter. There was, then, a bond that grew out of shared hardships; no hostility, rather an eagerness to talk to someone from a part of the world where many had been sent, as a kind of extension of experience. I, too, had had family and friends fighting that war, in Africa, in Burma, the Middle East and Europe. Not many still remember that India had the largest volunteer army in two world wars.[6]

Well aware of the animus toward Asian immigrants prevalent in England later, Hosain testifies to a brief moment of openness and welcome among Londoners recovering from war.[7] It was in this London, Hosain states, that she turned to fiction writing, encouraged by a white Jewish woman friend 'whose family and friends had been refugees from the Nazis', who 'liked [Hosain's] stories', and who introduced her to a community of writers and publishers (including Leonard Woolf and Cecil Day Lewis).[8]

Hosain's comments on post-war London also serve as an important reminder that people from the British colonies not only contributed to the war effort, but also fought for their colonizers in wars that were not their own.[9] Inevitably, the impact of war was profoundly gendered, experienced very differently by Indian women than men.[10] It is often forgotten that *Sunlight* (1961) finally reveals that Laila, the narrator-protagonist, is a war widow, and that her beloved husband Ameer joins the Second World War in 1942 and dies fighting for the British in the Middle East. If the primary thrust of this *Bildungsroman* is to show how Laila fights for independence from family and custom, emerges from purdah, gets an education, and marries the man she loves despite family opposition, its end also suggests the partial destruction of those hopes and dreams. Though she keeps her independence, Laila loses Ameer to a war between European empire-states and is left to raise her child alone as a single mother. *Sunlight* makes visible another key point. Women in the colonies at mid-century were impacted not just by the war, but also by the political turmoil produced by colonialism, including the nationalist movements that rose to combat it, led by Gandhi and Nehru; the consequences of British efforts to suppress the struggle for independence; and the changes in education and opportunities for women that arose as various social changes and progressive efforts grew in conjunction with nationalism.

Sunlight further highlights how South Asia was indirectly but forcefully impacted by the Second World War in another way: through the hastened and disorganized rush to grant independence to British India in 1947, which led to catastrophic Partition violence. Weakened by the war, the British withdrew from India much earlier than planned, without adequate preparation.[11] Hurried, arbitrary lines of division were drawn by inexpert officials to create independent India and Pakistan, precipitating the horrific violence, sexual and non-sexual, that broke out at the borders, and leading to the national traumas and silences that still persist.[12] While independence from colonialism was what Indian nationalists passionately desired, independence did not necessitate Partition, and Partition did not necessitate violence. The experiences of women in the colonies were thus very much shaped not just by the war but by the interconnected web of historic events precipitated by the war. *Sunlight* ends with Laila reflecting on the devastation and division of her family as a result of Partition, looking ahead to a mitigated future.[13]

Hosain's fiction is clearly infused by the impacts of European 'world' wars on colonized Indians. But from the beginning, her writing focuses *both* on British colonialism in India *and* on patriarchal Indian Muslim practices and their impact on women: she simultaneously critiques the impacts of gender oppression from within Indian society and of colonialism from without. She explores how Indian women can participate in politics and the public sphere in an environment where Muslim women were mostly cloistered by the purdah system, and where many women were called to join the nationalist movement against British rule. Attia Hosain's writing thus connected anti-imperialism and feminism and challenged the gendered public/private, personal/political divide in British India from the very start.

In an early essay, published around 1935, the young Hosain makes a forceful case against the system of purdah (the segregation and seclusion of women) because, she argues, it bars women from the 'body politic', from participating fully as citizens in a democracy or (as imperial subjects living under British law), and from joining in the fight for freedom:

> Purdah has been the greatest hindrance to the political development of Indian women. Under the new constitution they have been given a greater degree of political rights than they enjoy at present. Those rights can be of no value while conditions exist which have divorced women from politics and left them with little knowledge of their rights and duties as citizens. Moreover, merely having the right to vote does not constitute the sum and substance of political rights. The value of the vote lies in the power to use it as an unhindered expression of free and independent thought. Democracy demands a political education which purdah women are denied. It is chiefly purdah which has prevented all but a few pioneers among women from representing their interests and taking their place in legislatures and other political organizations.[14]

Hosain understood politics in both senses, as governmental activity and as the distribution and operation of power across intersecting axes of identity. She also understood intersectionality before the term was invented – that multiple vectors of identity such as class, gender, race, ethnicity, nationality, age, and ability intersect to constitute human experience. In this essay, she argues powerfully against the divide that relegated middle- and upper-class Indian women to the private, interior, domestic space of the home, disallowing their full participation in nationalist politics either as informed, educated citizens, or as elected officials. Women's equality (and humanity), she suggests, depends on breaking that divide, on enabling women to emerge from purdah. Moreover, she suggests, this exclusion from politics is itself political: it is premised upon the cultural and social disempowerment of women as a class vis-à-vis men. Hosain's fiction likewise not only argues against purdah as a pernicious practice, but also makes a case more generally for the inextricability of the public and private, or the personal and the political, and for the personal or private as political.

From her college days onward, Hosain was influenced by her friends in the Progressive Writers' Movement, who viewed their mission as necessarily political and public, as combating, through literature, retrogressive social practices in the supposedly private sphere. Years, later, in a BBC broadcast from London, Attia Hosain reflected on this time:

> The climate of opinion and the system of education that created this situation was the result of all sorts of complicated forces – political, economic and social ... the relationship between rulers and ruled was changing rapidly ... western influences were beginning to penetrate established ways of living and thinking.[15]

In her fiction as well, Hosain addresses this intersection of Indian women's experiences as at once colonized, racialized, and gendered subjects, at home and abroad, and suggests the value of integrating a western education with the struggle for independence.

Distant Traveller includes Hosain's essay 'Deep Roots', excerpts from her unfinished novel 'No New Lands, No New Seas' (about South Asians of various class backgrounds living in post-war Britain), six previously unpublished short stories, one story that was previously published in India, and a selection of eight stories (of twelve) originally published in *Phoenix Fled* (1953). The previously unpublished stories, mostly set in India, show remarkable range as they focus on characters marginalized because of their class status, gender, sexuality, race, age, ability, or religion (or some combination thereof). They trouble the conventional divide between the private or domestic and the public or political, suggesting that what may seem to be problems of stymied individual lives in fact involve a politics of oppression that should be national and social concerns. Even stories that seem limited to the private and domestic implicitly argue for the need to recognize the politics of division and segregation. In the next section, I focus on 'The Leader of Women', a previously unpublished short story, to examine how Hosain portrays an older upper-class Indian Muslim woman who negotiates the conflicting imperatives of Indian cultural norms of wifehood and her commitment to nationalist and feminist politics.

Anti-colonial nationalism and feminism: 'The Leader of Women'

In the 1930s, Hosain's mother-in-law Inam Fatima 'was actively encouraged by her husband ... into more "westernized society"' and was among the first generation of Indian Muslim women who broke from tradition and began to participate in nationalist politics.[16] 'The Leader of Women' is based on what Hosain observed both of 'her mother-in-law's political career within the dynamic of the household' and of the 1933 All India Women's Conference in Calcutta.[17]

In this story, Hosain presents a woman who is 'an acknowledged leader' in the Indian women's movement and who publicly announces 'her hitherto secret adherence to the nationalist cause' even though her own husband is a high-ranking official in the (British colonial) 'government'.[18] Hosain thus explores how a woman could be pulled in opposite directions by the conflicting demands of proper wifehood and her own political commitments, and how she might negotiate them. On the one hand, this leader publicly joins the anti-colonial movement, and is made much of in the Indian press for supporting a cause against a government in which her husband is a prominent official. On the other hand, she refrains from actions that would compromise or undermine his position: 'It was unfortunate that during the militant period of civil disobedience she was prevented by a mysterious but persistent illness from joining in active demonstration.'[19] While other Indian women demonstrated in the streets, and were subject to the punitive repercussions of colonial retaliation and repression – the arrests and police violence that Hosain described in her novel *Sunlight* – this 'leader of women', as a good wife, draws upon a transparent excuse to retreat into the home and not jeopardize her husband's career, making sure 'there was no cause for government to complain of her involvement'.[20]

In a similar contradiction, she gives up her fancy outfits and wears simple 'khaddar clothes [that] made her an outstanding figure in all social gatherings'.[21] Wearing khaddar emblazons her membership in the anti-colonial nationalist movement; as part of the protest against the British, many Indians, led by Gandhi, began to weave their own cotton cloth and refused to wear or buy the expensive imported silks and synthetic fabrics manufactured in Britain. They thus refused to support the imperial British textile economy and protested the colonial extraction of Indian resources and the destruction of the Indian textile industry.[22] And yet, as a dutiful wife, the 'leader of women' attends these social gatherings and hosts 'famous receptions' 'forced on her under protest by her position as her husband's wife', where, despite her khaddar, she 'blazed with jewels' that 'were heirlooms and worn as a tribute to past [Indian] traditions'.[23] This contradiction between her nationalism and attendance at British government events is, however, carefully considered: 'Not war but cooperation between the classes was her creed; compromise the principle of her life.'[24] The leader explicitly voices her principles: 'To all she talked of moderation, of the dangers of too rapid a change, of the necessity of accepting and mingling the best of the West and the best of the East.'[25] Hosain offers a nuanced understanding of how this prominent woman successfully negotiates conflicting demands and suggests that women's participation in politics in such contexts might necessitate a strategic syncretism, not the single-minded opposition that western feminists or anti-colonialists focused on a single category of identity might expect.

The first-person narrator, a young woman who describes herself as proud to go down in history as 'her secretary', clearly admires this eclectic spirit of judicious selectivity from West and East, and lauds the 'leader of women' as someone who refuses the kind of nationalism that rests upon easy binary oppositions and absolutist, uncompromising rejection of all things western. Hosain likewise presents as admirable this leader's unusual mode of circumventing the private/public divide: 'Her household duties were only one form of expressing her belief that a woman's place is in her home. The wider interpretation of the phrase made her serve her larger home – her country.'[26] With this stunning declaration – that her home is actually her country – this woman brilliantly undoes the usual division of home/world, private/public by radically transforming (and expanding) the idea of the home and locating the domestic in the public sphere of the postcolonial nation itself. The 'leader' thus legitimizes women's participation in anti-colonial nationalism by redefining it as acceptable within the norms of traditional womanhood, as service to the nation that is her home. She strategically and successfully uses accepted norms to reshape gender roles while maintaining the appearance of proper womanhood.

'The Leader of Women' ends with a note from Hosain: '*Unfinished – because I don't know what I was driving at really. What can I do to this?*'[27] Perhaps Hosain wanted to revise and add more action to what is effectively a portrait. However, I would argue, this story is not incomplete, in the sense that it does not lack an ending. It concludes with a twist. The leader of women is elected to public office. Persuaded to 'stand for election' despite her demurrals and claims of 'not being educated enough', she allows herself to be photographed 'among the simple and poor people, eating with their women, sitting and joking with them'.[28] Demonstrating that she is 'dignified and different', she responds to attacks from opponents with a restraint that wins her favour in the public eye. Here is the story's final sentence: 'Her admirable humility drew so many towards her that with the help of the friendly section of the press she was elected to the council, unopposed.'[29] Hosain thus presents the imaginative possibility of a woman who tactically deploys the conventional decorum expected of high-ranking Indian women to undo conventional gender roles and enters fully into the public and political sphere, serving the cause of both the women's movement of her time and of anti-colonial nationalism.

South Asians in Britain

Hosain's second novel, 'No New Lands, No New Seas', turns to the experiences of diasporic Indians living, like herself, in post-war England and explores the costs and benefits that migrant South Asians of different intersectional identities face in making new homes in England. Hosain began writing this novel in the 1960s; why did she leave it unfinished? In her foreword, Shama Habibullah suggests that the 'rising racism' of the time, 'exemplified in Enoch Powell's "rivers of blood" speech' of 1968, made it too painful for Hosain to continue.[30] For someone who chose to live in England to escape the divisiveness and sectarianism that led to the partition of pre-Independence India, the prejudice, 'the advocacy of political and social exclusions', and 'spectre of deep division' again in Britain was too devastating.[31] To dwell on present-day prejudice was to revisit past trauma. Only 'some chapters' of this 'lost novel' were found after Hosain's death.[32] It is unknown how many of those have been selected by the editors of *Distant Traveller* to make public as 'excerpts' in what they have titled 'No New Lands, No New Seas'.

The central protagonist of this unfinished novel is Murad, a wealthy, progressive, 'westernized Indian' Muslim aristocrat who decides to return to Lucknow after living in London for ten years, sick of the daily indignities and racism he experiences there.[33] The excerpts suggest an episodic structure, a series of encounters between Murad and four South Asians in London to whom he bids farewell. Murad's decision to leave England thus becomes almost a pretext, and a point of comparison, for the complex stories of others who choose to stay. 'No New Lands' explores the different reasons why each of these individuals chooses, despite the difficulties they face, not to return to their country of origin. Hosain compares a range of immigrant stories in this novel, each shaped by the intersection of each individual's class, gender, race/ethnicity, or nationality. She shows how class and gender are key elements in immigrants' decisions to stay or return and highlights the agency each exercises in making their choices.

The novel begins with Murad almost falling out of a bus he is exiting, as the 'scowling conductor' rings the bell for the bus to restart too soon. Seething with 'ineffectual anger' at what he knows is covert racism, and at his loss of 'dignity', Murad reflects: 'Who or what was he to anyone here? For ten years now the consciousness of this "who" or "what" had been hammered into him, on each new occasion another nail locking him into the coffin of anonymity.'[34] Aware that he is becoming affected by a 'retaliatory hatred', and hearing the conductor's bell as symbolic, a signal to depart from where he is unwelcome, Murad thinks, 'The time has come for me to leave. The bell has rung for me. I must go home.'[35] The enormity of his decision to leave is heightened by Murad's awareness that he came to England to escape from the claustrophobia of his eminence as a high-ranking Indian male. He remembers how 'that warmth had wrapped him to the point of suffocation; [how] that concern had assaulted his privacy; that tribal family love had choked his individuality'.[36] Now he realizes he wants to return, disillusioned by the fake 'liberation' that London offered, the 'ever-receding mirages' that left him 'alone in a void'.[37]

This powerful indictment of England's treatment of South Asian immigrants is complicated and nuanced because Hosain also shows that Murad can choose to return to India because of the greater privileges he has there and because others who lack those privileges and who suffer worse hardships in England still choose to stay. Unlike Murad, the working-class or middle-class South Asians Murad knows in London find England to be the lesser of evils. We first hear of Isa, Murad's friend, who died trying to stop a fight between another Indian man and a white man over a white woman.[38] Isa, we learn, was also from Lucknow, but from the lower middle class. After Partition, his family migrated to Pakistan, and his arranged marriage to Aziza, a very traditional, uneducated woman, was unhappy. In London, despite their different socio-economic backgrounds, Murad and Isa had 'been drawn together by the discovery that they came from the same town, spoke its language, loved its special culture ... the sense of brotherhood that resulted ... [was] forged by their grievous loneliness during those early years of uprootedness'.[39] Anticipating later writers, Hosain emphasizes how in the diaspora, Indians from disparate classes and nation-states come together in ways not possible back in South Asia, bonding over shared loss and pain.[40]

But Murad also recalls the tensions in this diasporic friendship and the resentments that Isa carried. He recalls that the reasons Isa came to England, and chose to stay, were very different from his own. Isa had fought for India's freedom from the British, but faced, after Partition, a Hobson's choice: when his homeland was split in two, and he could not bear to choose Pakistan over India, England offered a neutral space. Yet though he became a British citizen, he felt he had no country to call his own. As he said to Murad:

> 'You who have a country, tell me. ... I brandished banners against Colonialism. My father was beaten and imprisoned for his country's freedom from the country I have sworn loyalty to. We were poor and my mother suffered when my father took to going in and out of jail. You wouldn't know what it was like, with your people comfortably bargaining for equality in drawing rooms with English guests over a glass of whisky ... But when freedom came, where was I? When the country cracked apart I was on the other side of a bloody chasm. And I swore loyalty to the background of a cry of hate against my father's country, against your country, against my country that was. Tell me then, who I am, what I am, with no roots attached to any piece of earth.'[41]

In this astonishing speech riddled with pain, Isa remembers his familial heritage of anti-colonial struggle. He mourns the home he lost when his family migrated to Pakistan and when, amidst the hate-filled violence of Partition, he swore loyalty to Pakistan and enmity to India, which became the land of no return. Now he feels he has no identity, no 'roots'. Hence the bitter irony, he notes, that he has to thank Britain for providing him with refuge from the bitter opposition of India and Pakistan, from the conflicts created by British colonial policies of divide and conquer:

> 'Thank you, Britannia, for giving me shelter. I have no land, no home, no people – because you have bloody well taught your lessons too well and they have turned against each other. Now pay back the debts you owe me and my father and my father's father.'[42]

But amidst his resentment of Britain, Isa also voices his resentment of elite Indians like Murad whom he accuses of not making similar sacrifices, of not suffering the costs of the anti-colonial struggle, and whose families either colluded with or engaged on terms of relative equality with the English. Isa therefore also reminds Murad of the privileges Murad has – as an Indian Muslim who can return to India to a wealth and comfort that Isa never had. Class and class resentment divide them, despite their shared love of their home city, and shape their choices for the future.

Hosain sets up a comparison not only between Murad and Isa, but also between Murad, Isa's widow Aziza, and Isa, to show how intersecting gender and class differences further complicate immigrants' choices. After Isa's death, when Murad visits Aziza to condole, he finds her to be as conventional and unappealing as he remembered. But when he asks her if she will go back home, he is surprised by her response.

> 'Go back? Where? To what? To whom? Only my brother is in Lahore [in Pakistan]. My father, you know, is in India. I cannot go to him. My brother has his own family to support. What is a widow's life in another home, however close he may be. I have two children to bring up, to educate.'[43]

Hosain gives Aziza a distinctive and powerful voice. Aziza challenges Murad's assumption that she cannot survive on her own in England. Her family, she points out, was divided by Partition, so that turning to one relative would mean foregoing the other and choosing either Pakistan or India. For her as for Isa, England provides a neutral space, as it did for Hosain herself. As Aziza knows, the sexist, patriarchal system operative in South Asia means that neither her father nor brother would willingly support her as a widow; her 'home' is not with them, and she would have to become a dependent burdened by obligation to whichever male relative she appealed. Instead, Aziza has chosen another future and another community – in England. Though she performs the conventional melodramatic mourning expected of her – 'We are exiles in a desolated world', she laments – nonetheless, she makes clear what material and legal advantages she has in the imperial metropolis compared to either postcolonial state: 'This house is my only home', she asserts.[44] Isa bought the tiny house in London in which she now lives, and which now belongs to her. And, as she explains, in England her son is 'being educated', whereas she could not afford his school fees if they went back; here she gets 'an allowance for the baby, while there [she] would feel dependent on [her] relatives' charity'.[45] Furthermore, in England, Aziza notes, she has found a larger South Asian community: 'people from [*both*] Pakistan and India'.[46] Unlike Murad, this multiply disadvantaged but clear-sighted woman chooses to remain in England because it provides social services and opportunities that neither India nor Pakistan can offer her. Hosain thus suggests the benefits of the public solution over the private one: the social democracy of the British state provides publicly funded benefits for a widow and her children, unlike the postcolonial state that leaves her dependent on individual, private solutions, such as help from family. But Hosain also makes clear that England has the resources to do so because it has accumulated wealth from centuries of imperialism, in contrast to two fledgling postcolonial states whose resources have been thereby depleted.[47]

In this implicit comparison, Hosain makes clear that whereas Murad has land and wealth to return to, and knowledge of a comfortable future, lower-middle-class immigrants like Isa and Aziza do not. Their choices are shaped by their socio-economic positions and their consequent sense of unbelonging and dispossession in the homelands they left behind. Hosain thus offers an implicit explanation for why the first generation of post-war South Asian immigrants to Britain was predominantly an impoverished underclass of landless peasants and workers who arrived in the 1950s and 1960s, fleeing post-Partition turmoil in their newly created home nations. She therefore emphasizes class as a significant factor in this migration, even as she proposes the possibility of cross-class affiliations in the diaspora.

But Hosain also sets up an intersectional comparison that reveals gendered differences between Aziza and Isa, between the husband and wife's situations and choices. As Murad takes his leave of Aziza, amazed that the woman he had perceived as 'commonplace, uneducated, old fashioned, an appendage to her husband' was now 'emerging as an individual, as if his death had released her', he remembers that, unlike Aziza, Isa chose England as an escape, not as a refuge, in a decision tinged with bitterness.[48] Where Isa looked to the past, focused on nation and Partition, his wife looks pragmatically to the future and thinks instead of her children and her independence from patriarchy. Isa's masculine pride and sense of identity were tied up in carrying the wounds of colonization and an independence struggle that turned so bloody that he had to flee to the very colonizer whose actions dispossessed him of his home. But Aziza seems not to carry that burden. She is focused more on what England can provide for her and her children. Hosain thus emphasizes powerful differences of gender even for immigrants of the same class and shows how men and women might differ in their views based on their different histories and intersectional identities.

Highlighting further differences of class and gender among South Asians, 'No New Lands' also provides encounters between Murad and two working-class men who choose England. Both work in an Indian restaurant. Chaudhary, the proprietor of 'The Pride of Asia', Murad's favourite Indian restaurant in London, was 'once an impoverished peasant in East Bengal, then a cook's help on a P & O liner'. Chaudhary too is a victim of Partition, of what Hosain highlights as the cruel arbitrariness of hastily created new borders: 'the boundary sliced his insignificant village; it placed his home in Pakistan, his brother's in India, and ran right through others so that children played in one country and slept in another'.[49] Hosain emphasizes how the changing politics of the homeland continue to affect the material conditions and safety of the struggling expatriate in England. Over the years, Chaudhary has sought Murad's advice on what to name his restaurant. Before Independence, he called it 'The British Indian Restaurant', which worked until 1942 when the Quit India Movement began and his Indian customers taunted him for having no 'national pride'; after Independence, he changed the name to 'The Great Indian Restaurant', which in turn evoked charges of betrayal.[50] Trying to appease his changing customers, he changed the name to 'The Great Indo-Pakistan Restaurant', but that produced accusations that he was 'sitting on the fence'.[51] Murad finally suggested 'The Pride of Asia', signalling a region without colonialist or nationalist overtones and appealing to a broad base. Hosain thus presents a decade-long relationship between Murad and Chaudhary that developed despite their class differences, where Chaudhary sought Murad's advice and Murad offered benign patronage, contributing to Chaudhary's success.

Hosain writes that Indian working-class (male) characters turn to Murad because they perceive him rightly as a 'sympathetic human being' who 'had an intense desire to know everyone with whom he came in contact as human individuals, no matter who they were'.[52] In England, because he is not in India where his rank would be a barrier, Murad can be open to different classes and show his interest in his fellow expatriates. Hence Murad had befriended Chaudhary from the start and actually helped him rename himself. Upon discovering that his given name was 'Khadim-e-Allah' (which means 'server of God'), Murad recognized the problems that this name would pose in England – it was long and could not be shortened to either Khadim or Allah. 'You are no slave or servant', Murad declared, and warned that calling oneself 'Allah' would obviously be 'dangerous'.[53] Murad then suggested 'Chaudhary' (headman; of a village) as a new name and identity.[54] Hosain thus calls attention both to the necessary adaptations that diasporic individuals must make to survive in a new place, and to the importance of solidarity and support among diasporic individuals in ensuring that new arrivals survive and thrive. Murad has used his privilege – his know-how and familiarity with the host country – to help others who needed and benefitted from the help. Hosain thereby suggests that privilege is not in itself suspect if those with privilege are self-aware and use that privilege to benefit others who lack such privilege. Hosain does not imply that all Indians with the privileges of wealth and education are like Murad, but she does offer an imaginative utopian possibility through the figure of Murad.

Chaudhary's decision to remain in England, then, is different from that of Isa or Aziza. Coming from even lower-class origins than them, he has chosen to settle where he could build a prosperous livelihood while maintaining ties to the homeland that cannot offer him similar opportunity. His life is divided, much as his village was once divided. In England, he has found happiness with an Irish woman. But Chaudhary also has a wife and children in his village in (what is now) Bangladesh, whom he supports but does not bring to England. He has the privilege to leave them behind. In this unfinished novel, Hosain is clearly interested not only in women but also in men, and in contrasting their differently gendered and classed diasporic experiences.

Even among working-class Indian Muslims, there are further gradations, as Hosain reminds her readers through the multiplicity of her characters.

She next introduces Munnay, an even more impoverished young man whose Bengali family migrated from Delhi to Dacca in 1947, and who migrated (yet again) to England and works in Chaudhary's restaurant. Murad and Munnay have connected because they recognized in each other a shared understanding of Urdu, their mother tongue. Away from home, Murad picks up Munnay's use of 'the polite Urdu term for home –"sharifkhana"', so that a 'bond had been established by inflections of language in spite of differences in circumstances'.[55] For Murad, the workers at the restaurant provide a sense of home away from home, the welcome, 'the solidity, the warmth, the inescapable reality of human relationships' that he cannot find among English people.[56] In a marvellous expression, suggestive of her own experience, Hosain describes Murad's sense of alienation in England, where he 'lived among people as emotionally elusive as mist, as cold as fog, as warm as the sun shining through it', where he cannot enjoy food in English restaurants because it is 'eaten in an aspic of aloofness'.[57] For the newly arrived Munnay (whose name literally means 'young one' and who is described as 'a frightened child'), Murad provides the guidance of an experienced elder: 'In his own country Munnay would have looked up to Murad as a master more than normally kind, but here he thought of him as an elder, wise in guidance.'[58] Empathetically and poignantly, Hosain describes how Munnay is 'getting used to the elusiveness of the sun, the permanence of the damp, the wonder of affluence, the bewilderment of machines and speed, the human ordinariness of the whites. But inside him were areas of fear, traps and tunnels and chasms.'[59] It is these challenges of living in mid-century England that Hosain understands, and that, she suggests, Murad helps Munnay to navigate. Diaspora changes the tenor of relationships that would in South Asia be shaped differently by mutual awareness of class differences. That awareness is not dissipated by being abroad, but it is changed. For these South Asian men in England, barriers of class are mitigated, though not overcome, by solidarities created by race, region, language, and gender.

Even though incomplete, 'No New Lands' achieves a great deal. Through the varied stories of these diasporic characters, Hosain gives voice to the South Asian immigrant underclass, where Murad becomes a utopian substitute for herself. Murad is the wanderer in the city who can connect more with the working-class man because of his gender, despite his class.

'Journey to No End'

If this unfinished novel 'No New Lands', written in the 1960s, imagines the possibility of return, at least for the wealthy scion of an aristocratic Indian Muslim family, that possibility seems less viable for the Indian Muslim male narrator of Hosain's short story 'Journey to No End'.⁶⁰ Placed at the end of the collection In *Distant Traveller*, this story examines the costs of settling in Britain and the tragic yearning for a lost home. The ageing narrator, living alone in London, longs to return to India but is painfully aware that return has become impossible because of the animosity towards Muslims that has intensified since Partition. The story opens with this unnamed narrator in his lonely apartment in London, unable to perceive his present-day surroundings without overlaying them with memories of a past landscape that he continues to mourn. Hosain's writing merges descriptions of the present (the grey skies, the rain over crowded buildings that he sees from his window) with those of the past that he seems to see more clearly in his mind's eye (the 'ghostly orchard' of orange trees, his childhood laughter as he ran upon a terrace) as if to emphasize their indistinguishability for him.⁶¹ 'I am here by the window. Yet always I am going back through years and space; and there is no way of stopping this scattering of myself.'⁶² This story becomes an attempt, then, to gather this scattered self, or to excavate the reasons for its scattering.

'Home' and 'roots' are key words that recur in Hosain's writing about diaspora. 'I have known what it is to be a stranger among friends', this narrator reflects, as he describes his past eagerness to return: 'I did not believe it when I first went home; I had too much to give, to measure what I received.'⁶³ But then he catches himself, and questions with some bitterness that notion of home: 'Went home? I have never left it though I am not there. But I have no home. I have to repeat the thought to myself to believe in it, because it is incredible.'⁶⁴ He cannot believe that what has taken 'root' for generations of his family in India could be so easily 'torn out'.⁶⁵ His repeated organic metaphor of roots suggests wrenching pain and a determination to claim belonging: 'The roots leave fine tendrils that cling firmly round each particle of soil.'⁶⁶

The home he longs for, we learn, is that of his childhood in India, shared with a Hindu friend. They had played together, studied together, eaten together. But when he visited, though welcomed by old servants, the narrator found that this friend, now an important politician, was embarrassed by him:

> He was in the room he used as an office, where once we had helped each other with our studies. It had not changed. ...
> There were four men in the room with him and they looked at me with a coldness that did not burn me as his look of surprised embarrassment did.⁶⁷

The room had not changed, but the friend had. The friend subsequently offered weak excuses for his reaction: 'these men, they're ignorant but

'Some other land, some other sea' 217

– influential. You know how it is now – your very name ...'[68] The friend could not finish his sentence, leaving unnamed what was obvious to them both: that the narrator's name conveyed his Muslim identity. As a politician, the friend could not be seen socializing with a Muslim. Hosain's writing is elliptical, leaving gaps for the reader to fill in. But she leaves no doubt of what distances the narrator from his childhood friend in postcolonial India: 'My name, his name, our pain. Only our names ... indications of different faiths.'[69] He recalls then 'the shadows of fear-filled violence' that lie between them (namely Partition): 'Between him and me the shadow of shadows.'[70] The story ends with the narrator's poignant yearning for an India to which he cannot return, for the maturing fruit he cannot pick: 'The oranges must be ripe in the orchard.'[71] The joys of Independence are not for him, lost forever in the betwixt and between.[72] Nor can England, his resting place, be home.

'Journey to No End' suggests dismally that there is no purpose, no final destination, no end to the journey for the distant traveller, no home that the diasporic Indian Muslim can find in England or in India. But that is not necessarily the final implication of Hosain's work in *Distant Traveller*. The pessimistic title of her unfinished novel 'No New Land, No New Seas' was assigned posthumously by the editors, based on a poem by the Greek poet Cavafy that Hosain 'carefully recorded in her journals' just before her death, with the heading 'Lucknow for Me':

You tell yourself: I'll be gone
To some other land, some other sea,
To a city far lovelier than this
Could ever have been or hoped to be –
 You will find no other lands, no other seas.[73]

Hosain's extract speaks powerfully of a similar sense of exile, of a lost home that cannot be recovered, replaced, or forgotten: that home city will haunt one forever. But though Hosain's title, 'Lucknow for Me', suggests that this may be her personal experience or feeling, her unfinished novel suggests her awareness that that is not necessarily generalizable to others in the diaspora. In 'No New Lands', in a marvellous tribute to the South Asian diasporic community (which anticipates later ones such as Jhumpa Lahiri's story 'The Third and Final Continent'), Hosain also presents Murad's admiration for men like Munnay, distant travellers whose adjustments are necessarily tougher and more successful than any Murad himself has had to make:

Murad was filled with wonder and speculation about these intrepid explorers, these adventurers who came like conquistadors in search of wealth but ill-equipped; ill-armed, lured, seduced, lost, deceived on their Odysseys, coping with hazards, reaching points of vantage more successfully than such as he who had mapped the terrain, charted the course, studied, copied, befriended the inhabitants.[74]

Such a passage suggests both the strength and resilience of a less privileged, younger generation like Munnay, Chaudhary, and Aziza, and the admiration of an older generation for their intrepidity and willingness to take risks and face challenges, settle in a new land, and make it a second home. It also suggests more optimism. Drawing upon the same poem, my title for this chapter, 'Some Other Land, Some Other Sea', suggests that Hosain's fiction does offer some hope, that it looks forward to the possibility that for some at least, who cannot return to India or Pakistan, England will in fact become a home, for themselves and, in the future, for their descendants.

Conclusion

Hosain writes as a cosmopolitan, transnational, British South Asian postcolonial writer who made England her home for over fifty years. Disillusioned both by the aftermath of Independence and by the racist turn in the postimperial metropolis towards the British Empire's formerly colonized non-white subjects, Hosain nonetheless does not seem despairing. Her unfinished novel suggests the possibility of diasporic South Asians of different classes and backgrounds making new homes in this new land. As a chronicler and analyst of diasporic experience far ahead of her time, she was cognizant of the work – emotional and otherwise – immigrants get done, in and for postimperial Britain. In his afterword, Aamer Hussein describes her as 'a pioneering anglophone Indian woman writer' whose 'handwritten manuscripts ... show Hosain entering a new raw and radical phase of expression. Powerful and poetic, [these chapters] prove that Attia Hosain was one of the first writers to imagine into being the crude realities of a migrant existence long, long before such fiction became fashionable.'[75] *Distant Traveller* presents a range of Hosain's work, from the beginning of her career to the end. It shows how she started out as a young woman challenging the gendered and colonial politics of British subjects in pre-Independence India, before becoming a public commentator and intersectional analyst of mid-century life in Britain. It ends with her under-recognized writing about South Asians in Britain, demonstrating yet again how she made the private public, delved into heartbreak and anguish, and highlighted courage and achievements in the hope of bringing about more public awareness and social and political change.

Notes

1. Much of this biographical information is included in Shama Habibullah's Foreword in Attia Hosain, *Distant Traveller*, ed. Aamer Hussein and Shama Habibullah (New Delhi: Women Unlimited, Kali for Women, 2013). See also Antoinette Burton, *Dwelling in the Archive: Women Writing House, Home, and History in Late Colonial India* (New York: Oxford University Press, 2003), pp. 108–9. Unlike her brother, Hosain was not allowed to continue her college education at Cambridge University. As her legacy, the Attia Hosain Trust Fund at Newnham College now funds public lectures on multiculturalism and an annual scholarship to enable a South Asian woman to continue her education at Cambridge University.
2. As Shama Habibullah elaborates, in the 1950s, Hosain earned her living working for the BBC in London, in Urdu for the Eastern Service, and in English for the BBC Third Programme. 'Foreword', in *Distant Traveller*, pp. 11–12. Hosain also appeared on television and the West End stage. Bawna Singh, 'Attia Hosain: A Radical Muslim Writer and Archivist of the Partition', *Feminism in India* (29 July 2019), https://feminisminindia.com/2019/07/29/attia-hosain-radical-muslim-writer-archivist-partition/ (accessed 7 January 2023).
3. See Anuradha Dingwaney Needham, 'Multiple Forms of (National) Belonging: Attia Hosain's *Sunlight on a Broken Column*', *Modern Fiction Studies* 39.1 (1993), pp. 93–111; Susheila Nasta, *Home Truths: Fictions of the South Asian Diaspora in Britain* (New York: Palgrave, 2002); and Burton, *Dwelling in the Archive*.
4. I do not mean to imply that women in colonial India could not see their own double oppression. Indeed, Hosain's early Indian writings, as her essay about purdah and politics shows, did precisely that. But distance in space and time enabled a longer viewpoint.
5. Hosain, 'Deep Roots', in *Distant Traveller*, p. 20.
6. *Ibid.*, pp. 20–1.
7. This reception was undoubtedly shaped by Hosain's highly educated, upper-class status, and would differ for other immigrants from other backgrounds. Nonetheless, even after fifty years in England, Hosain never lost a sense of being an outsider. As she adds, 'I was always an observer, watching through glass, never really made to feel at home as in the eastern tradition. … I could not penetrate that invisible barrier …' 'Deep Roots', p. 26.
8. *Ibid.*, p. 22. This is not to say that Hosain saw only the after-effects of the Second World War. In India, Hosain and her family experienced its direct impacts. In her foreword, Hosain's daughter describes how her parents moved to Bombay but left the children in Lucknow for a year because Bombay was not considered safe, liable to be invaded by Japan. These fears, she writes, were not unfounded: 'Our first childhood memories of Bombay were of anti-aircraft barrage balloons over Breach Candy where we lived, and the explosion of the *Fort Stikine*, when my father was blown under his desk in Ballard Pier Habibullah.' Habibullah, 'Foreword', p. 8.

220   *Women beyond the nation*

9 Historian Yasmin Khan reports, 'Two-and-a-half million Indian soldiers served in the Second World War, over 24,000 were killed and 64,000 wounded. ... Partition emerged from a cauldron of social disorder. ... The Second World War and Partition bled into each other.' Yasmin Kahn, *The Great Partition: The Making of India and Pakistan* (New Haven, CT: Yale University Press, 2007), p. 17.
10 In her short story 'Time is Unredeemable' (1953), Hosain evokes the negative impact of the Second World War even on Indian women living in India. Bano, a young bride, lives for nine years with her in-laws, waiting for her husband to return from university in England. His return is delayed because of the war. When he returns, he rejects her because the time lost is 'unredeemable', and they have grown too far apart. In Attia Hosain, *Phoenix Fled* (London: Penguin, 1988), pp. 57–77.
11 See Khan, *The Great Partition*, p. 13.
12 Khan notes that the British government announced its plan to partition India on 3 June 1947, two months before independence in August 1947: 'the plan – for all its superficial complexity and detail – was wafer thin and left numerous critical aspects unexamined and unclear'. Despite the imperial promises of a 'smooth and seamless transfer of power', the whole process was 'disorderly' and 'threatened the very existence of the two new states'. She concludes, 'the British government's most grievous failure was the shoddy way in which the plan was implemented'. Kahn, *The Great Partition*, pp. 4–5, 208.
13 It is worth noting that the presence of Indians in Britain and Hosain's own decision to stay in England were themselves indirect consequences of the war. After the labour shortage created by the war, Britain invited workers from the colonies to migrate to Britain. Hosain did not go there to work, but after Partition she decided to stay in Britain because from there she did not have to choose between India and Pakistan. As her daughter puts it, 'Though she never did accept Partition, by taking British nationality she was free to travel between countries.' Habibullah, 'Foreword', p. 10.
14 Attia Habibullah, 'Seclusion of Women', in *Our Cause: A Symposium by Indian Women*, ed. Shyam Kumari Nehru (Allahabad: Kitabistan, c.1935), pp. 206–7.
15 Quoted by Shama Habibullah, 'Foreword', p. 7.
16 *Ibid.*, p. 6.
17 *Ibid.*, p. 6.
18 Hosain, 'The Leader of Women', in *Distant Traveller*, p. 96.
19 *Ibid.*
20 *Ibid.*, p. 97.
21 *Ibid.*
22 In the 1920s, instead of protests that could turn violent, Gandhi 'proposed what he called constructive work ... such as the uplift of "untouchables", khadi production ... the boycott of British goods and the public burning of foreign cloth'. Burton Stein, *A History of India* (Oxford: Blackwell, 1998), p. 323. Indian women joined in: 'In the mass movements of the 1920s and

1930s, women's participation was much in evidence in certain acts such as the khadi campaigns (to wear homespun cloth), in the picketing of shops selling foreign goods, and the Salt March of 1930.' Kumari Jayawardena, *Feminism and Nationalism in the Third World* (London: Zed Books, 1986), p. 99.
23 Hosain, *Distant Traveller*, p. 97.
24 *Ibid.*, p. 97.
25 *Ibid.*, p. 98.
26 *Ibid.*, pp. 96, 98.
27 *Ibid.*, p. 99.
28 *Ibid.*, pp. 98, 99.
29 *Ibid.*, p. 99.
30 Habibullah, 'Foreword', pp. 12–13.
31 *Ibid.*, p. 13.
32 *Ibid.*
33 Hosain, 'No New Lands', in *Distant Traveller*, p. 35.
34 *Ibid.*, p. 29.
35 *Ibid.*, p. 30.
36 *Ibid.*, p. 31.
37 *Ibid.*
38 Here is an occasion where the unfinished nature of the novel seems apparent. Hosain provides no further details of this event.
39 *Ibid.*, p. 36.
40 See for instance Jhumpa Lahiri's story 'When Mr. Pirzada Came to Dine', in *The Interpreter of Maladies* (New York: Houghton Mifflin, 1999), pp.23–42.
41 Hosain, 'No New Lands', pp. 52–3. Italics in the original.
42 *Ibid.*, p. 53. Italics in the original.
43 *Ibid.*, p. 43.
44 *Ibid.*, p. 44, 45.
45 *Ibid.*, p. 45.
46 *Ibid.*
47 Hosain hence implies that the immigrants are not taking what they have no right to claim: they are in London because of what the British have taken from them, because of the damage inflicted by British colonialism in India. In a memorable moment in Michele Cliff's novel, when racists demonstrate against black immigrants in England, the immigrants push back, responding 'WE ARE HERE BECAUSE YOU WERE THERE.' *No Telephone to Heaven* (New York: Vintage, 1987), p. 137 (capitalized in the original). The formerly colonized arrive in the metropolitan centre seeking resources that were taken from them. As one character says in Kiran Desai's novel, 'Your father came to *my* country and took *my* bread and now I have to come to *your* country to get *my* bread back.' *The Inheritance of Loss* (New York: Grove Press, 2006), p. 150.
48 Hosain, 'No New Lands', p. 45.
49 *Ibid.*, p. 56. Khan describes how these borders were 'devised from a distance; the land, villages and communities to be divided were not visited or inspected by the imperial map-maker, the British judge, Cyril Radcliffe, who arrived in

India on 8 July to carry out the task and stayed in the country only six weeks'. *The Great Partition*, p. 3.
50 Hosain, 'No New Lands', p. 56.
51 *Ibid.*, p. 57.
52 *Ibid.*
53 *Ibid.*
54 *Ibid.*, p. 58.
55 *Ibid.*, p. 63.
56 *Ibid.*, p. 61.
57 *Ibid.*, pp. 61, 55.
58 *Ibid.*, p. 64.
59 *Ibid.*
60 This story was first published in the magazine *Wasafiri* 26 (Autumn 1997), pp. 64–5, just before Attia Hosain died. It is set after Partition. Aamer Hussein writes that, upon the request of the editor, Susheila Nasta, Hosain agreed to relinquish this 'delicate' story for the twenty-fifth anniversary of India's independence, and that it 'emerged from a box of unpublished writings'. 'Afterword', in *Distant Traveller*, p. 231. It seems likely that Hosain had written it much earlier and revised it for publication in 1997.
61 Hosain, 'Journey to No End', in *Distant Traveller*, p. 212.
62 *Ibid.*, p. 213.
63 *Ibid.*, p. 214.
64 *Ibid.*
65 *Ibid.*, p. 215.
66 *Ibid.*
67 *Ibid.*, pp. 217–18.
68 *Ibid.*, p. 218.
69 *Ibid.*
70 *Ibid.*
71 *Ibid.*
72 Hosain did in fact return to India several times with her adult children, but only as a visitor.
73 Habibullah, 'Foreword', p. 16.
74 Hosain, 'No New Lands', p. 67.
75 Hussain, 'Afterword', pp. 228, 232.

Bibliography

Adam, Ruth. *A Woman's Place: 1910–1975*. London: Persephone Books, 2000.
Aguiree, Mercedes. 'History and Myth in *After the Death of Don Juan*'. *The Journal of the Sylvia Townsend Warner Society* 15.1 (2014): 76–90.
Ahmed, Sara. *The Cultural Politics of Emotion*. Edinburgh: Edinburgh University Press, 2015.
Alexander, Stephen. *Exile and Otherness*. Bern: Peter Lang, 2005.
Anders, Jaroslaw. 'Hansel and Gretel in Belarus'. *The New York Review of Books* LXVIII (10 June 2010): 39–41.
Anon. 'General Medical Council: Disciplinary Cases'. *British Medical Journal Supplement* (19 June 1937): 398.
Anon. 'MGM Drops Story Prize'. *New York Times* (26 May 1948): 29.
Anon. 'Numbers of the Profession'. *British Medical Journal* (3 September 1938): 488–9.
Anon. 'Women in Medicine'. *British Medical Journal* (3 September 1938): 523–5.
Arendt, Hannah. *The Human Condition*. Chicago, IL: University of Chicago Press, 1998.
Bagchi, Jasodhara, and Subhoranjan Dasgupta. *The Trauma and the Triumph: Gender and Partition in Eastern India*. Kolkata: Bhatkal & Son, 2003.
Bailkin, Jordanna. *The Afterlife of Empire*. Berkeley, CA: Global, Area, and International Archive, University of California Press, 2012.
Baldwin, M. Page. 'Subject to Empire: Married Women and the British Nationality and Status of Aliens Act'. *The Journal of British Studies* 40.4 (2001): 522–56.
Baxell, Richard. *Unlikely Warriors: The British in the Spanish Civil War and the Struggle Against Fascism*. London: Aurum, 2012.
Beauman, Nicola. *The Other Elizabeth Taylor*. London: Persephone Books, 2009.
Beaumont, Caitríona. *Housewives and Citizens: Domesticity and the Women's Movement in England, 1928–64*. Manchester: Manchester University Press, 2013.
Beers, Laura. *Red Ellen: The Life of Ellen Wilkinson, Socialist, Feminist, Internationalist*. Cambridge, MA: Harvard University Press, 2016.
Beveridge, Sir William. 'Social Insurance and Allied Services'. *The Bulletin of the World Health Organization* 78.6 (2000): 847–55.
Bhattacharya, Sudheshna. 'The Making of a Popular Base for the Quit India Movement: The Impact of the Pacific War on the People and the Colonial State in India (1941–42)'. *Proceedings of the Indian History Congress* 63 (2002): 683–94.

Bluemel, Kristin. 'The Aftermath of War', in *The History of British Women's Writing 1945–1975*, edited by Clare Hanson and Susan Watkins, 142–56. London: Palgrave, 2017.

Bluemel, Kristin. 'Introduction: What is Intermodernism?', in *Intermodernism: Literary Culture in Mid-Twentieth-Century Britain*, edited by Kristin Bluemel, 1–20. Edinburgh: Edinburgh University Press, 2009.

Bock, Gisela. 'Racism and Sexism in Nazi Germany: Motherhood, Compulsory Sterilization, and The State', in *Different Voices: Women and the Holocaust*, edited by Carol Rittner and John K. Roth, 161–86. New York: Paragon House, 1993.

Bottome, Phyllis. *Survival*. Boston, MA: Little Brown, 1943.

Bowen, Elizabeth. 'Review of *A Wreath of Roses*', in *The Weight of a World of Feeling: Reviews and Essays by Elizabeth Bowen*, edited by Alan Hepburn, 236–38. Evanston, IL: Northwestern University Press, 2017.

Brecht, Bertolt. 'Fragen eines lesenden Arbeiters', in *Gesammelte Werke*, vol. 9, 656–7. Frankfurt am Main: Suhrkamp Verlag, 1967.

Brenner, Rachel. *The Ethics of Witnessing: The Holocaust in Polish Writers' Diaries from Warsaw, 1939–1945*. Evanston, IL: Northwestern University Press, 2014.

Briganti, Chiara, and Kathy Mezei. 'Introduction: Living with Strangers', in *Living with Strangers: Bedsits and Boarding Houses in Modern English Life, Literature and Film*, edited by Chiara Briganti and Kathy Mezei, 1–24. London: Routledge, 2020.

Briggs, Austin. 'Rebecca West v. James Joyce, Samuel Beckett, and William Carlos Williams', in *Joyce in the Hibernian Metropolis: Essays*, edited by Morris Beja and David Norris, 83–102. Columbus, OH: Ohio State University Press, 1996.

Brothers, Barbara. 'Writing against the Grain: Sylvia Townsend Warner and the Spanish Civil War', in *Women's Writing in Exile*, edited by Mary Lynn Broe and Angela Ingram, 349–68. Chapel Hill, NC: University of North Carolina Press, 1989.

Brown, Susan, Patricia Clements, and Isobel Grundy, eds. 'Marghanita Laski Entry: Life & Writing Screen', in *Orlando: Women's Writing in the British Isles from the Beginnings to the Present*. Cambridge: Cambridge University Press, 2006.

Bunting, Madeleine. *Labours of Love: The Crisis of Care*. London: Granta, 2020.

Burdekin, Katharine. *Swastika Night*. London: Gollancz, 1985.

Burton, Antoinette. *Dwelling in the Archive: Women Writing House, Home, and History in Late Colonial India*. New York: Oxford University Press, 2003.

Calder, Angus. *The Myth of the Blitz*. 1991; London: Pimlico, 1992.

'Celia Fremlin'. *The Times* (9 September 2009): 66.

Centre for Jewish Studies. 'Moses Gaster Projects'. University of Manchester. www.manchesterjewishstudies.org/moses-gaster-project/

Chakraborty, Paulomi. *The Refugee Woman: Partition of Bengal, Women, and the Everyday of the Nation*. Edmonton, AB: University of Alberta, 2009.

Chattapadhyay, Gouranga. 'Translator's Note', in *Nabankur: The Seedling's Tale*. Kolkata: Stree, 2001.

Chatzidakis, Andreas, Jamie Hakim, Jo Littler, Catherine Rottenberg, and Lynne Segal. *The Care Manifesto: The Politics of Interdependence*. London: Verso, 2020.

Cho, Sumi, Kimberlé Williams, and Leslie McCall. 'Intersectionality: Theorizing Power, Empowering Theory'. *Signs* 38.4 (2013): 795–810.
Chowdhury, Elora Halim and Liz Philipose, eds. 'Introduction', in *Dissident Friendships: Feminism, Imperialism, and Transnational Solidarity*, 11–16. Champaign, IL: University of Illinois Press, 2016.
Clarke, Steve. 'Scorning the Dread of Night'. *Evening Standard* (22 January 1987): 23.
Cliff, Michelle. *No Telephone to Heaven*. New York: Vintage, 1987.
Cohen, Debra Rae. 'Rebecca West's Palimpsestic Praxis: Crafting the Intermodern Voice of Witness', in *Intermodernism: Literary Culture in Mid-Twentieth-Century Britain*, edited by Kristen Bluemel, 150–67. Edinburgh: Edinburgh University Press, 2009.
Cohen, Debra Rae. 'Sheepish Modernism: Rebecca West, the Adam Brothers, and the Taxonomies of Criticism', in *Rebecca West Today: Contemporary Critical Approaches*, edited by Bernard Schweizer, 143–56. Newark, DE: University of Delaware Press, 2006.
Collier, Patrick. *Modern Print Artefacts: Textual Materiality and Literary Value in British Print Culture, 1890–1930s*. Edinburgh: Edinburgh University Press, 2016.
Conradi, Peter J. *Iris Murdoch: A Writer at War, Letters and Diaries 1938–46*. London: Short Books, 2010.
Cooper, Katherine. 'Figures on the Threshold: Refugees and the Politics of Hospitality, 1930–51', *Literature and History* 27.2 (2018): 189–204.
Cooper, Katherine. '"His Dearest Property": Women, Nation and Displacement in Storm Jameson's *Cloudless May*', in *War and Displacement in the Twentieth Century*, edited by Angela K. Smith and Sandra Barkof, 168–82. Abingdon: Routledge, 2014.
Critchley, Simon. 'Mystical Anarchism'. *Critical Horizons: A Journal of Philosophy and Social Theory* 10.2 (2009): 272–306.
Crouch, Julia. 'Foreword: Notes from a Genre Bender', in *Domestic Noir: The New Face of 21st Century Crime Fiction*, edited by Laura Joyce and Henry Sutton, v–viii. Cham: Palgrave Macmillan, 2018.
Cunard, Nancy, ed. *Authors Take Sides on the Spanish War*. London: Left Review, 1936.
Cunningham, Valentine. *British Writers of the Thirties*. Oxford: Oxford University Press, 1988.
Davidoff, Leonore. 'Gender and the Great Divide: Public and Private in British Gender History'. *Journal of Women's History* 15.1 (Spring 2003): 11–27.
Davis, Kathy. 'Toward a Feminist Rhetoric: The Gilligan Debate Revisited'. *Women's Studies International Forum* 15.2 (1992): 219–31.
Davis, Thomas. *The Extinct Scene: Late Modernism and Everyday Life*. New York: Columbia University Press, 2016.
Day, Chris. 'The Beveridge Report and the Foundations of the Welfare State'. The National Archives (7 December 2017). blog.nationalarchives.gov.uk/beveridge-report-foundations-welfare-state/
Deer, Patrick. *Culture in Camouflage: War, Empire, and Modern British Literature*. New York: Oxford University Press, 2009.

Dennis, Ferdinand, and Naseem Khan, eds. *Voices of the Crossing: The Impact of Britain on Writers from Asia, the Caribbean and Africa*. London: Serpent's Tale, 2000.
Derdiger, Paula. *Reconstruction Fiction: Housing and Realist Literature in Postwar Britain*. Columbus, OH: Ohio State University Press, 2020.
Desai, Kiran. *The Inheritance of Loss*. New York: Grove Press, 2006.
Dinsman, Melissa. 'Mrs. Miniver Builds the Home Front: Architecture and Household Objects as Wartime Propaganda'. *Modernism/Modernity Print Plus* 3.1 (2018), https://doi.org/10.26597/mod.0049
Dudziak, Mary L. *War Time: An Idea, Its History, Its Consequences*. New York: Oxford University Press, 2012.
du Maurier, Daphne. *The Birds and Other Stories*. London: Virago, 2004.
'Editorial'. *Chronicle of the Berkhamsted School for Girls* (July 1937): 1–3.
Egan, Jesi. 'Cultural Futurity and the Politics of Recovery: Mary Renault's Ambivalent Romances'. *Modern Fiction Studies* 62.3 (2016): 462–80.
Eksteins, Modris. *Rites of Spring: The Great War and the Birth of the Modern Age*. New York: Doubleday, 1989.
Ellmann, Maud. 'After the Death of Don Juan: Sylvia Townsend Warner's Spanish Novel'. *The Journal of the Sylvia Townsend Warner Society* 17.2 (2017): 1–26.
England, Suzanne E. and Carol Ganzer. 'The Micropolitics of Elder Care in *Memento Mori*, *Diary of a Good Neighbour* and *A Taste for Death*'. *International Journal of Health Services* 24.2 (1994): 355–69.
Faragher, Megan. *Public Opinion Polling in Mid-Century British Literature: The Psychographic Turn*. Oxford: Oxford University Press, 2021.
Favret, Mary. *War at a Distance: Romanticism and the Making of Modern Wartime*. Princeton:, NJ Princeton University Press, 2009.
Finch, Janet, and Penny Summerfield. 'Social Reconstruction and the Emergence of Companionate Marriage, 1945–59', in *The Sociology of the Family: A Reader*, edited by Graham Allan, 12–34. Malden, MA: Blackwell, 1999.
Folbre, Nancy. *The Invisible Heart: Economics and Family Values*. New York: New Press, 2001.
Folbre, Nancy. *Who Cares? A Feminist Critique of the Care Economy*. New York: Rosa Luxembourg Stiftung, 2014.
Ford, Sachelle M. 'Revolution', in *Gender: Love*, edited by Jennifer C. Nash, vii–x. New York: Macmillan, 2016.
Forster, Margaret. *Daphne du Maurier*. London: Arrow Books, 2007.
Foucault, Michel. *The History of Sexuality*, *Volume 1: An Introduction*, translated by Robert Hurley. London: Penguin, 1990.
Fraser, Nancy. 'Contradictions of Capital and Care'. *New Left Review* 100 (2016): 99–117.
Freeborn, Diane. '"Is It Time We Move Through or Space?": Literary Anachronism and Anachorism in the Novels of Elizabeth Taylor'. University of East Anglia, PhD Thesis, 2014. 213–28. https://ueaeprints.uea.ac.uk/id/eprint/49756/1/2014FreebornDPhD.pdf
'Freedom Is in Peril. Defend It with All Your Might'. 1939. Imperial War Museum Poster Collection. Art.IWM PST 14789. www.iwm.org.uk/collections/item/object/32267

Fremlin, Celia. 'A Housewife Looks at Affluence'. *Ethical Record* 71.3 (1966): 10–11.

Fremlin, Celia. 'Preface to the Cresset Library Edition', in *War Factory*. London: The Cresset Library, 1987: vii–ix.

Fremlin, Celia. Preface to *The Hours before Dawn*. London: Pandora, 1988: vii–viii.

Fremlin, John, and Margaret Fremlin. *There Isn't a Snake in the Cupboard: A Review of the Life of J. H. Fremlin*. http://margaret.fremlin.org/book.html

Friedman, Susan Stanford. *Mappings: Feminism and the Cultural Geographies of Encounter*. Princeton, NJ: Princeton University Press, 1998.

Gandhi, Leela. *Affective Communities: Anticolonial Thought, Fin-de-Siècle Radicalism, and the Politics of Friendship*. Durham, NC: Duke University Press, 2006.

Garrity, Jane. *Step-Daughters of England: British Women Modernists and the National Imaginary*. Manchester: Manchester University Press, 2003.

Gatrell, Peter. *The Making of the Modern Refugee*. Oxford: Oxford University Press, 2013.

Giles, Judy. *The Parlour and the Suburb: Domestic Identities, Class, Femininity and Modernity*. Oxford: Berg, 2004.

Gilliat, Sidney, and Frank Launder. *Millions Like Us*, performed by Patricia Roc, Anne Crawford, and Basil Radford. Gainsborough Pictures, 1943.

Gilligan, Carol. *In a Different Voice: Psychological Theory and Women's Development*. Cambridge, MA: Harvard University Press, 1993.

Gilman, Sander. *Jewish Self-Hatred and the Language of the Jews*. Baltimore, MD: Johns Hopkins University Press, 1990.

Gmeyner, Anna. *Manja: The Story of Five Children*, translated by Kate Phillips. London: Persephone Books, 2003.

Goller, Celia. 'Methods of Mass-Observation, with Particular Reference to Housing'. *Agenda: A Quarterly Journal of Reconstruction* (August 1943): 255–65.

Gordon, Colin. 'Governmental Rationality: An Introduction', in *The Foucault Effect: Studies in Governmentality with Two Lectures and an Interview with Michel Foucault*, edited by Graham Burchell, Colin Gordon, and Peter Miller, 1–52. Chicago, IL: University of Chicago Press, 1991.

Govind, Nikhil. 'Pluralizing Nationalism: Narrative, Politics and the Figure of the Revolutionary in the Hindi Novel from the 1930s to the 1950s'. PhD thesis, University of California Berkeley, 2011. https://escholarship.org/content/qt2hm2q00n/qt2hm2q00n_noSplash_7cf02c2ebff9c587041b0968c15db29a.pdf

Graham, Robert, ed. *Anarchism: A Documentary History of Libertarian Ideas, Volume One, From Anarchy to Anarchism (300 CE to 1939)*. Montreal, QC: Black Rose Books, 2005.

Grant, Rachel. 'Sources of Gender Bias in International Relations Theory', in *Gender and International Relations*, edited by Rachel Grant and Kathleen Newland, 8–26. Milton Keynes: Open University Press, 1991.

Graves, Robert and Alan Hodge. *The Long Week-End: A Social History of Great Britain, 1918–1939*. New York: Norton, 1994.

Greenwood, Walter. *Love on the Dole*. London: Vintage, 1993.

Grewal, Inderpal, and Caren Kaplan. 'Introduction: Transnational Feminist Practices and Questions of Postmodernity', in *Scattered Hegemonies: Postmodernity and*

Transnational Feminist Practices, edited by Inderpal Grewal and Caren Kaplan, 1–27. Minneapolis, MN: University of Minnesota Press, 1994.

Grove, Robin. 'From the Island: Elizabeth Taylor's Novels'. *Studies in the Literary Imagination* 11.2 (1978): 79–95.

Guevara, Che. 'Socialism and Man in Cuba', in *Che Guevara Reader: Writings on Politics and Revolution*, edited by David Deutschmann, 212–28. Melbourne, Australia: Ocean Books, 2003.

Habibullah, Attia. 'Seclusion of Women', in *Our Cause: A Symposium by Indian Women*, edited by Shyam Kumari Nehru, 205–11. Allahabad: Kitabistan, c.1935.

Habibullah, Shama. 'Foreword', in *Distant Traveller*, edited by Aamer Hussein and Shama Habibullah, 1–17. New Delhi: Women Unlimited, Kali for Women, 2013.

Hammell, Andrea. *Everyday Life as Alternative Space in Exile Writing: The Novels of Anna Gmeyner, Selma Kahn, Hilde Spiel, Martina Wied and Hermynia Zur Mühlen*. Oxford: Oxford University Press, 2008.

Hammell, Andrea. 'Idealized and Demonized: Representations of Jewish Motherhood by Anna Gmeyner and Selma Kahn', in *'Not an Essence but a Positioning': German-Jewish Women Writers*, edited by Andrea Hammell and Godela Weiss-Sussex, 95–112. Munich: Martin Meidenbauer Verlagsbuchhandlung, 2009.

Hammell, Andrea. 'Negotiating the "I" and the "We": Aspects of Modernism in the Exile Novels of Anna Gmeyner and Martina Wied'. *Leo Baeck Institute Year Book* 63.1 (2018): 35–154.

Hanson, Clare. *Hysterical Fictions: The 'Woman's Novel' in the Twentieth Century*. Basingstoke: Palgrave, 2000.

Harman, Claire. *Sylvia Townsend Warner: A Biography*. London: Penguin, 1989.

Harrisson, Tom. 'Industrial Survey', in *War Factory*, 5–11. London: Faber and Faber, 2009.

Harrisson, Tom. *Living through the Blitz*. Faber and Faber: London, 2010.

Hepburn, Allan. *Around 1945: Literature, Citizenship, Rights*. Montreal, QC: McGill-Queens University Press, 2009.

Hepburn, Allan. '*Memento Mori* and Gerontography'. *Textual Practice* 32.9 (2018): 1495–1511.

Heyes, Cressida J. 'Anti-Essentialism in Practice: Carol Gilligan and Feminist Philosophy'. *Hypatia* 12.3 (1997): 142–63.

Hinton, James. *The Mass Observers: A History, 1937–1949*. Oxford: Oxford University Press, 2013.

Hirsch, Pam. *The Constant Liberal: The Life and Work of Phyllis Bottome*. London: Quartet, 2010.

Hobbes, Thomas. *Leviathan*. New York: Dover Publications, 2006.

Hochschild, Arlie Russell. *The Managed Heart: Commercialization of Human Feeling*. Berkeley, CA: University of California Press, 2012.

Hosain, Attia. *Distant Traveller*, edited by Aamer Hussein and Shama Habibullah. New Delhi: Women Unlimited, Kali for Women, 2013.

Hosain, Attia. *Phoenix Fled*. London: Penguin, 1988.

Hosain, Attia. *Sunlight on a Broken Column*. London: Penguin, 1988.

Humble, Nicola. *The Feminine Middlebrow Novel, 1920s to 1950s: Class, Domesticity, and Bohemianism*. Oxford: Oxford University Press, 2001.
Hussein, Aamer. 'Afterword', in *Distant Traveller*, edited by Aamer Hussein and Shama Habibullah, 220–34. New Delhi: Women Unlimited, Kali for Women, 2013.
Ibbotson, Eva. 'Preface', in *Manja: The Story of Five Children*, by Anna Gmeyner, v–xiv. London: Persephone Books, 2003.
Jackson, Angela. *British Women and the Spanish Civil War*. London: Routledge, 2002.
James, P.D. 'Preface', in *The Victorian Chaise-Longue*, by Marghanita Laski, v–ix. London: Persephone Press, 1999.
Jameson, Storm. *In the Second Year*. New York: Macmillan, 1936.
Jordan, June. 'Where Is the Love?', in *Civil Wars*, 140–6. Boston, MA: Beacon Press, 1981.
'Keep Calm and Carry On'. 1939. Imperial War Museum Poster Collection. Art.IWM PST 14843. www.iwm.org.uk/collections/item/object/32305
Kennedy, Sue. '"The Lure of Pleasure": Sex and the Married Girl in Marghanita Laski's *To Bed with Grand Music* (1946)', in *British Women's Writing, 1930 to 1960: Between the Waves*, edited by Sue Kennedy and Jane Thomas, 73–90. Liverpool: Liverpool University Press, 2020.
Kennedy, Sue, and Jane Thomas. 'Introduction', in *British Women's Writing, 1930 to 1960: Between the Waves*, edited by Sue Kennedy and Jane Thomas, 1–16. Liverpool: Liverpool University Press, 2020.
Kettlewell, Margaret. 'Other Lives: Celia Fremlin'. *Guardian* (6 September 2009). www.theguardian.com/theguardian/2009/sep/06/celia-fremlin-obituary
Khan, Yasmin. *The Great Partition: The Making of India and Pakistan*. New Haven, CT: Yale University Press, 2007.
Kynaston, David. *Austerity Britain, 1945–51*. New York: Walker & Co., 2008.
Lahiri, Jhumpa. 'The Third and Final Continent', in *The Interpreter of Maladies*, 173–98. New York: Houghton Mifflin, 1999.
Lane, Margaret. 'Life or Death for Your Doctor'. *Daily Mail* (27 May 1937): 12.
Laski, Marghanita. *Little Boy Lost*. London: Persephone Press, 2008.
Laski, Marghanita. *Love on the Super Tax*. London: Cresset, 1945.
Laski, Marghanita. *To Bed with Grand Music*. London: Persephone Press, 2012.
Laski, Marghanita. *Tory Heaven or Thunder on the Right*. London: Persephone Press, 2018.
Laski, Marghanita. *The Victorian Chaise-Longue*. London: Persephone Press, 1999.
Laski, Marghanita. *The Village*. London: Persephone Press, 2004.
Lassner, Phyllis. *British Women Writers of World War II: Battlegrounds of Their Own*. Basingstoke: Macmillan, 1998.
Lawrence, Karen R. '"Twenty Pockets Aren't Enough for Their Lies": Pocketed Objects as Props for Bloom's Masculinity in *Ulysses*', in *Masculinities in Joyce: Postcolonial Constructions*, edited by Christine van Boheemen-Saaf and Colleen Lamos, 163–76. Amsterdam: Rodopi, 2001.
Leclercq, Florence. *Elizabeth Taylor*. Boston, MA: Twayne Publishers, 1985.

Leeson, Miles. 'The Engendered and Dis-Engendered Other in Iris Murdoch's Early Fiction', in *Cross-Gendered Literary Voices: Appropriating, Resisting, Embracing*, edited by Kim Rina and Claire Westall, 113–27. London: Palgrave Macmillan, 2012.

Leeson, Miles. *Iris Murdoch: Philosophical Novelist*. London: Continuum, 2011.

Lewis, Jane. *Women in Britain Since 1945: Women, Family, Work and the State in the Post-War Years*. Oxford: Blackwell, 1992.

Lister, Ruth. *Citizenship: Feminist Perspectives*. Basingstoke: Macmillan, 1997.

Love, Heather K. *Feeling Backward: Loss and the Politics of Queer History*. Cambridge, MA: Harvard University Press, 2007.

Lowe, Rodney. 'The Second World War, Consensus, and the Foundation of the Welfare State'. *Twentieth Century British History* 1.2 (1990): 152–82.

Lugones, Maria. 'Heterosexualism and the Colonial/Modern Gender System'. *Hypatia* 22.1 (2007): 186–209.

Mackay, Marina, and Lyndsey Stonebridge, eds. 'Introduction', in *British Fiction After Modernism: The Novel at Mid-Century*, 1–16. New York: Palgrave Macmillan, 2007.

Majumder, Supriti. 'India's Women Workers', in *Shaping the Discourse: Women's Writing in Bengali Periodical 1865–1947*, edited by Ipshita Chanda and Jayeeta Bagchi, 367–71. Kolkata: Stree, 2014.

Mallet, Isabelle. 'It Simply Isn't Done'. *New York Times* (1 June 1952): BR5.

Mandal, Renuka. 'Indian Women's Movement', in *Shaping the Discourse: Women's Writing in Bengali Periodical 1865–1947*, edited by Ipshita Chanda and Jayeeta Bagchi, 282–7. Kolkata: Stree, 2014.

Martin, Cyril. 'Struck-Off Doctor Leaves His Home'. *Daily Mail* (31 May 1937): 13–14.

McCarthy, Helen. 'Women, Marriage and Paid Work in Post-War Britain'. *Women's History Review* 26.1 (2017): 46–61.

Misra, Jahnavi. 'Exploration of Ethical Debates Through Desai's *The Inheritance of Loss*, Ishiguro's *Never Let Me Go* and Smith's *On Beauty*'. *Journal of Medical Humanities* 35.3 (2014): 335–48.

'The Model Family: Women and the Welfare State'. Poster Collection 1975–1985. LSE Finding Aid. TWL.2004.1014. archives.lse.ac.uk/Record.aspx?src=CalmView.Catalog&pos=1

Morgan, Kenneth O. *Labour in Power: 1945–1951*. Oxford: Oxford University Press, 1984.

Mosse, George L. *Fallen Soldiers: Reshaping the Memory of the World Wars*. Oxford: Oxford University Press, 1990.

Mosse, George L. *Nationalism and Sexuality: Middle-Class Morality and Sexual Norms in Modern Europe*. Madison, WI: University of Wisconsin Press, 1985.

Mulford, Wendy. *This Narrow Place: Sylvia Townsend Warner and Valentine Ackland: Life, Letters and Politics, 1930–1951*. London: Pandora, 1988.

Mulford, Wendy. 'Introduction', in *After the Death of Don Juan*, by Sylvia Townsend Warner, v–xvii. London: Virago, 1989.

Murdoch, Iris. *The Flight from the Enchanter*. London: Triad/Panther, 1976.

Murdoch, Iris. *Living on Paper: Letters from Iris Murdoch, 1934–1995*, edited by Avril Horner and Anne Rowe. London: Chatto and Windus, 2015.
Nasta, Susheila. *Home Truths: Fictions of the South Asian Diaspora in Britain*. New York: Palgrave, 2002.
Newitt, Hilary. *Women Must Choose: The Position of Women in Europe Today*. London: Gollancz: 1937.
Noakes, Lucy. *War and the British: Gender, Memory and National Identity*. London & New York: I.B. Tauris Publishers, 1998.
Okano, Yayo. 'Why Has the Ethics of Care Become an Issue of Global Concern?' *International Journal of Japanese Sociology* 25.1 (2016): 85–99.
Orwell, George. 'Boys' Weeklies', in *The Complete Works of George Orwell: A Patriot After All, 1940–1940 (XII)*, edited by Peter Davison, 57–79. London: Secker and Warburg, 1998.
'Oxonians'. 'Old Girls' News and College Letters: News from Oxford'. *Chronicle of the Berkhamsted School for Girls* (July 1938): 62.
Panter-Downes, Mollie. 'In Clover'. *New Yorker* (13 April 1940): 15–16.
Panter-Downes, Mollie. 'Letter from London'. *New Yorker* (28 September 1940): 40, 42.
Panter-Downes, Mollie. 'Letter from London'. *New Yorker* (5 October 1940): 37–8.
Panter-Downes, Mollie. 'Lunch with Mr. Biddle'. *New Yorker* (7 December 1940): 31–3.
Petersen, Kirsten Holst, and Anna Rutherford. *A Double Colonization: Colonial and Post-Colonial Women's Writing*. Oxford: Dangaroo Press, 1986.
Philips, Deborah and Ian Haywood. *Brave New Causes: Women in British Postwar Fictions*. Leicester: Leicester University Press, 1998.
Pinfold, Debbie. *The Child's View of the Third Reich in German Literature: The Eye Among the Blind*. Oxford: Oxford University Press, 2001.
Plain, Gill. *British Literature in Transition, 1940–1960: Postwar*. Cambridge: Cambridge University Press, 2019.
Plain, Gill. *Literature of the 1940s*: War, *Postwar and 'Peace'*. Edinburgh: Edinburgh University Press, 2013.
Pong, Beryl. *British Literature and Culture in Second World Wartime: For the Duration* (New York: Oxford University Press, 2020).
Pong, Beryl. 'Wartime'. *Modernism/Modernity Print Plus* 5.2 (2020). https://doi.org/10.26597/mod.0145
Preston, Paul. *The Spanish Civil War: Reaction, Revolution and Revenge*. New York: Norton, 2006.
Price, Leah. 'B-Sides: Celia Fremlin's "The Hours before Dawn"'. Public Books. www.publicbooks.org/pb-staff-favorites-2017-b-sides-celia-fremlins-hours-dawn/
'Prizes and Certificates'. *Chronicle of the Berkhamsted School for Girls* (July 1934): 10–12.
Prokhovnik, Raia. 'Public and Private Citizenship: From Gender Invisibility to Feminist Inclusiveness'. *Feminist Review* 60 (1998): 84–104.
Raguer, Hilari. *Gunpowder and Incense: The Catholic Church and the Spanish Civil War*, translated by Gerald Howson. London: Routledge, 2007.

Reeve, N.H. *Elizabeth Taylor*. Tavistock: Northcote House Publishers, 2008.
Remarque, Erich. *Flotsam*. New York: Random House, 2017.
Renault, Mary. *Kind Are Her Answers*. London: Virago, 2014.
Renault, Mary. *Return to Night*. London: Virago, 2014.
Riley, Denise. *War in the Nursery: Theories of the Child and Mother*. London: Virago Press, 1983.
Robinson, Roxana. 'Introduction', in *A View of the Harbour*, edited by Elizabeth Taylor, vii–xii. New York: New York Review Books, 2015.
Robson, W.W. *Modern English Literature*. Oxford: Oxford University Press, 1970.
Rollyson, Carl. *Rebecca West: A Life*. New York: Scribner's, 1996.
Rose, Nikolas. *Governing the Soul: The Shaping of the Private Self*. London: Free Association Books, 1999.
Rose, Sonya O. *Which People's War? National Identity and Citizenship in Britain 1939–1945*. Oxford: Oxford University Press, 2003.
Roy, Sabitri. *Harvest Song: A Novel on the Tebhaga Movement*. Kolkata: Stree, 2006.
Sadleir, Michael. 'A La Carte'. *Sunday Times* (31 August 1947): 3.
Salvadó, Francisco J. Romero. *The Foundations of Civil War: Revolution, Social Conflict and Reaction in Liberal Spain, 1916–1923*. New York: Routledge, 2008.
Sangari, Kumkum, and Sudesh Vaid. *Recasting Women: Essays in Indian Colonial History*. New Brunswick, NJ: Rutgers University Press, 1990.
Sanyal, Sulekha. *Nabankur: The Seedling's Tale*. Kolkata: Stree, 2001.
Sarkar, Tanika. 'Foreword', in *Harvest Song: A Novel on the Tebhaga Movement*, by Sabitri Roy, v–xi. Kolkata: Stree, 2006.
Schmidt, Michael, and Val Warner. 'Sylvia Townsend Warner in Conversation'. *PN Review 23* 8.3 (1982): 35–7.
Schwarz, Benjamin. 'The Other Elizabeth Taylor'. *Atlantic Monthly* (September 2007): 109–11.
Scott, Bonnie Kime, ed. *Selected Letters of Rebecca West*. New Haven, CT: Yale University Press, 2000.
Seaber, Luke. *Incognito Social Investigation in British Literature: Certainties in Degradation*. Cham: Palgrave Macmillan, 2017.
Seaber, Luke. 'Kings in Disguise and "Pure Ellen Kellond": Literary Social Passing in the Early Twentieth Century', in *Working-Class Writing: Theory and Practice*, edited by Ben Clarke and Nick Hubble, 81–98. Cham: Palgrave Macmillan, 2018.
Seaber, Luke. 'Private Faces in Public Places: Auto-Intertextuality, Authority and 1930s Fiction', in *The 1930s: A Decade of British Fiction*, edited by Nick Hubble, Luke Seaber, and Elinor Taylor, 183–206. London: Bloomsbury Academic, 2021.
Sen, Mandira and Mausumi Bhowmik. 'Publishing Women's Studies in India: Stree's Experience'. *Women's Studies International Forum* 25.2 (2022): 185–92.
Shandilya, Krupa. 'The Widow, the Wife, and the Courtesan: A Comparative Study of Social Reform in Premchand's *Sevasadan* and the Late Nineteenth-Century Bengali and Urdu Novel'. *Comparative Literature Studies* 53.2 (2016): 272–88.
Simmons, Chris. 'Preface', in *Uncle Paul*, by Celia Fremlin, 1–6. London: Faber and Faber, 2014.

Singh, Bhawna. 'Attia Hosain: A Radical Muslim Writer and Archivist of the Partition'. *Feminism in India* (29 July 2019). https://feminisminindia.com/2019/07/29/attia-hosain-radical-muslim-writer-archivist-partition/

Snyder, Timothy. 'Commemorative Causality'. *Modernism/Modernity* 20.1 (2013): 77–94.

Spark, Muriel. *Memento Mori*. London: Virago, 2009.

Stec, Loretta. 'Female Sacrifice: Gender and Nostalgic Nationalism in Rebecca West's *Black Lamb and Grey Falcon*', in *Narratives of Nostalgia, Gender, and Nationalism*, edited by Jean Pickering and Suzanne Kehde, 138–58. New York: New York University Press, 1997.

Stewart, Victoria. 'Objects, Things and Clues in Early Twentieth-Century Fiction'. *Modernist Cultures* 14.2 (2019): 172–92.

Stonebridge, Lyndsey. *The Judicial Imagination: Writing After Nuremburg*. Edinburgh: Edinburgh University Press, 2011.

Summers-Bremner, Eluned. '"Another World Than This": Muriel Spark's Postwar Investigations'. *The Yearbook of English Studies* 42 (2012): 151–67.

Sweetman, David. *Mary Renault: A Biography*. London: Pimlico, 1994.

Taylor, Elizabeth. *A View of the Harbour*. London: Virago, 2006.

Taylor, Elizabeth. *Mrs Palfrey at the Claremont*. London: Virago, 2013.

Taylor, Elizabeth. *The Soul of Kindness*. London: Virago, 2010.

Taylor, Elizabeth. *A Wreath of Roses*. London: Peter Davies, 1949.

Tharu, Susie. 'Foreword', in *Nabankur: The Seedling's Tale*, by Sulekha Sanyal, vii–viii. Kolkata: Stree, 2001.

Thomson, Elaine. 'Between Separate Spheres: Medical Women, Moral Hygiene and the Edinburgh Hospital for Women and Children', in *Medicine, Health and the Public Sphere in Britain, 1600–2000*, edited by Steve Sturdy, 107–22. London: Taylor & Francis, 2002.

Warner, Sylvia Townsend. *After the Death of Don Juan*. London: Penguin Classics, 2021.

Warner, Sylvia Townsend. *Letters*, edited by William Maxwell. London: Chatto & Windus, 1982.

Wasserstein, Bernard. *On the Eve: The Jews of Europe Before the Second World War*. New York: Simon and Schuster, 2012.

Waters, Sarah. 'Introduction', in *A View of the Harbour*, by Elizabeth Taylor, 1–8. London: Virago Press, 2006.

Waugh, Evelyn. *Brideshead Revisited*. New York: Back Bay, 2012.

West, Rebecca. 'A Reporter at Large: A Day in Town'. *New Yorker* (25 January 1941): 36, 38–40.

West, Rebecca. 'A Reporter at Large: Housewife's Nightmare'. *New Yorker* (14 December 1940): 50, 52, 55–62.

West, Rebecca. 'Around Us the Wail of Sirens'. *Saturday Evening Post* (8 February 1941): 27, 48–51, 53.

West, Rebecca. *Black Lamb and Grey Falcon: A Journey Through Yugoslavia*. 1941; New York: Penguin, 1982.

West, Rebecca. 'The Bright Face of Danger'. *Reader's Digest* (October 1940): 77–8.

West, Rebecca. 'Dinner for the Man Who Came to Dinner'. *Harper's* (December 1942). 20–7.
West, Rebecca. 'Enemy'. *New Yorker* (1 March 1941): 21–4, 27.
West, Rebecca. 'The First Fortnight'. *Ladies' Home Journal* (January 1940): 12, 68–9.
West, Rebecca. 'Little Horror of War'. *New Yorker* (15 November 1941): 29–34.
West, Rebecca. 'Notes on the Way'. *Time and Tide* (9 March 1940): 237–8.
West, Rebecca. 'Notes on the Way'. *Time and Tide* (6 December 1941): 1053–4.
West, Rebecca. *The Return of the Soldier*. 1918; New York: Penguin, 1998.
West, Rebecca. 'Shocking'. *Saturday Evening Post* (26 October 1940): 16, 48, 50.
West, Rebecca. 'The Strange Necessity', in *The Strange Necessity: Essays and Reviews*, 13–198. 1928; London: Virago, 1987.
Wisker, Gina. 'Undermining the Everyday: Daphne du Maurier's Gothic Horror'. *Revue Lisa* 19.52 (2021). https://journals-openedition.org.nuigalway.idm.oclc.org/lisa/13590#quotation
Wolfe, Peter. *Rebecca West: Artist and Thinker*. Carbondale, IL: Southern Illinois University Press, 1971.
Woolf, Virginia. *Three Guineas*. Oxford: Oxford University Press, 2015.
Yeatman, Anna. 'Feminism and Citizenship', in *Politics and Culture: A Theory, Culture & Society Series: Culture and Citizenship*, edited by N. Stevenson, 138–52. London: SAGE Publications Ltd, 2001.
'Your Courage, Your Cheerfulness, Your Resolution – Will Bring Us Victory'. 1939. Imperial War Museum Poster Collection. Art.IWM PST 14792. www.iwm.org.uk/collections/item/object/32270

Index

Note: 'n' indicates chapter endnotes. Literary works can be found under authors' names.

Ackland, Valentine 146, 147
activism 52, 61, 129–32 passim, 136–41 passim, 146–7, 158, 168, 188
  anti-fascist 61, 146, 147
  legislative 129
  literary 130
  socialist 132, 140
  suffrage 169
Adam, Ruth 123n8
affect 54–5, 66, 73, 78, 136
  see also care
agency 3, 52, 95, 104, 128, 140–1, 143, 174, 176, 178, 181, 210
Age of Consent Bill (1892) 129
Aguirre, Mercedes 157
Ahmed, Sara 70
alienation 167, 171, 177, 182, 215
allegory 149, 153–4
anarchism 87, 146–51 passim, 158, 190n8
  mystical 151, 158
Anders, Jaroslaw 197
anti-colonialism 131, 133, 134, 136, 139, 141, 143
anti-fascism 61, 87, 146–8, 159, 175
antisemitism 2, 97, 168, 188, 192, 193, 196
archive 43, 94
Arendt, Hannah 3
Attlee, Clement 2, 86, 90, 94
Austen, Jane: *Emma* 72

Bailkin, Jordanna 76
Baldwin, M. Page 169
Bannerjee, Sumanta 129

Baxell, Richard 146
Beauman, Nicola 5
Beauvoir, Simone de 79
Beer, Gillian 148
Bengal 128–43
  literature of 87, 128–9, 132, 139
  women in 87, 128, 133–4, 139, 141–2
  women writers in 128, 132, 142
Bentley, Phyllis 171
Beveridge, Sir William 86, 93
Bhattacharya, Chandrima 142
Bildungsroman 133, 196, 200n61, 204
biopolitics 78
Blitz, the 19, 51, 55, 58, 119
Bluemel, Kristin 9, 12n16, 89
Bottome, Phyllis 165–7, 171–5, 177, 181–2, 187
  Mortal Storm, The 187
  Within the Cup 167, 173–7
Bowen, Elizabeth 9, 12n16, 89
Brenner, Rachel 186
Briganti, Chiara 5–6
British Nationality and Status of Aliens Act (1914) 167–70, 181
Brittain, Vera 8, 171
Brothers, Barbara 152
Burdekin, Katherine: *Swastika Night* 187
Burton, Antoinette 202

Calder, Angus 47n16, 58
canonicity 4–5, 11, 18, 35–8, 47n20, 85
  exclusion 35, 37–8
capitalism 18, 67–8, 70, 72, 74, 78, 136

care 3, 17–19, 23–4, 27–9, 66–79, 136, 140, 179, 182
  and capital 18, 67–8, 72–4, 78, 136
  as critique 68–70
  ethics of 78
  and gender 10, 18, 78
Care Collective: *Care Manifesto* 78
catastrophe 185–97
Catholicism 87, 146, 149–50, 154, 199n25
  Spanish Catholic Church 146, 154
Cavafy 217
Chakraborty, Paulomi 141
Chamberlain, Neville 2, 40
Chattopadhyay, Bankim Chandra 142, 143n1
  Anandamath 143n1
Chattopadhyay, Gouranga 142
Christianity 31, 149–55
Churchill, Winston 2, 93, 97, 104
citizenship 3–4, 12n6, 89–104, 128, 167–72, 176–8, 181–2, 193
  women's 92, 169–72, 182
class 21, 38, 57, 58, 77, 85, 86, 89, 90, 118, 129–43 *passim*, 157, 159, 165, 177, 179, 203, 206, 210, 213, 215
  consciousness 98, 99
  cross-class affiliations 167, 194, 213
  dissolution of 96
  middle- 5, 21, 37, 38, 41–2, 91, 93, 96, 100–4, 105n15, 129–31, 134, 165
  resentment 211
  ruling 150–4
  upper- 38, 93, 138, 150, 153, 157, 159, 175, 206–7, 219n7
  working- 21, 29, 32, 90, 92, 98–9, 105n15, 117, 135, 155, 210, 214
Clay, Catherine 8
Cliff, Michele: *No Telephone to Heaven* 221n47
climate change 11
Collier, Patrick 35
colonialism 2, 87, 128–9, 138, 141, 167–8, 203–5, 211, 221n47
  and ideology 129
  see also anti-colonialism; empire; imperialism
communism 99, 109, 148
  British Communist Party 109, 146–8
  Communist Party of India 131–3, 136, 140, 141
  fear of 90, 93, 199n21

consensus 86, 108, 116, 119, 121, 122, 123n2, 126n65
  critique of 108, 122
Cooper, Katherine 59
Critchley, Simon 151
Crosland, Margaret 5
Crouch, Julia 42
Cunard, Nancy 149, 155, 160n8
  Authors Take Sides on the Spanish War 155, 160n8
Cunningham, Valentine 4–5, 37

Davidoff, Leonore 6
Davis, Kathy 78
Davis, Thomas 6
Day, Chris 93
democracy 76, 90, 100, 123, 165, 167–8, 185–7, 190, 205, 212
Derdiger, Paula 6, 109
Desai, Kiran: *Inheritance of Loss, The* 221n47
diaries 1
diasporic writing 166, 167, 203, 209, 217–18
Dinsman, Melissa 63n25
domestic fiction 7, 86
domesticity 1, 54, 73, 89, 104, 109, 112, 116, 128, 129, 132, 133, 142
  and anxiety 18, 76, 104
  critique of 70, 85, 87, 110–11, 113, 116, 152
  and politics 1
  see also domestic sphere; work, domestic
domestic noir 18, 42
domestic sphere 2–10, 12, 17–21, 54, 67, 69–72, 85–7, 109, 117, 129–41 *passim*, 152, 168, 206
  and medical work 21–4
  see also domesticity; home; privacy; work, domestic

Egan, Jesi 30
Ehrenreich, Barbara: *Nickel and Dimed* 38
Eksteins, Modris 190, 194
Ellmann, Maud 149
empire 2, 5, 52–3, 57, 101, 104, 131, 169, 171, 189, 218
  and Bengal 128
  declining 1, 8, 90, 185

England, Suzanne E. 77
equality 137–8, 141, 157, 182, 193, 211
  gender 129, 134, 136, 143n1,
    159, 206
Esty, Jed 4–5
everyday, the 5–7, 18–19, 142
exile 172, 178, 180, 185–90 *passim*,
    198n5, 212, 217

family 42, 87, 90–8 *passim*, 103, 108,
    110, 117, 123n4, 131, 136–7,
    150, 152, 155, 166–7, 175,
    187–91, 195–6, 204–5, 210–16
    passim
Famine of Bengal (1943) 87, 128,
    133–4, 136
Faragher, Megan 35
fascism 2, 7, 10, 87, 146, 149, 150,
    153, 168, 177, 185, 187, 200n48
  British Union of Fascists 2, 146, 187
  Spanish 149, 150, 153–7
  see also anti-fascism
Favret, Mary 54
feminism 9–11, 78, 90, 98, 150, 154,
    205
  and anti-colonial nationalism 207–9
  intersectional 11
  radical 154
  second-wave 12n16
  spatial 9
  third-wave 78
fiction 64n54, 125n31, 165, 185
  crime 49n44
  historical 154, 158
  limits of 59
  literary 18
  middlebrow 6, 89
  post-war 17, 109, 115
  realist 185
  women's 7
  writing 112, 114, 204
First World War 7, 39, 146, 150, 169,
    171, 186, 187, 190, 194, 203
Folbre, Nancy 69, 70
Ford, Sachelle 134, 138
form
  collectivist 150
  experimental 9, 153
  hybrid 149
  modernist 5
  montage 153, 155
  narrative 159

Forster, E.M. 171
Forster, Margaret 69
Foucault, Michel 78
Franco, Francisco 2, 87, 147, 149,
    154–6, 161n35
Fraser, Nancy 67, 68, 70, 73
Freeborn, Diane 74, 79
freedom 2, 3, 11, 22, 23, 31, 66, 78,
    85, 86, 97–9, 120, 130, 134,
    140–3, 151, 165, 167–9, 171,
    186, 205, 211
Fremlin, Celia 17–19, 35–46, 48n33,
    48n37, 49n44, 49n50, 49n53
  Appointment with Yesterday 42
  biography of 36–8, 41
  and domestic service 38
  Hours before Dawn, The 18, 38, 41,
    42, 46
  King of the World 41
  at Mass-Observation 36, 38–44
  Mugging and the Myths, The 43
  Seven Chars of Chelsea, The 38, 42
  sociological work of 19, 40, 42
  War Factory: A Report 39–45
Freud, Sigmund 190, 192
Friedman, Susan Stanford 9–10
friendship
  female 86–101 *passim*, 120–2, 129,
    133–40 *passim*

Gandhi, Leela 134
Gandhi, Mahatma 204, 207,
    220n22
Ganzer, Carol 77
Gaster, Moses 90
Gatrell, Peter 173
General Medical Council (GMC) 175
genocide 7, 167
  see also war
German Expressionism 186, 191
Gibbons, Stella: *Cold Comfort Farm* 72
Giles, Judy 42
Gilligan, Carol 67, 78
Gilman, Sander 192
Gmeyner, Anna: *Manja* 165–8 passim,
    185–97
gothic fiction 18, 23, 68, 79
Govind, Nikhil 139
Grant, Rebecca 170
Graves, Robert 31
Greenwood, Walter: *Love on the
    Dole* 91

Index

Habibullah, Shama 202, 209, 212n1, 212n3
Hammell, Andrea 194–5
Hanisch, Carol 133
Harman, Claire 146, 147
Harrisson, Tom 38–40, 43–6, 47n21
  Living through the Blitz 39
Hartwell, Jenny 7
Hepburn, Allan 181–2
Hilzinger, Sonja 198n5
Hirsch, Pam 173, 175
Hitler, Adolf 2, 51, 54, 59, 61, 168, 173, 185–8 *passim*, 196
Hobbes, Thomas 170
Hochschild, Arlie Russell 66, 73–4
Hodge, Alan 31
Holocaust, the 2, 166, 175, 185
home 3, 6–10 *passim*, 24, 42, 78, 85–6, 89, 92, 109, 167, 206–11 *passim*, 216
  see also domesticity; domestic sphere; privacy
Hosain, Attia 165–8 *passim*, 202–18, 219n1, 219n2, 220n10, 222n60
  'Deep Roots' 203, 206, 219n7
  Distant Traveller 166, 202–3, 206, 209, 216–18
  'Journey to No End' 215–17
  'Leader of Women, The' 207–9
  'No New Lands, No New Seas' 209–15
  Phoenix Fled 202, 206
  Sunlight on a Broken Column 202, 204–5
  'Time is Unredeemable' 220n10
hospitality 170
  see also home
housewives 41, 42, 45, 94, 105n26
housework see work
Hubble, Nick 6
Humble, Nicola 5, 20, 89
Hussein, Aamer 202, 218, 222n60

identity formation 87, 128, 130, 134, 182
ideology 158, 191, 193
  colonial 129, 143
  corporate 73
  nationalist 128
  political 167, 168
  racial 195
  religious 159
  of separate spheres 67
  see also propaganda
immigrants 168, 198n9, 204, 210–13, 218, 219, 221n47
  see also refugees
imperialism 10, 138, 140, 168, 203, 212
  see also colonialism
Indian Independence (1947) 2, 85, 128, 130–1, 133, 142, 203–5, 213, 217–18, 220n12
Indo-Pakistani War (1947–48) 2
Intermodernism 1, 9, 13
intersectionality 11, 132, 141, 143, 165, 203, 205, 213, 218
Israel: establishment of 2

Jackson, Angela 147
Jahoda, Marie 43
James, P.D. 91
Jameson, Storm 8, 171–3, 182, 186–7
  In the Second Year 187
Joannou, Maroula 4, 12n15
Jordan, June 138
journalism 1, 18, 19, 51–61, 146, 186
  New Journalism 58
  wartime 19, 51–61
Joyce, James 55, 63n31, 80n22
  Ulysses 80n22

Kennedy, Sue 4, 12n16, 91
Khan, Yasmin 220n9, 220n12, 221n49
Kremer, Michael 37
Kropotkin, Pyotr 158
Kynaston, David 99, 101, 108

labour see work
Labour Party 2, 86, 89–94, 97, 99, 102, 106n52, 108, 169
Lahiri, Jhumpa: 'Third and Final Continent, The' 217
Lahiri, Ramtanu 131
Laski, Marghanita 86, 89–104
  Little Boy Lost 91
  Love on the Super Tax 91
  To Bed with Grand Music 91
  Tory Heaven 91
  Victorian Chaise-Longue, The 91
  Village, The 86, 89–90, 95–104
Lassner, Phyllis 7, 165–7, 174–5
Lawrence, Karen R. 80n22

Index

Leclerq, Florence 124n16
Leeson, Miles 178
letters 1, 26, 55, 58, 74, 109, 119, 140, 148–9, 156, 171
Light, Alison 5
Lister, Ruth 170
London, Jack: *People of the Abyss* 38
Lorenz, Dagmar 198n11
love 58, 71–5 *passim*, 86, 87, 97–8, 102–3, 112, 115, 119, 128–40 *passim*, 151, 154, 157–9, 194–5, 210
  communal 157–9
  family 210
  revolutionary 86, 87, 129, 133–41
Love, Heather K. 158

McKay, Marina 5
Majumder, Supriti 130
Mandal, Renuka 130
Mann, Thomas: *Buddenbrooks* 189
Mansfield, Katherine: 'Bliss' 72
marginalization 3, 10, 12, 35, 39, 43, 49, 110, 117, 122, 132, 140, 198, 206
  see also canonicity, exclusion
marriage
  and assimilation 192
  bar 7
  companionate 110, 120, 125n23
  laws 141
  plot 89, 97, 104, 110
  and redemption 52
  and work 53
masculinity 4, 166, 179, 197
  crises of 166
Mass-Observation 6, 18, 36, 38–45, 95
Maurier, Daphne du 17, 18, 19, 66–9, 72, 75–9 *passim*
  Rebecca 18, 68–70
medicine 17, 19–32, 76, 146, 176
  ethics of 24, 78
melodrama 68, 85, 212
#MeToo movement 11
Mezei, Kathy 5–6
Mieszkowski, Jan 54
migration 20, 137, 166, 185, 191, 213
  see also refugees
Miller, Tyrus 4–5
Mitchison, Naomi 8, 187
  We Have Been Warned 187

modernism 1, 4–9, 185
  high 4–5, 9
  late 5–7, 9
  see also Intermodernism
montage 153, 155
Morgan, Kenneth O. 93–4, 106n52, 123n2, 126n65
Mosley, Oswald 2, 187, 200n48
Mosse, George 192, 194
Mozart, Wolfgang Amadeus 149, 151–2
  Don Giovanni 151
Mukherjee, Adrita 142
Mukhopadhyay, Arati 130
Mulford, Wendy 153, 161n63
Mullholland, Terri 7
Murdoch, Iris 165–7, 171–4, 177–82
  Flight from the Enchanter, The 167, 177–81

Nasta, Susheila 202
nationalism 1, 10, 52, 85, 86, 102, 128, 136, 146, 149, 150, 204
  anti-colonial 207–9
  British 102
  feminist 136
  Indian 128, 204
  religious 85, 87
  Spanish 146, 149, 150
  see also ideology; propaganda
Nazism 167, 173, 177, 185–95 *passim*
  see also fascism
Needham, Anuradha Dingwaney 202
Newitt, Hilary 182
New World women 89–104
non-fiction 1, 203
novel, the
  domestic 5, 104
  as genre 143n1
Nuremburg Trials 2

Orwell, George 32, 38
  'Boys' Weeklies' 32
  Down and Out in Paris and London 38

Pabst, Georg Wilhelm 186
Panter-Downes, Mollie 58
Partition (of India) 166, 168, 202, 204–5, 210–17 *passim*, 220n9, 220n12, 222n60

patriarchy 86–7, 128–30, 133–9, 141, 150–1, 166–7, 171, 174–7, 180, 182, 195, 203, 205, 212–13
Pemán, José María 149
Petersen, Kirsten Holst 203
Pinfold, Debbie 199n24, 200n61
Pistol, Rachel 198n9
Plain, Gill 7, 8, 109, 115
Plock, Martina 7
poetry 1, 55, 146
political theology 87, 149–52, 159
Pong, Beryl 54, 63n25
postcolonialism 128–9, 137, 143, 167, 202–3, 208, 212, 217
Priestley, J.B. 171
privacy 3, 17, 22, 23, 210
privation 17–19, 194
professionalization 10, 17–19, 73
   caregiving 3, 10, 17–19, 23–4, 27–9, 66–79, 136, 140, 179, 182
   de- 39, 40, 43
   journalism 10, 18–19
   medicine 10, 17, 19–21, 24–7, 32
   sociology 10, 17, 19, 35, 42
Prokhovnik, Raia 3
propaganda 58, 63n25, 91, 97, 102, 149, 154, 171, 173
public and private divide 1, 3, 6, 67, 70–1, 137, 203, 205, 206, 208
public sphere 2–7 *passim*, 10, 12n6, 17, 128–31, 134, 137, 139, 166, 205

queerness 150, 154, 159
   and longing 158
   and politics 150

racism 168, 209, 210
realism 32, 85, 109, 149, 158, 159
reconstruction 6, 8, 39, 85, 108, 109
refugees 8, 54, 60, 91, 148, 165–8 *passim*, 171–82 *passim*, 186, 188, 196, 198n5, 204
Reichstag Fire, the (1933) 146, 190, 199n21
Remarque, Erich Maria 177, 180
Renault, Mary 17–32 *passim*
   Funeral Games 20
   Kind Are Her Answers 17, 18, 19, 20–8 *passim*, 30–1
   Last of the Wine, The 20
   Purposes of Love 20, 30
   Return to Night 17, 19, 21–4, 26–31

Resolution of Native Female Education (1868) 129
rights
   electoral 130
   human 77, 128, 134, 141, 165, 170–2, 175, 178, 180–2, 188, 205
   LGBTQ+ 11
   parental 139
   reproductive 11
   social 126n65, 130
   women's 1, 11, 128, 138, 169–72, 182
   see also Universal Declaration of Human Rights (1914)
Riley, Denise 123n4
Ritchie, J.M. 198n6
Robson, W.W. 91
Rollyson, Carl 52, 63n31
Rose, Nikolas 67
Rose, Sonya O. 4, 89
Roy, Sabitri 87, 128, 131–3, 137–41
   biography 132–3
   Harvest Song 137–41
Rutherford, Anna 203

Sadleir, Michael 31–2
Salvadó, Francisco J. Romero 147
Sanyal, Sulekha 87, 128–34, 136, 141–3
   biography 131–2
   Seedling's Tale, The 133–7
Sarkar, Tanika 132
Sati, ban on (1829) 129
Scarry, Elaine 58
Schneider, Karen 7
Schwarz, Benjamin 124n10
Second World War 1–10 *passim*, 63n25, 66, 67, 71, 73, 85–92 *passim*, 104–9 *passim*, 131, 134, 135, 166–74 *passim*, 186, 203–4, 219n8, 220n9, 220n10
Sen, Mandira 142
sex 20, 42
sexuality 1, 158, 197, 206
Simmons, Chris 36, 37
Singer, I.J.: *Family Carnovsky, The* 189
Smith, Adam 68
Snyder, Timothy 62n17, 186
social epics 189
Social Insurance and Allied Services Report (Beveridge Report) 2, 85–6, 92–5, 97, 104, 108
socialism 132

social welfare 17, 67, 74, 76, 94, 123n2, 136
  see also welfare state
sociology 10, 17, 19, 35, 39–45 *passim*
  see also Mass-Observation
Son, Nirajbasini 130
Spanish Civil War, the 2, 85, 87, 146–59
Spark, Muriel 17, 19, 52, 66–7, 75–7, 79
  Memento Mori 67, 68, 75–7
  Prime of Miss Jean Brodie, The 76
statelessness *see* exile
Stec, Loretta 62n12
Stonebridge, Lyndsey 109, 178
Stree Publishing 142
Sweetman, David 27, 31

Taylor, Elizabeth 17–19, 66–7, 71–5, 77, 79
  'Apple Tree' 18, 66–8, 79n9
  Mrs Palfrey at the Claremont 17, 66, 67
  Soul of Kindness, The 67, 71–4, 79
  View of the Harbour, A 86, 109–14, 116–20, 122, 125n31
  Wreath of Roses, A 86, 109, 110, 114–16, 119–22
Tebhaga Movement 87, 128, 133, 137, 145n25
Tharu, Susie 131–2
Thomas, Jane 4, 12n16
Thomson, Elaine 21
translation 129, 141–3
transnationalism 10, 142–3, 153, 185, 218
trauma 109, 115, 119, 165, 166, 185, 190, 205, 209

Universal Declaration of Human Rights (1914) 181

Victorian culture 20, 23, 26, 32, 91
violence 2, 7, 11, 115, 119, 128, 131, 135, 137, 139, 147, 149, 155, 165–7, 172, 177, 179, 180, 189, 192, 194, 204, 217
  administrative 177, 181
  domestic 131
  ideological 135, 165
  nationalist 149, 204, 205, 211
  patriarchal 128, 139, 167, 180, 194, 217

  religious 156
  sexual 11, 137, 205
  state 189

war
  and domesticity 1, 54, 73, 89, 109, 116
  and myth 55–6
  see also First World War; journalism, wartime; propaganda; Second World War; trauma; violence
Warner, Sylvia Townsend 85–7, 146–59
  After the Death of Don Juan 87, 149–59
  Lolly Willowes 150, 154
  Mr. Fortune's Maggot 150
  Summer Will Show 158
Warren, Elizabeth 53, 62n15
Wasserstein, Bernard 188, 193
Waters, Sarah 125n31
welfare state 2, 7, 67, 74, 76–7, 90, 94, 103, 106n52, 109, 123n2
  see also care; social welfare
Wells, H.G. 171
West, Anthony 31
West, Rebecca 17–19, 51–61, 62n12, 171
  'Around Us the Wail of Sirens' 59, 60
  Black Lamb and Grey Falcon 51–4, 59–61
  'Bright Face of Danger, The' 60
  'Day in Town, A' 57
  'Dinner for the Man Who Came to Dinner' 60
  'Enemy' 60–1, 64n54
  'Little Horror of War' 60
  Return of the Soldier, The 57
  'Shocking' 60
  'Strange Necessity, The' 55–6
  and wartime journalism 51–61
Widow Remarriage Act (1856) 129
Wilkinson, Ellen 169, 170, 183n5
Willcock, H.D. 40, 48n33
Windrush Generation 2
Wisker, Gina 79
witnessing 51, 59, 110, 119, 134, 142, 146, 151, 153, 156, 187
women's magazines 7, 109

Woolf, Virginia 3, 6, 7, 124n16,
  125n33, 170
 Room of One's Own, A 6
 Three Guineas 170
 To the Lighthouse 125n33
work
 affective 66, 78
 clerical 146
 domestic 20, 24, 38, 41, 45–6, 51,
  55–6, 66, 70, 85, 92, 95, 98,
  105n15, 111, 125n23, 141, 177,
  198n5, 208
 invisible 19, 35–46
 medical 17, 19, 20–5 *passim*, 27, 31,
  32, 146, 176
 privation of 17–19, 194
 professional 10, 17–19, 28–9, 35,
  72–3
 social 18
 wartime 4
 women's 18, 39, 45, 87, 130, 133,
  136, 141
 writing 17, 45, 111
 see also care; professionalization

Yeatman, Anna 170